BLUEPRINTS

Environmental Education
Education
Key Stage 2

Joy A Palmer

Stanley Thornes (Publishers) Ltd

BLUEPRINTS – HOW TO GET MORE INFORMATION

The following titles are currently available. New titles are being added every year.

Topics
Assemblies
Writing
Science 5–7 Teacher's Resource Book
Science 5–7 Pupils' Copymasters
Science 7–11 Teacher's Resource Book
Science 7–11 Pupils' Copymasters
English Key Stage 1 Teacher's Resource Book
English Key Stage 1 Pupils' Copymasters
English Key Stage 2 Teacher's Resource Book
English Key Stage 2 Pupils' Copymasters
History Key Stage 1 Teacher's Resource Book
History Key Stage 1 Pupils' Copymasters
History Key Stage 2 Teacher's Resource Book
History Key Stage 2 Pupils' Copymasters
Environmental Education Key Stage 1
Environmental Education Key Stage 2

Geography Key Stage 1 Teacher's Resource Book
Geography Key Stage 1 Pupils' Copymasters
Geography Key Stage 2 Teacher's Resource Book
Geography Key Stage 2 Pupils' Copymasters
Technology Key Stage 1
Technology Key Stage 2
Health Education Key Stage 1 Teacher's Resource Book
Health Education Key Stage 1 Pupils' Copymasters
Health Education Key Stage 2 Teacher's Resource Book
Health Education Key Stage 2 Pupils' Copymasters
Maths Key Stage 1 Teacher's Resource Book
Maths Key Stage 1 Pupils' Copymasters
Maths Key Stage 2 Teacher's Resource Book
Maths Key Stage 2 Pupils' Copymasters

Books may be bought by credit card over the telephone and information obtained on (0242) 228888. Alternatively, photocopy and return this FREEPOST form for further information.

Photocopiable

Please send further information on BLUEPRINTS to:

Name _____

Address_____

_____

_____

Postcode_____

To: Marketing Services Dept., Stanley Thornes Publishers, FREEPOST (GR 782), Cheltenham, Glos. GL53 1BR

Text © J A Palmer 1992

Original line illustrations © ST(P) Ltd 1992

First published in 1992 by:
Stanley Thornes (Publishers) Ltd
Old Station Drive
Leckhampton
CHELTENHAM GL53 0DN

A catalogue record for this book is available from the British Library.

ISBN 0–7487–1392–1

Typeset by Tech-Set, Gateshead, Tyne & Wear
Printed in Great Britain at The Bath Press, Avon

CONTENTS

INTRODUCTION

WHAT IS BLUEPRINTS *ENVIRONMENTAL EDUCATION?*

The publication of **Blueprints** *Environmental Education* is in response to the ever increasing awareness of the great importance of Environmental Education as a curriculum area, and its recognition as a cross-curricular theme of the National Curriculum for schools.

Blueprints *Environmental Education* is a practical teacher's resource written to fulfill all the requirements of Environmental Education as a cross-curricular theme of the National Curriculum at primary level. It is intended to be used flexibly either as an ideas bank for individual teachers developing cross-curricular topics which include elements of Environmental Education, or as a key resource for those wishing to implement topics which have a central, discernible core of environmental content. **Blueprints** *Environmental Education* consists of a book for each of the primary key stages. Together they can be used to provide a complete, structured resource for Environmental Education work in the primary school.

Each book provides teacher's resource material, hundreds of practical and relevant ideas and activities, and 54 photocopiable copymasters linked to the other activities in the book. These copymasters reinforce and extend activities already undertaken and provide opportunities to build up a record of the pupils' work in Environmental Education. They may also be seen as a resource for teacher assessment of the pupils' progress.

Complete coverage of the National Curriculum demands for Environmental Education is provided through the same nine topics at both Key Stage 1 and Key Stage 2 and the structure throughout is completely cross-curricular. The nine topics in each book are:

Weather
Farms
Ponds
Energy
Trees
Food
Waste
Work
Oceans.

You will find that ideas within these topics can also resource a wide range of other key primary topics. With the help of the chart on page 10 and the information on the first page of each topic, you can identify environmental work relevant to other particular topics you may be doing.

Taken together the topics at the two key stages provide a coherent continuous resource for Environmental Education in the primary years. Each topic at each level covers clearly-stated learning objectives within the seven areas of study outlined in *Curriculum Guidance 7: Environmental Education* (Climate; Soils, Rocks and Minerals; Water; Materials and Resources, including Energy; Plants and Animals; People and their Communities; Buildings, Industrialisation and Waste). The chart on page 9 shows how the topics cover these areas of study.

The activities in the books pay due attention to the importance of individual investigation, enquiry and communication, aiming to provide ways in which you can help children to develop field work skills and investigate environmental topics on their own. A wide variety of opportunities are provided for asking questions, choosing sources for investigations, collecting and recording information, and for presenting results orally, visually and in writing. Due attention is paid to cross-curricular skills such as problem-solving, investigating and communicating.

The ideas for work in each topic are not age-specific but are designed to fit in with and span the general range of expectations for the key stage. No attempt has been made to grade the activities formally or to identify specific Levels of Attainment in related core and foundation subjects. The emphasis of the book is on helpful flexibility. No doubt you will wish to draw upon and modify ideas and suggestions to suit the needs of individual situations and learners. In so doing, it is hoped that the theme of Environmental Education genuinely permeates Attainment Targets and Programmes of Study in other areas, thus providing a sound cross-curricular framework. You will find that the activities for each topic are explicitly structured around particular curriculum areas throughout.

WHY STUDY ENVIRONMENTAL EDUCATION?

Environmental Education is a cross-curricular theme and part of the whole curriculum. As such, it is considered to be part of every pupil's entitlement. The structure and approach of the book is designed to provide a comprehensive resource that will cover all the key requirements of the theme.

However, beyond the constraints of Attainment Targets and Programmes of Study lies the fundamental need for all children to develop an enjoyment of the world around them, an appreciation of our planet, and a concern for its future. The activities suggested are intended also to help meet this larger need, thus helping children to enjoy an interest in the environment whilst acquiring appropriate attitudes of concern and respect for it. It is hoped that the activities that follow are both educational and enjoyable!

ENVIRONMENTAL EDUCATION AS A CROSS-CURRICULAR THEME

Environmental Education fits within the overall curriculum framework as one of a number of particular themes which are under the general umbrella of cross-curricular issues as shown in Figure 1.

As such it must be regarded as part of every pupil's entitlement. It is not a statutory subject in its own right, but must be viewed as being complementary to and permeating all of the core and foundation subjects. The matching of the published guidelines for Environmental Education (*Curriculum Guidance 7: Environmental Education, National Curriculum Council, 1990*) to the core and foundation subjects can be done with reference to the published core subject material, and a great deal of the content can be delivered through the Attainment Targets and Programmes of Study of these statutory subject areas. This will require an overarching and cross-referenced structure, which is reflected in the way **Blueprints** *Environmental Education* is organised to deliver the subject across the whole curriculum.

It is also important to relate Environmental Education to the other cross-curricular themes (Health Education, Careers Education and Guidance, Economic and Industrial Understanding and Education for Citizenship) as well as to the core and foundation subjects. In this way it should be possible to adopt an integrated approach to curriculum development which allows for a coherent programme of cross-curricular work.

Issues		
Skills	Dimensions	Themes
Communication Numeracy Study Problem Solving Personal and Social Information Technology	Equal Opportunities Gender Issues Multicultural Perspectives	Economic and Industrial Understanding Careers Education & Guidance Health Education Education for Citizenship Environmental Education

Source: *The Curriculum Guidance 3: the Whole Curriculum*, NCC 1990

Figure 1   Cross-curricular issues of the National Curriculum

A GUIDE TO THE NON-STATUTORY GUIDANCE ON ENVIRONMENTAL EDUCATION

The following is a concise summary of the non-statutory guidance on Environmental Education as set out in *Curriculum Guidance 7: Environmental Education*.

The *objectives* necessary to develop an environmental curriculum include knowledge, skills and attitudes. *Knowledge* and understanding of the following areas should be developed:

● the natural processes which take place in the environment.

● the impact of human activities on the environment
● different environments, both past and present
● environmental issues such as the greenhouse effect, acid rain, air pollution
● local, national and international legislative controls; how policies and decisions are made about the environment
● the environmental inter-dependence of individuals, groups, communities and nations

• how human lives and livelihoods are dependent on the environment
• the conflicts which can arise about environmental issues
• how the environment has been affected by past decisions and actions
• the importance of planning, design and aesthetic considerations
• the importance of effective action to protect and manage the environment.

Skills of a cross-curricular kind can be developed through Environmental Education, including:

• Communication skills
• Numeracy skills
• Study skills
• Problem-solving skills
• Personal and social skills
• Information technology skills.

Attitudes and personal qualities should be developed, including:

• appreciation of, and care and concern for, the environment and for other living things
• independence of thought on environmental issues
• a respect for the beliefs and opinions of others
• a respect for evidence and rational argument
• tolerance and open-mindedness.

Planning framework for the inclusion of Environmental Education in the curriculum includes three linked components as shown in Figure 2.

• Education *about* the environment: that is, knowledge and understanding through environmentally-related content in other core and foundation subjects, notably Science, Geography, History and Technology.
• Education *for* the environment: that is, values, attitudes and positive action. Education for the environment is concerned with finding ways of ensuring caring use of the environment now and in the future; finding solutions to environmental problems, taking into account the fact that there are conflicting interests and different cultural perspectives; and informing the choices which have to be made.
• Education *in* and *through* the environment: that is, using the environment as a resource for the development of skills; for direct experience, enquiry and investigation.

Seven topics or areas of study are recommended for the development of basic knowledge and understanding of the environment:

• Climate
• Soils, Rocks and Minerals
• Water
• Materials and Resources, including Energy
• Plants and Animals
• People and their Communities
• Buildings, Industrialisation and Waste.

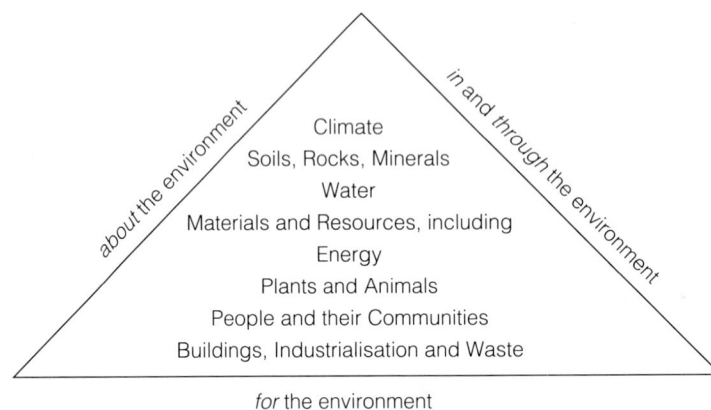

Figure 2 Environmental Education: three dimensions to a topic-based approach

ORGANISING ENVIRONMENTAL EDUCATION

No single approach to the organisation of the curriculum or teaching methodology for Environmental Education is recommended. Indeed it is believed that it is best to use a variety of approaches. The NCC identifies five possible timetabling arrangements for the inclusion of cross-curricular themes:

A. Taught through National Curriculum and other subjects.
B. Whole-curriculum planning leading to blocks of

activities (for example, a series of subject-based topics lasting for varying periods of time).
C. Separately timetabled themes.
D. Taught through separately timetabled Personal and Social Education.
E. Long-block timetabling (for example, activity week).

Without doubt, approaches A and B are particularly relevant to primary schools. Together they provide an efficient and effective way of including cross-curricular themes through both National Curriculum subjects and through approaches to organisation that are already in place in most schools and have been proved to be successful. Primary schools have a long tradition of curriculum organisation that is integrated and cross-curricular in nature. Topic work is well-established as an effective means of enabling meaningful learning that draws on a number of areas of the curriculum. It is perhaps the most appropriate way of ensuring the

inclusion of cross-curricular elements in Key Stages 1 and 2. Topics may be subject-based, incorporating cross-curricular issues, or the actual focus of a topic could be taken from one of the cross-curricular themes such as Environmental Education.

The suggestions in **Blueprints** *Environmental Education* are based on the topic work approach. They are full of ideas for practical activities and investigations to promote the teaching and learning of Environmental Education arising from topics.

USING BLUEPRINTS *ENVIRONMENTAL EDUCATION*

Blueprints *Environmental Education* is structured around topics, so that Environmental Education may be related to the whole of the primary curriculum. The same topics appear at both key stages to provide complete continuity and progression of learning, should you want to use the books as a coherent core resource. You will find that each topic in this book provides you with the following clear, basic planning information to enable you to do this in a flexible way.

1. Information showing how the topic links in with the seven areas of study outlined in the *Cross-Curriculum guidance 7*. Usually the topic covers principally one or two areas of study, and several others to a lesser extent. The context of each topic is also identified. This context may be, for example, local to global, aesthetic aspects, historical aspects, etc. The example below is from the Weather topic on page 12.

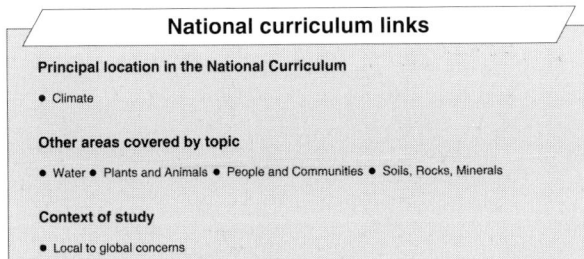

National curriculum links

Principal location in the National Curriculum

- Climate

Other areas covered by topic

- Water ● Plants and Animals ● People and Communities ● Soils, Rocks, Minerals

Context of study

- Local to global concerns

2. Within each **Blueprints** *Environmental Education* topic there is potential for several other common primary sub-topics which may be a natural starting point for environmental work. These are identified clearly at the start of each topic. The example below is from the Weather topic on page 12.

Suggested sub-topics and their location in areas of study of curriculum guidelines for Environmental Education

Sub-topic	Areas of Study in the National Curriculum						
	Climate	Soils, Rocks, Minerals	Water	Materials, Resources, Energy	Plants and Animals	People and Communities	Buildings, Industrialisation, Waste
Acid rain	●	○	●		○	○	○
Global warming	●	○	●	○	●	●	○
Global habitats	●	○	●	○	●	●	
Pollution	●	○	●	○	○	○	○

Key ● Principal location   ○ Part coverage

3. There is an overview of the cross-curricular coverage of all the topics at both key stages on page 11, and at the start of each topic there is a web showing cross-curicular coverage in detail. The example below is from the Weather topic on page 13.

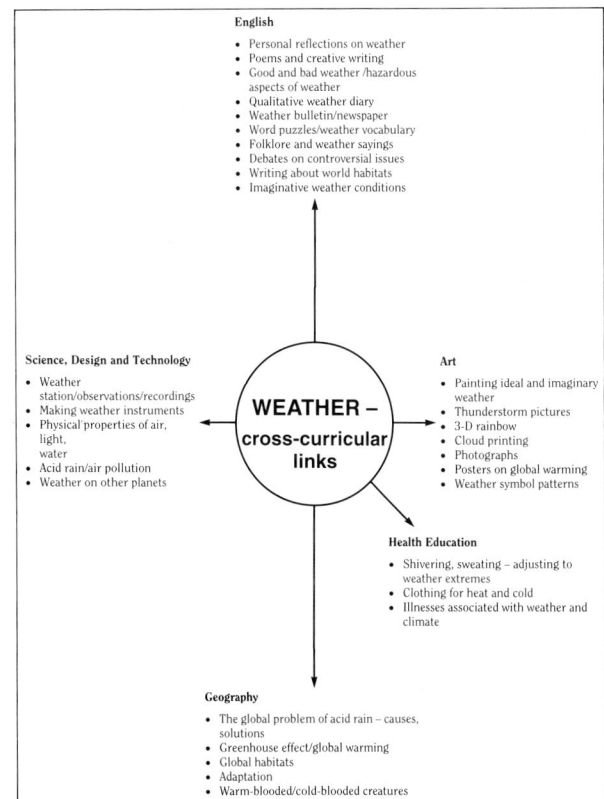

English
- Personal reflections on weather
- Poems and creative writing
- Good and bad weather /hazardous aspects of weather
- Qualitative weather diary
- Weather bulletin/newspaper
- Word puzzles/weather vocabulary
- Folklore and weather sayings
- Debates on controversial issues
- Writing about world habitats
- Imaginative weather conditions

Science, Design and Technology
- Weather station/observations/recordings
- Making weather instruments
- Physical properties of air, light, water
- Acid rain/air pollution
- Weather on other planets

WEATHER – cross-curricular links

Art
- Painting ideal and imaginary weather
- Thunderstorm pictures
- 3-D rainbow
- Cloud printing
- Photographs
- Posters on global warming
- Weather symbol patterns

Health Education
- Shivering, sweating – adjusting to weather extremes
- Clothing for heat and cold
- Illnesses associated with weather and climate

Geography
- The global problem of acid rain – causes, solutions
- Greenhouse effect/global warming
- Global habitats
- Adaptation
- Warm-blooded/cold-blooded creatures

4. There is a guide to the environmental learning covered by the topic. The example below is from the Weather topic on page 14.

Basics to be developed throughout the topic

Concepts

- Weather as a scientific phenomenon that can be measured, recorded, predicted
- Weather as part of global climate
- Changes in weather and climate
- The importance of weather and climate to all forms of life on Earth, including human life
- Weather and mood – the aesthetic dimension

Attitudes

- Appreciation of, and care and concern for, the environment and life within it
- Care and concern for conservation of resources
- Respect for empirical evidence and scientific facts

Environmental issues

- Climatic effects on vegetation and all forms of life
- Effects of pollution on climate and on water supply
- Water conservation and problems of water supply

Within each topic, you will find a starting point for the topic, then suggestions for activities which are always delivered across the curriculum in clearly identified sections. The example below is from the Weather topic on page 14.

ENGLISH ACTIVITIES

The numbers on the right of these headings identify the copymasters that you can use to support the learning. The activities in the book provide ideas for approaching topics from many different starting points, allowing you scope for individual interpretation and development. The photocopiable copymasters contain a wealth of ideas and activities that can be used to complement the topics in the book. They allow plenty of scope for flexibility and individual use and interpretation.

The structure of the book allows you to access and use the materials in many different ways. We are conscious that no topic can be prescribed in its entirety and that individual needs, enthusiasms and detailed organisation will inevitably shape the way any topic proceeds in practice.

However it may be useful to highlight one or two general points relating to the development of topic work for, whilst any topic needs to be well planned and implemented, this is perhaps especially true for wide-ranging topics that might arise from a cross-curricular theme such as Environmental Education.

First and foremost, a topic must be coherent. Without detailed planning, or if too many elements are included, fragmentation and incoherence will invariably result. A cross-curricular topic will include aspects of a variety of subject areas but it is certainly not necessary to include all areas of the curriculum in any one topic. Indeed it would be foolish to attempt to 'drag in' those subjects which have no meaningful links. It is very likely that a single topic will cover one or more curriculum areas, for example History or Science, as a particular focus. Other subjects may readily be integrated. Some may not. A well organised curriculum will take account of the differing strengths of a variety of topics across the year with a view to balance and breadth, rather than trying to cover everything on every occasion. The topic webs at the start of each topic reflect this principle.

Secondly, it is important to give thought to the appropriate duration of a topic. Often a theme may become tedious and repetitive when it is perhaps better to move on to new areas while children remain motivated and enthusiastic. A shift in emphasis might be sufficient: the broad topics outlined in this book suggest various sub-topics which may be developed.

Thirdly, it is necessary to take account of all elements of children's learning when planning topic work. While content is important (drawing on the knowledge and understanding of various subject areas), so too are other elements of learning such as the acquisition of concepts, skills and attitudes.

Finally, due consideration should be given to the particular approach to teaching and learning which is to be adopted. The most important basis for this in Environmental Education is task-based learning, derived from children's direct experiences and investigations of their surroundings both inside and outside the classroom.

However you choose to integrate Environmental Education into your classroom work, you will find that **Blueprints** *Environmental Education* will give you structured ideas for planning and teaching children in a clear, practical, flexible and enjoyable way.

Matrix of topics and their location in the areas of study of curriculum guidelines for Environmental Education

Sub-topic	Areas of Study in the National Curriculum						
	Climate	Soils, Rocks, Minerals	Water	Materials, Resources, Energy	Plants and Animals	People and Communities	Buildings, Industrialisation, Waste
Weather	●	○	○		○	○	
Farms	○	●	○		●	○	
Ponds	○		●		●		
Energy		○	○	●	○	○	○
Trees	○	○	○	○	●	○	
Food	○	○	○	○	●	●	
Waste		○	○	○		○	●
Work				○		●	○
Oceans	○		●	○	○	○	○

Key ● Principal location ○ Part coverage

9

Topic index

	Oceans	Work	Waste	Food	Trees	Energy	Ponds	Farms	Weather
Climate/Habitat	✓			✓	✓		✓	✓	✓
Plants	✓		✓	✓		✓	✓	✓	✓
Animals	✓		✓	✓		✓	✓	✓	✓
Buildings	✓	✓				✓			
Water	✓		✓	✓	✓	✓	✓	✓	✓
Pollution	✓					✓	✓		✓
Waste	✓	✓				✓			
Business/Trade		✓		✓					
Power/Fuels		✓	✓			✓			
Leisure		✓							
Soil/rocks			✓	✓				✓	✓
Recycling			✓						
Farms				✓					
Keeping healthy				✓					
Forests/Woods					✓				
Meat						✓			
Change							✓		
Work								✓	
Seasons								✓	✓
Machines						✓		✓	
Food			✓					✓	

Use this index to see how the main topics in the book can resource a wider range of common primary topics.

Matrix of topics and links with national curriculum core and foundation subjects

	English	Maths	Science	History	Geog	D&T	PE	Music	Art	RE
Weather KS1	✓	✓	✓		✓	✓	✓	✓		✓
Weather KS2	✓		✓		✓	✓			✓	
Farms KS1	✓	✓	✓		✓			✓	✓	
Farms KS2	✓	✓	✓	✓	✓				✓	
Ponds KS1	✓	✓	✓		✓		✓		✓	
Ponds KS2	✓	✓	✓	✓	✓	✓	✓	✓		
Energy KS1	✓	✓	✓	✓		✓	✓		✓	
Energy KS2	✓	✓	✓	✓	✓	✓	✓			
Trees KS1	✓	✓	✓	✓	✓		✓	✓	✓	
Trees KS2	✓	✓	✓		✓				✓	✓
Food KS1	✓	✓	✓		✓					✓
Foods KS2	✓	✓	✓	✓	✓			✓		
Waste KS1	✓	✓	✓			✓	✓	✓	✓	
Waste KS2	✓	✓	✓	✓	✓	✓			✓	
Work KS1	✓	✓	✓	✓			✓	✓		
Work KS2	✓	✓	✓	✓	✓		✓		✓	✓
Oceans KS1	✓	✓	✓		✓				✓	✓
Oceans KS2	✓	✓	✓		✓	✓	✓			

Note Other cross-curricular themes, such as Health Education, Economic and Industrial Understanding and Citizenship also permeate topics where appropriate.

WEATHER

National curriculum links

Principal location in the National Curriculum

- Climate

Other areas covered by topic

- Water ● Plants and Animals ● People and Communities ● Soils, Rocks, Minerals

Context of study

- Local to global concerns

Suggested sub-topics and their location in areas of study of curriculum guidelines for Environmental Education

Sub-topic	Areas of Study in the National Curriculum						
	Climate	Soils, Rocks, Minerals	Water	Materials, Resources, Energy	Plants and Animals	People and Communities	Buildings, Industrialis-ation, Waste
Acid rain	●	○	●		○	○	○
Global warming	●	○	●	○	●	●	○
Global habitats	●	○	●	○	●	●	
Pollution	●	○	●	○	○	○	○

Key ● Principal location ○ Part coverage

English

- Personal reflections on weather
- Poems and creative writing
- Good and bad weather /hazardous aspects of weather
- Qualitative weather diary
- Weather bulletin/newspaper
- Word puzzles/weather vocabulary
- Folklore and weather sayings
- Debates on controversial issues
- Writing about world habitats
- Imaginative weather conditions

Science, Design and Technology

- Weather station/observations/recordings
- Making weather instruments
- Physical properties of air, light, water
- Acid rain/air pollution
- Weather on other planets

WEATHER – cross-curricular links

Art

- Painting ideal and imaginary weather
- Thunderstorm pictures
- 3-D rainbow
- Cloud printing
- Photographs
- Posters on global warming
- Weather symbol patterns

Health Education

- Shivering, sweating – adjusting to weather extremes
- Clothing for heat and cold
- Illnesses associated with weather and climate

Geography

- The global problem of acid rain – causes, solutions
- Greenhouse effect/global warming
- Global habitats
- Adaptation
- Warm-blooded/cold-blooded creatures

Basics to be developed throughout the topic

Concepts

- Weather as a scientific phenomenon that can be measured, recorded, predicted
- Weather as part of global climate
- Changes in weather and climate
- The importance of weather and climate to all forms of life on Earth, including human life
- Weather and mood – the aesthetic dimension

Attitudes

- Appreciation of, and care and concern for, the environment and life within it
- Care and concern for conservation of resources
- Respect for empirical evidence and scientific facts

Environmental issues

- Climatic effects on vegetation and all forms of life
- Effects of pollution on climate and on water supply
- Water conservation and problems of water supply

STARTING POINTS

- Talk about the aesthetic aspects of weather – the weather and our moods. Think and talk about how the weather affects our feelings – the personal dimension.

- Collect instruments for measuring and recording the weather, and materials for making your own instruments.

- Set up a weather station. Teach skills of measurement, prediction, recording, forecasting.

- Make a collection of stories which have aspects of weather as a central theme (storms, snow, etc.), particularly those of distant lands which will lead into sub-topics on world habitats.

- The topic is best started at the beginning of a school year, so that observations and recordings can be made over an extended period of time. First-hand experiences of seasonal changes in weather patterns are essential for a worthwhile topic. Daily recordings can continue throughout the year without taking up vast amounts of time. Cross-curricular development and sub-topics can be undertaken at appropriate stages throughout the year.

ENGLISH ACTIVITIES
C1–2

1 Start when there is an interesting or dramatic occurrence in the weather, perhaps a thunderstorm, a ferociously windy day, a dense fog or an early frost. Encourage the children to talk about the experience and write down words to describe it. How does it make them feel? Do they enjoy what they see? Discussion should reveal interestingly different perspectives and personal views. To some a thunderstorm may be threatening, scary, frightening; to others it may be exciting, dramatic, thrilling.

2 Ask the children to write poems and personal reflections based on these discussions and experiences. Such personal involvement is very important as it raises awareness of weather, its pleasures and problems, which we often take for granted.

3 Ask the children to write an account of good and bad aspects of the weather in our country. Once again, this activity is designed to raise awareness of how weather affects people's lives.

WEATHER

The Good . . .

We can lie in the sun and play games outdoors.

Rain feels cool on a hot day.
It keeps plants alive and supplies water for us.

Snow is fun for games.

We can fly kites in the wind.

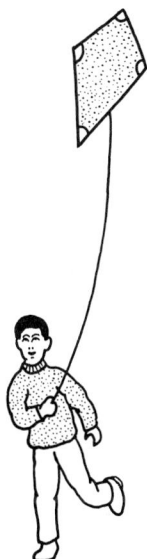

The Bad . . .

Icy roads cause motor accidents,

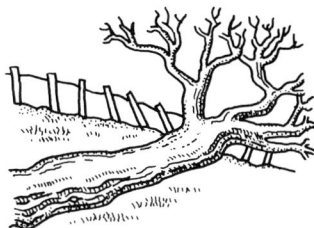

Lightning strikes and may kill.

Pipes burst in freezing temperatures.

Strong winds cause damage to trees and buildings.

4 Divide the class into groups and ask each group to study the effects of weather on the work of different people in the community. For example, there could be study of the fire service, hospital casualty department, park keepers, farmers, shopkeepers, road cleaners and the Electricity and Water Boards.

Wherever possible, interview people concerned and find out to what extent weather affects their day to day routines. Each group should report back so that a wide-ranging overview of 'Weather and our community' can be built up.

5 Help the children keep a qualitative diary of the weather. Again, feelings and impressions have a valuable role to play alongside more scientific recordings. The diary could include a daily written account of the weather, personal reflections on this, drawings, photographs, and reference to any event of significance that has occurred as a result of, or been affected by, weather conditions.

6 With the children, publish a weather report or newsletter for the rest of the school to read. This could be a weekly bulletin containing extracts from diaries about weather events of the week, drawings, poems, facts and figures, and a forecast for the coming week.

7 Help the children build up a vocabulary of weather which they will be able to use for qualitative, imaginative writing and which will be essential for scientific investigations.

8 **Copymaster 1** (Weather words) is a crossword designed to explain or reinforce weather words. Necessary vocabulary to be introduced and used with children will include the names of various elements of the weather (snow, frost, wind, ice, hail, fog, cloud types, etc.), the language of weather forecasting (for example, cold fronts, warm fronts, low and high air pressure), the names of weather station instruments (thermometer, barometer, rain gauge, anemometer, hygrometer) and topical words relating to world issues such as acid rain, the greenhouse effect, global warming and the ozone layer. All of these can be the subject of puzzles and vocabulary exercises.

9   Help the children find out about weather folklore and sayings: for example,

'Red sky at night, shepherd's delight,
Red sky in the morning, shepherd's warning.'

'Wet before seven, fine before eleven.'

Make up an illustrated book of such predictions. Encourage the children to ask older people whether, in their experience, such sayings are true. Test them.

10   Organise classroom debates on controversial climatic issues, for example 'The world is getting to be a warmer place'. Present arguments for and against.

11   Consider weather in other parts of the world. **Copymaster 2** (Through the icebergs) is a simple maze and vocabulary puzzle, which asks children to plot the path of the polar bear through the ice to find food. Ask the children to think of words associated with polar lands and to write one word on each iceberg. Ask them to colour the icebergs which have names in blue and icebergs which have describing words in red. This activity is a useful complement to studies of distant lands (see Geography activities, page 21).

12   Ask the children to write imaginative stories about changing the weather. What would they do if they could make any changes they desired? Ask them to illustrate their stories. Use the stories as a basis for discussion. For example, what would it really be like to live in a world of permanent sunshine or snow?

Would a world of permanent sunshine be ideal?

SCIENCE, DESIGN AND TECHNOLOGY ACTIVITIES   C3–6

1   Set up a weather station. This may be a commercially produced Stephenson screen, or your own collection of instruments secured in suitable places.

Teach children how to use a maximum and minimum thermometer, hygrometer, barometer, rain gauge, anemometer or wind vane. Numerous books are available for consultation on the science of weather

recording, and educational suppliers produce a wide range of instruments suitable for use in schools. It is important that children learn how to use accurate scientific equipment, but there is also a place for design and construction of home-made weather reading materials.

2   Help the children make a simple barometer (see picture at the bottom of page 17). It will demonstrate that changes in air pressure lead to good or bad weather.

You will need
- A balloon
- A plastic jar with a wide neck
- An elastic band
- Sellotape®
- A drinking straw
- Paper and pen.

What to do
- Blow up the balloon, then deflate it.
- Cut away a section of the balloon that can be stretched over the neck of the jar.
- Attach it with the elastic band.
- Sellotape® the straw on to the balloon over the top of the jar.
- Place the jar against a wall.
- Attach a sheet of paper to the wall behind it so that the straw points to the middle of the paper.

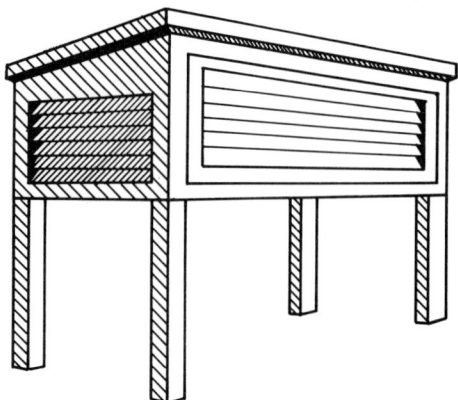

Stephenson screens are available in build-it-yourself kit form. They have the advantage of concealing instruments in a lockable, purpose-built container.

Five main instruments are needed for recording the weather.

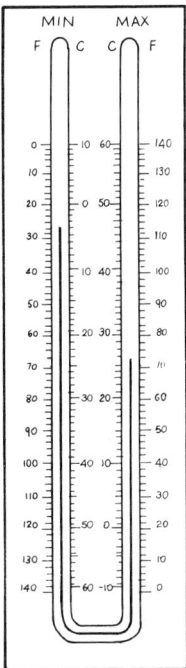

MIN	MAX			DRY	WET	

A maximum and minimum thermometer measures the day's highest and lowest temperatures.

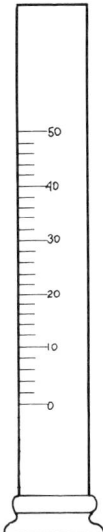

A rain gauge tells how much rain has fallen.

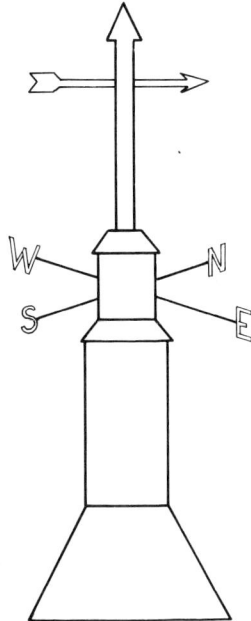

A wind vane tells which direction the wind is blowing from.

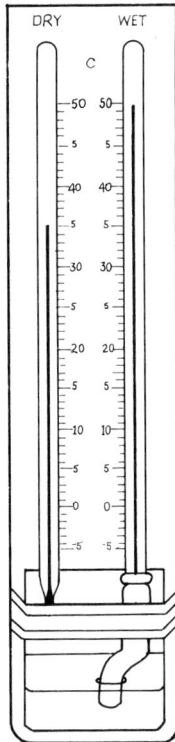

A hygrometer measures the amount of moisture in the air.

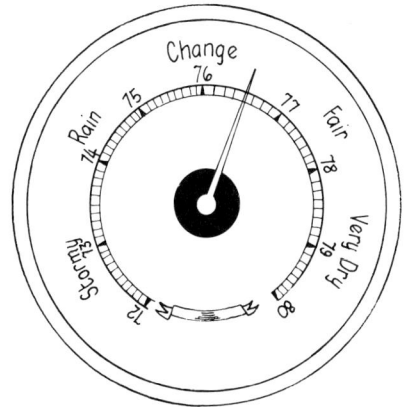

A barometer measures air pressure. Increasing pressures usually means good weather.

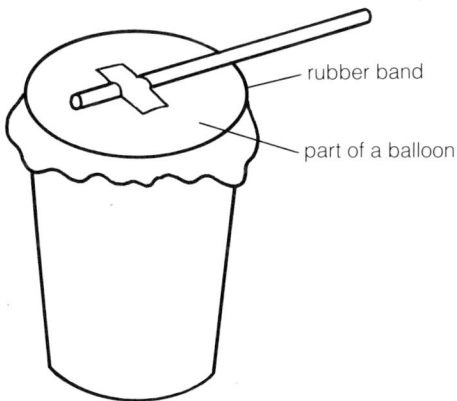

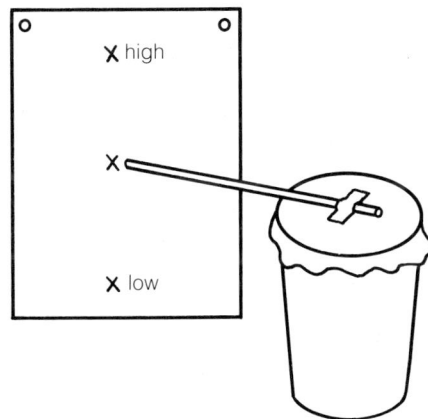

rubber band

part of a balloon

X high

X

X low

• Mark the position of the straw on the paper.

• Observe and record the position of the straw each day. Some days it will point higher, on other days it will be lower. Note what the weather is like as the straw changes position.

What makes it work?

Air pressing on the balloon makes it curve downwards. This makes the end of the straw point upwards. The more air pressure on the balloon, the higher the straw points.

3 Find out in which direction the wind is blowing. Winds are named according to where they come from. With the children, make a wind vane.

You will need
• A square block of wood
• A ruler
• A pen
• A hammer
• Glue
• 2 nails
• A cork
• A pen cap
• A feather
• A compass.

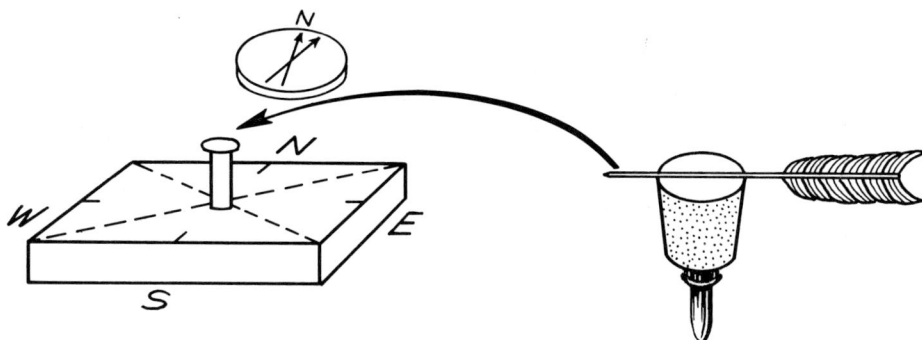

Home-made weather vane. The quill points into the wind.

What to do
- Take the wood block and measure the half-way point on the four sides. Label these North, South, East, West.
- Draw diagonals to find the midpoint on the block. Hammer one nail part-way into the wood at the midpoint. It should protrude about 6 cm.
- With the other nail, make a hole in the cork large enough to push the pen cap into. Glue it in place.
- Next, glue the feather across the top of the cork, laying it carefully across the middle.
- Place the cork, feather and pen cap over the protruding nail. Use the compass to line up North on the wind vane with magnetic North.

Watch the vane! The quill end of the feather will point into the wind so you can see which direction it is coming from.

[4] Help the children discover ways of recording sunshine and clouds, neither of which are easily measured by standard instruments. Count hours of sunshine each day. Give practice in estimation of cloud cover. This is usually done in eighths of the sky, but children can begin by estimating whether more than half or less than half of the sky is covered. The children may then progress to working with quarters and eighths.

Copymaster 3 (Weather record) is a basic recording sheet for use with a school weather station. It can be adapted or expanded to include space for maximum and minimum temperatures, air pressure and humidity. Alternatively, these could be put on separate charts. The record allows for a mixture of symbolic and numerical representation. It provides space for fourteen days of recording. Make enough photocopies of the copymaster for each two weeks of the intended project.

[5] With the children, do experiments and investigations to find out more about the physical properties of air, light and water. Make a rainbow. On a sunny day, take a small dish and fill it with water. Place a mirror in the water so that the sun shines on to it. Hold a piece of white paper above the dish so that the sun is reflected on to it. Rainbow colours should appear on the paper as illustrated below.

[6] Observe glass prisms to see the breaking up of light into rainbow colours.

[7] Use **copymaster 4** (What makes a rainbow?) to teach the correct order of colours of the rainbow, to think about the path of light through a water droplet and to consider what is happening. Children can colour the sheet accurately.

[8] Try and spot a 'moonbow'! On the night of a full moon when it rains shortly after the moon has risen, look carefully at the sky.

[9] Demonstrate to the children how to make rain. *Note:* For safety reasons the teacher should do this experiment.

You will need
- A kettle
- A tin can filled with ice
- Oven gloves or tongs for holding the can.

What to do
- Boil water in the kettle
- Hold the ice-filled can above the steam of the kettle
- Watch home-made rain fall from the bottom of the can.

Making a rainbow

clouds

condensation

Warm air, with lots of water vapour, rises to meet cold air in the sky.

Tiny drops of water collect to make a cloud.

If there is enough water in the clouds, it falls as rain.

streams

evaporation

land

sea

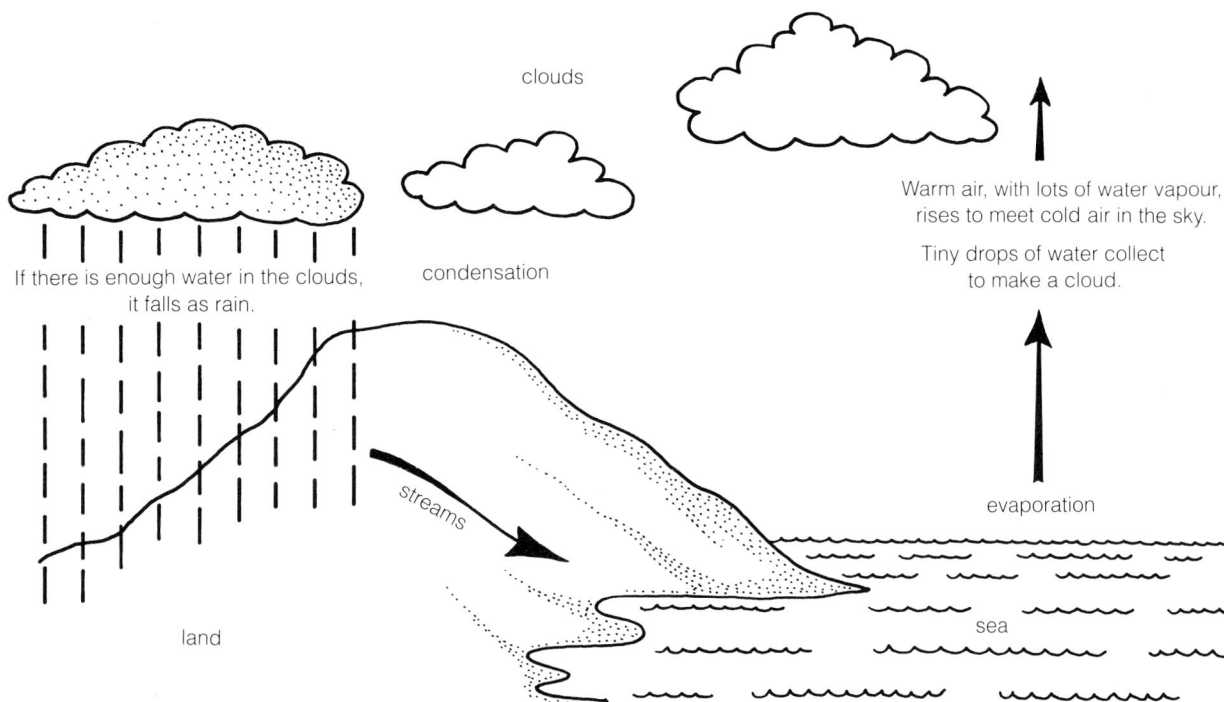

The natural water cycle

10 Relate the above experiment to the natural hydrological (water) cycle, by discussing the equivalent process in it.

11 Use **copymaster 5** (Name that cloud) to help teach the family names of clouds. The three main families are cumulus, cirrus and stratus. The copymaster can be used for an I-spy of clouds. When the children spot the different clouds they should write down the weather which is associated with them. They should also note cloud cover of the sky. This is a useful exercise in making predictions based on recorded information, which is the essence of weather forecasting. To link this with work in English and Art activities, ask the children to write vivid descriptions of various cloud types and paint them as backgrounds to weather pictures.

12 Help the children catch a snowflake.

You will need
- A microscope slide
- Tweezers
- A magnifying glass or microscope
- Spray-on lacquer or plastic.

What to do
- Place the clean slide and the spray in a freezer overnight.
- Remove slide with tweezers (do not touch it or your hands will make it warm!).
- Spray a thin layer of lacquer or plastic on to the slide.
- Put it outside when snow is falling.
- When a snowflake has landed on it, pick up the slide with tweezers and put it in an outdoor spot where it is protected. Leave it for an hour.
- Bring the slide into the classroom, and observe the snowflake's impression under a microscope or magnifier.

Impression of snowflakes on microscope slides

19

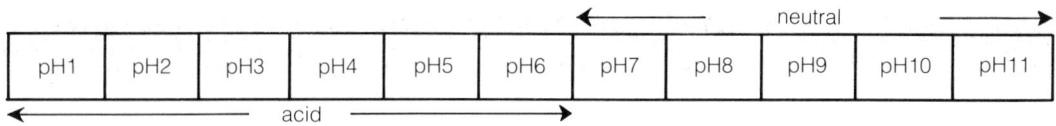

pH1	pH2	pH3	pH4	pH5	pH6	pH7	pH8	pH9	pH10	pH11

← acid →

neutral ← →

pH scale

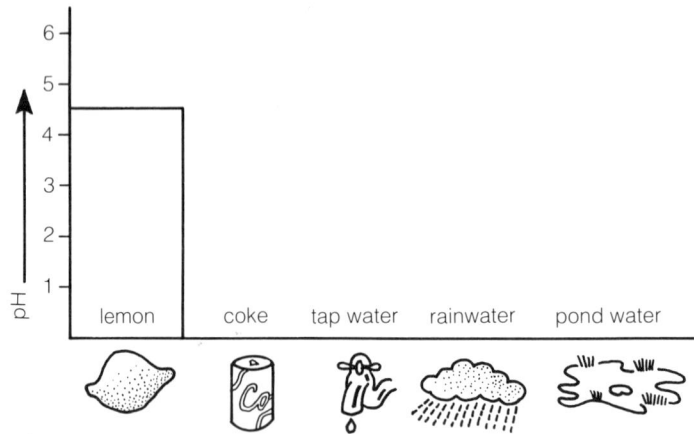

A graph of the acidity of various liquids

13 Help the children find out about acid rain. Use pH testing papers to test the acidity of various liquids, for example lemon juice, tap water, rainwater, cola, water from a pond or stream.

Acidity of rain is measured by its pH value. Pure rain has a value of 5.6. Acid rain is rain with a value below 5.6. Draw graphs to show the results of the investigations.

If too much acidity falls into a pond or lake, living things may not survive. Fish cannot live with a pH value below 4.5.

Ask the children to draw posters and write about the effects of acid rain on our Earth as in the example below.

14 With the children, consider ways to reduce acid rain, and relate the problem to the global issues of greenhouse effect and global warming (see Geography activities, page 21).

15 Consider the weather on other planets of the solar system. This will involve naming other planets and investigating their distances from the Sun. Ask the children to use the information provided on **copymaster 6** to rank planets according to their temperatures. They should rank them in terms of distance from the Sun and compare rankings. They can then plot the temperatures on a graph. Ask them to think about why the weather on Earth is so different from that on other planets. The main reasons are the Earth's distance from the Sun, and our atmosphere. We are not so far away from the Sun that we freeze, and our atmosphere acts as a blanket so that we do not burn up.

Relate this knowledge to the ozone layer and global warming debate.

16 Ask the children to write imaginative stories about 'holiday weather' on other planets. Which planet would they like to visit?

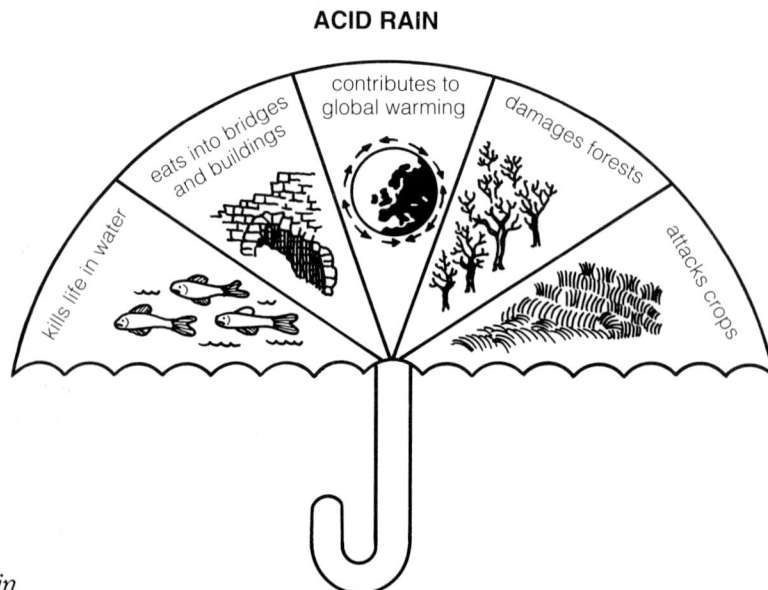

ACID RAIN

Some effects of acid rain

GEOGRAPHY ACTIVITIES

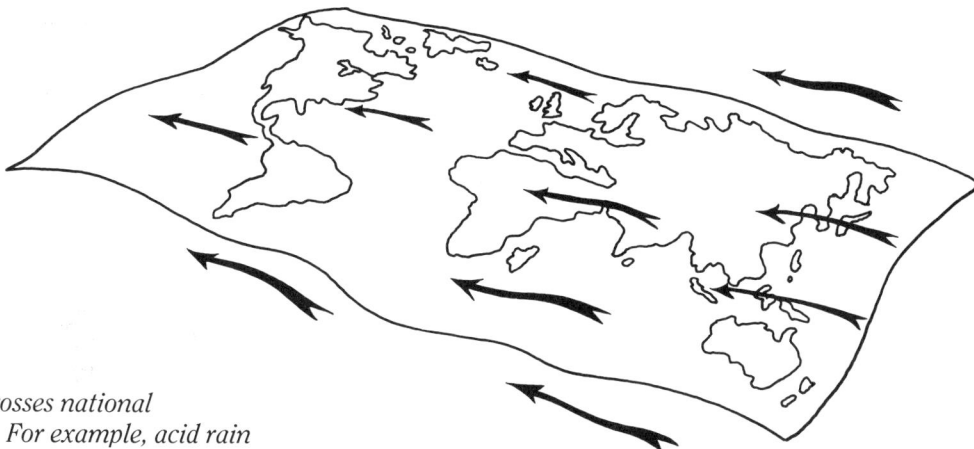

Acid rain crosses national boundaries. For example, acid rain produced in Canada falls in Scandinavia.

1. Investigate causes of and possible solutions to acid rain. Help the children understand that this is a global problem: it comes from chemicals in car exhausts and smoke derived from the burning of fossil fuels. Acid rain is made up of minute particles that can travel long distances in the air, carried along by the wind.

2. Help the children design posters about global air pollution. Encourage readers to 'clean up their act'.

3. Relate acid rain to the problems of the greenhouse effect and global warming.

Pollution → Greenhouse gases → Global warming

Discuss the more pleasant features of having a warmer world, for example doing away with the fur-lined boots and jackets. However, also discuss and encourage children to write about the serious negative features:

- Good farmland turned to deserts
- Water shortages: plants, trees and animals die
- Not enough water for people (or *too much* rain in other areas)
- Melting of ice caps, flooding of land by rising oceans.

4. Undertake sub-topics on global habitats which have extreme weather conditions or those very different from our own, notably hot deserts, cold deserts, polar lands and rain forests. Obtain facts and figures about climate, plants, animals and features of human life in these habitats. Draw comparative graphs of temperature and rainfall statistics to show how climate in these lands is very different from here.

5. Help the children find out how plants and animals adapt to cold, wet, dry or hot conditions. Differentiate between warm-blooded and cold-blooded creatures.

Warm-blooded animals, including humans, other mammals and birds have a body temperature that stays more or less the same, irrespective of the weather.

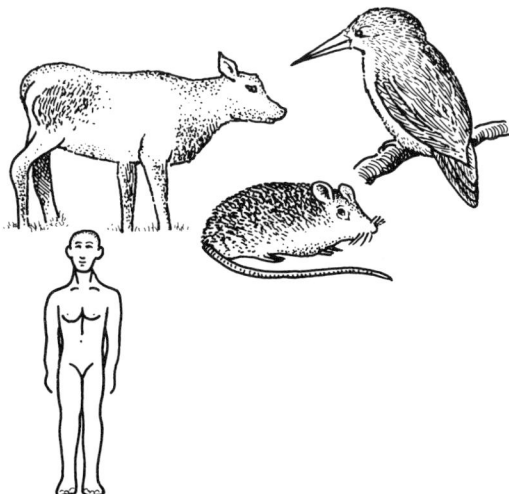

Our blood temperature is steady all through the year.

Cold-blooded animals, e.g. amphibians, reptiles and insects do not have a 'central heating' mechanism. They depend on the weather for their body heat.

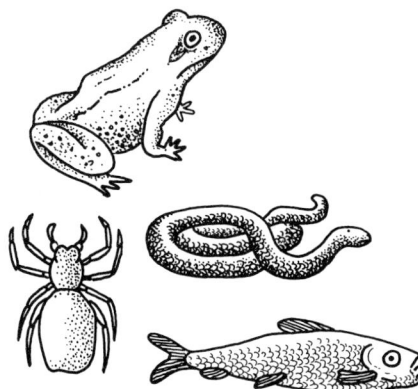

On cold days, they are cold.
On warm days, they are warm and move around more.

6 Ask the children to imagine what would happen if mammals became cold-blooded. They could write an imaginative account about being dependent on the Sun to warm up muscles to enable them to move!

7 Do an experiment to show how hot or cold weather affects a cold-blooded fly (it will not hurt the fly!).

What to do
- Take a fly and place it in a 'bug box' or pot with holes in the lid, so that it has air.
- Put the container in the refrigerator for half an hour, then remove it and observe the fly.
- Is the fly moving more slowly or faster than before it was put in there?
- Release the fly!

HEALTH EDUCATION ACTIVITIES ▶

1 Discuss the processes of shivering and sweating. Adjusting to extremes of weather is not easy for the human body. In very cold temperatures, our muscles have contractions which give off heat to warm us. This happens while we are shivering. In very hot temperatures, on the other hand, sweat pours off us. Heat from the body is carried out as water from sweat glands.

2 Relate the above facts to learning rules for survival in very hot and cold weather. Ask the children to write stories about 'Desert survival', 'Living in the Antarctic', that is fiction informed with scientific fact.

3 Do a sub-topic on clothing appropriate to various climatic conditions. Investigate the properties of insulation and its importance in keeping us fit and well. Take various materials, for example blankets, foil, paper, plastic, sheepskin; wrap them around children and ask them to say how they feel. Demonstrate that if we wear several thin layers, we are warmer than when wearing one thick layer. Discuss the importance of trapping air between layers; some fabrics have this built-in insulation. Submerge pieces of quilted material, fur and sheepskin in water and let the children watch to see if air bubbles rise.

Discuss appropriate winter clothing. Why do we wear hats, gloves and earmuffs?

4 Find out about illnesses that are related to weather and climate. Seasonal Affective Disorder, for example, affects people who are intolerant of low light levels in winter time. Sunstroke and skin cancer are hazards of receiving too much sun. Discuss ways in which we can do our utmost to keep healthy in both winter and summer.

Whew, it's hot!

Brr . . . it's cold!

When it's hot:

1 Do not do strenuous exercise. Muscles give off heat, and you don't need any more.

2 Drink lots of cold water to replace water lost through sweating.

3 Wear a hat to protect your head from the Sun.

When it's cold:

1 Eat lots of food that contains protein, to make more internal heat.

2 Wear a warm hat. Lots of body heat is lost through your head.

3 Take exercise to warm up.

ART ACTIVITIES

1 Ask the children to paint pictures of 'My ideal climate', and imaginary weather conditions, perhaps on other planets.

2 Make thunderstorm pictures. Flashes of silver foil make ideal lightning when stuck on to a painted background of threatening thunder clouds.

3 Help the children cut out and paint an enormous rainbow to suspend across the classroom ceiling, or use as the central feature of a wall frieze. Hang a three-dimensional sun, and rain droplet mobiles. Other weather hangings could be devised and added, to represent fog, snow, wind, and so on.

4 Show the children how to use polystyrene shapes to print clouds on to fabric. Use this fabric as a backcloth for superimposing foil raindrops.

5 Take photographs of weather phenomena: clouds, a rainbow, frost, etc. Display these alongside imaginative writing or scientific records.

6 Ask the children to make posters to persuade others to take individual action to help prevent the greenhouse effect and global warming.

7 Ask the children to design patterns, using repeated weather symbols and to print patterns out of potato or polystyrene blocks.

Patterns using repeated weather symbols

Weather words

CLUES

Across

2　Edge of a warm air mass
4　Its destruction leads to global warming
6　Measures air pressure
8　Results from the splitting of white light
9　Jack of the cold

Down

1　Light rain
3　Follows a cumulonimbus cloud
5　A prediction of weather
7　Stratus cloud on the ground

Through the icebergs

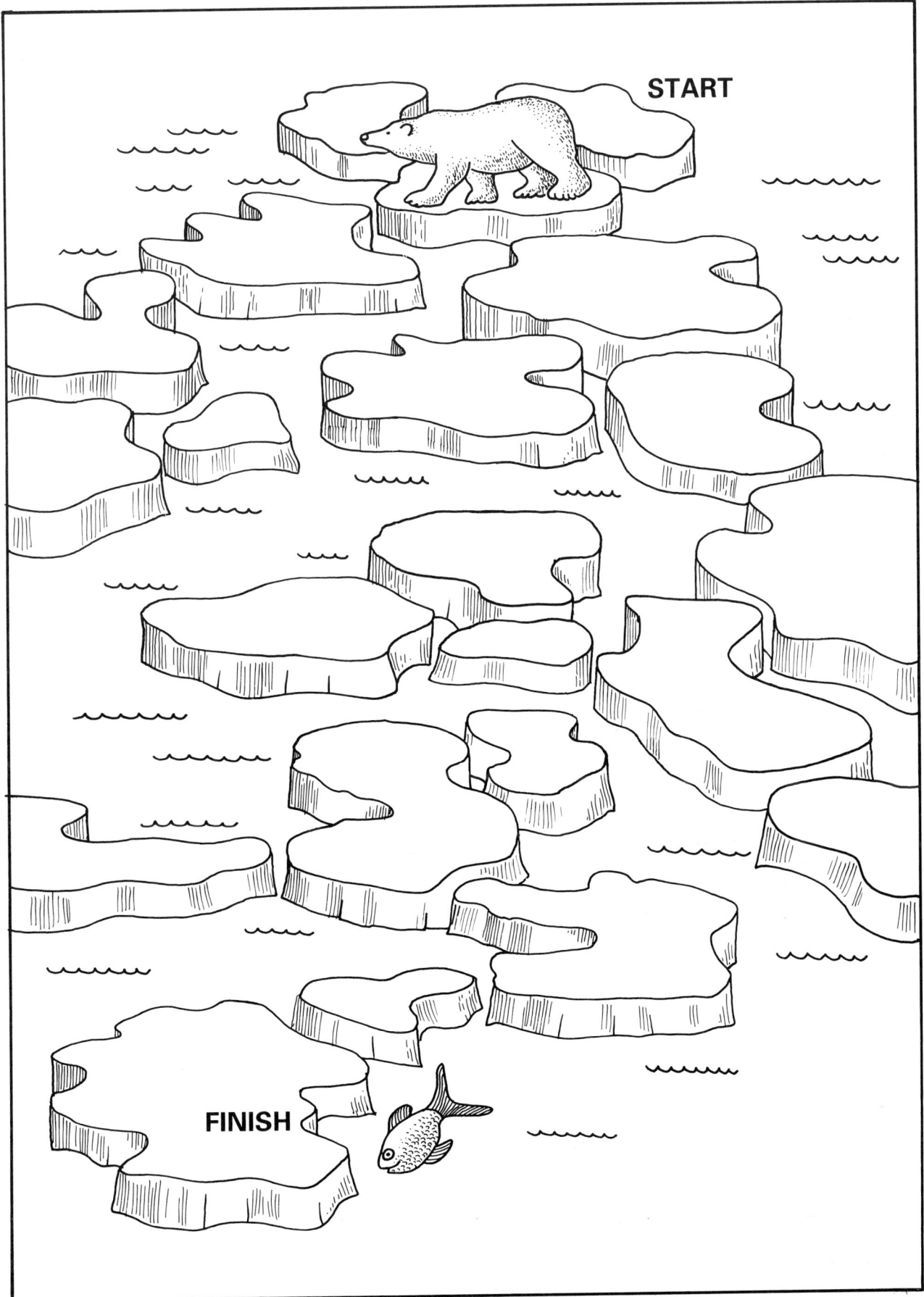

START

FINISH

Weather record

DATE	TEMPERATURE		RAINFALL	CLOUD COVER	WIND SPEED	WIND DIRECTION	OTHER ELEMENTS
	Max	Min					
1							
2							
3							
4							
5							
6							
7							
8							
9							
10							
11							
12							
13							
14							
TOTALS							

What makes a rainbow?

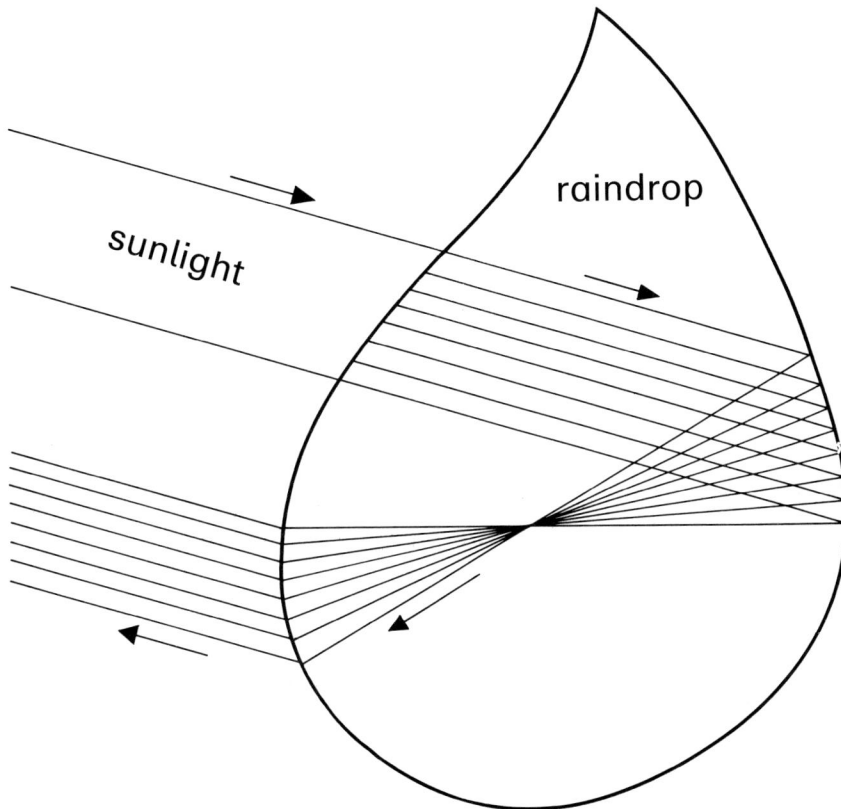

sunlight

raindrop

Trace the path of sunlight through the raindrop. White light is split into 7 colours. Unscramble their names.

1 e r d

2 r e o g n a

3 l e w o l y

4 e e n r g

____

_____

_____

_____

5 u b e l

6 n o i g i d

7 i l e t v o

____

_____

_____

Name that cloud

weather forecast:	weather forecast:
Cloud cover — 8	Cloud cover — 8

weather forecast:	weather forecast:
Cloud cover — 8	Cloud cover — 8

Weather on other planets

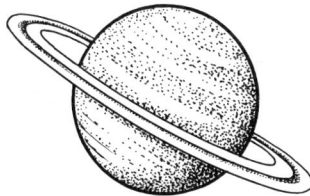

Neptune

Saturn

Uranus

Day time temperatures (approximates)	
Mercury	410° C
Venus	445° C
Earth	14° C
Mars	−125° C
Jupiter	−140° C
Saturn	−180° C
Uranus	−215° C
Neptune	−220° C
Pluto	−230° C

Mercury

Pluto

Venus

Mars

Earth

Jupiter

Why is Earth's weather so different?

FARMS

National curriculum links

Principal location in the National Curriculum

- Soils, Rocks, Minerals ● Plants and Animals

Other areas covered by topic

- Climate ● Water and Water Supplies ● People and Communities

Context of study

- Local to global concerns

Suggested sub-topics and their location in areas of study of curriculum guidelines for Environmental Education

Sub-topic	Areas of Study in the National Curriculum						
	Climate	Soils, Rocks, Minerals	Water	Materials, Resources, Energy	Plants and Animals	People and Communities	Buildings, Industrialisation, Waste
The seasons	●	O	O		●	O	
Life cycles	O	O	O		●	O	
World of work	O	O	O	O		●	O
Machines				●		O	●
Food for health	O	O	O		●	●	

Key   ● Principal location   O Part coverage

30

Geography

- Graphicacy – drawing and interpreting farm maps
- Concept of farm as a system
- Field work skills and techniques
- Seasonal changes – effects of climate, etc.
- Conflicting demands on land use
- Conservation

Mathematics

- Measuring farm buildings and distances between them
- Drawing plans of farm and buildings
- Calculations relating to growth rates of animals and plants, feeding production
- Cow calendars

Science

- Importance of soils
- Soils analysis/testing
- Decomposition
- Field operations
- Germination of seeds
- Growth of animals/plants
- Food chains/webs
- Interdependence of living things

FARMS – cross-curricular links

History

- Origins of breeds
- Historic farming methods
- Change through time – animals/machinery/farmer's tasks
- Visit a farm museum

Art and Craft

- Animal footprints
- Food chain mobiles
- Spinning, weaving, dyeing of sheep's wool
- Animal drawings based on field observations and sketches
- Collage/paintings of animals in bygone days
- Painting/needlecraft – a farm through the seasons
- Smocking
- Corn dolly making

English

- Creative writing
- Reportive writing – the visit
- Interview with farmer
- Listening to and reading poems and stories
- Vocabulary of the farm

Basics to be developed throughout the topic

Concepts

- Relationships between human life and the land
- Patterns in farming practice
- Relationships in farming practice, for example between arable and livestock elements
- A farm is a system with key inputs and outputs

Attitudes

- Appreciation of and care for living things
- Care and respect for the Earth on which we depend

Environmental issues

- Effects of climate on plant and animal life
- Management of resources
- Conservation
- Concern for living things and the Earth on which they depend

STARTING POINTS

- If at all possible, take the children on a farm visit. The National Curriculum requirements for Geography include an emphasis on field work and investigatory skills. A key element of environmental education is educating *in* or *through* the environment, that is using the environment as a resource.

Select a suitable farm depending on the type that you intend to use for the topic (small mixed farm, arable farm, dairy farm). Some of the key questions to consider are: Is the farmer willing to give up time to show round a party of children? Is the farm a safe place for the children? Will there be opportunities to study animals at close quarters? What is the main focus of the topic/sub-topics (animals, food, crops, machinery, soils)?

Checklist for topic planning
- Selecting an appropriate farm
- Preliminary visit by teacher
- Details of cost, transport, insurance, staffing of visit
- Information to and permission from parents
- Preparing the children: farm safety and Country Code
- What will the children do? (field work activities)
- Equipment needed on visit
- Developing the topic. Collect secondary resources if a visit is not possible.

GEOGRAPHY ACTIVITIES

C7–8

1 **Copymaster 7** (What goes in must come out) introduces the basic geographical idea of a *system*. The farm as a system has certain inputs and outputs. Discuss what are the basic needs of a farmer. Consider what would happen if we had no rain and sunshine. What is the importance of sunlight and the hydrological cycle? Discuss the range of goods that are sold from a farm. The children can colour the drawings and have a colour-coded key for labels: they can colour inputs in green and outputs in red. Lines can be turned into arrows to show inputs and outputs as illustrated on page 33.

2 Study life on a farm throughout the year. This can be done by interviewing the farmer on a visit, or from secondary resources. Ideally, the children should visit the same farm in different seasons of the year.

Copymaster 8 can be adapted for different uses. The title could remain general, or could be related to a specific enterprise, for example 'A year in the life of a sheep farmer'. The children can draw activities in the spaces and/or add key words of description. Further lines can be drawn to make a more precise division between months of the year, if required.

INPUTS

Natural
- sun
- rain
- soils

OUTPUTS

Animals
- calves to market
- chickens, etc.

Animal products
- milk to dairy
- eggs to market

THE FARM

Human impact
- management
- fertilisers
- pesticides
- machinery

Crops
- potatoes to market
- hay, silage for animal feed, etc.

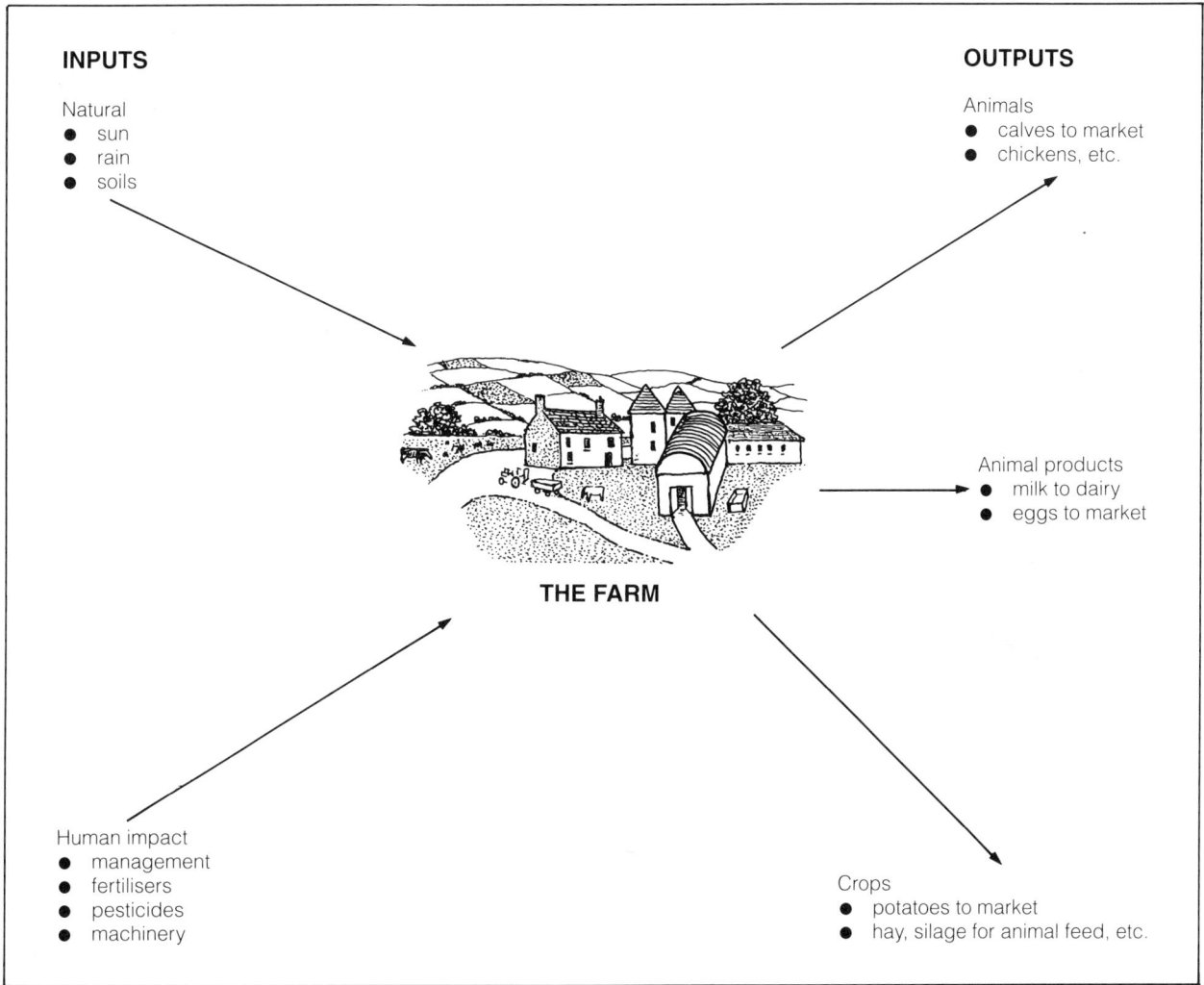

With the children, find out what species of wild plants are found on a farm and what wild animals are often found visiting or making their homes there. What attracts them? Help the children make a study of specific habitats: trees, hedgerows, ponds, streams, grasslands, buildings. Are these wild plants and animals a help or hindrance to the farmer?

Discover more about conservation on farmland, the importance of the Wildlife and Countryside Act and protecting natural habitats.

'Weeds' are wild plants that are growing in an inappropriate place. They use up valuable soil nutrients and take up space that other crops need.

Birds are beautiful to look at, but can be pests on a farm. They may eat valuable seeds in the ground or attack young animals.

Develop the children's skills of graphicacy, including practice in field measuring and the use of scale and keys. Obtain a map of the farm if possible. Ask the children to draw simple maps, not necessarily to scale, to show how the land is used and the location of buildings, ponds, hedges, etc.

MATHEMATICS ACTIVITIES

1 Help the children measure the farm buildings. Draw a simple scale plan of the farm house and main buildings. Find out from a map or from measurements, the area of the fields of the farm. Calculate the total area.

A wide range of calculations can be done on the number of animals kept, space per animal (indoors and outdoors), feed quantities, growth rates and reproduction rates.

2 Investigate a year in the life of a cow. The amount of milk a dairy cow produces varies throughout the year. She does not give any milk until after the first calf is born. Ask the children to make a calendar showing the milk yield over a year.

Charts can be drawn to show how fast animals grow. Growth rates can be related to feed quantities.

Cow: Jays Henry May
Breed: Jersey
Age: 2 years

Month	Diary	Milk yield
October	1st calf born	24
November		22
December		20
January	Mated with bull	18
February	Pregnant	12
March	Pregnant	14
April	Pregnant	14
May	Pregnant	12
June	Pregnant	10
July	Pregnant	6
August	Cow is 'dry'	0
September	'Steaming up'	0
October	2nd calf born	22

Note: Milk yield is the amount produced in one day of the month, measured in kilograms.

A new born piglet weighs around 1.3 kg.

A young pig, 10 weeks old, weighs 20 kg.

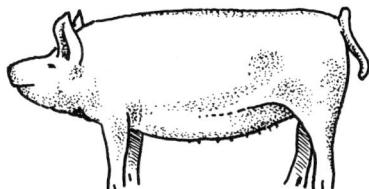

At $7\frac{1}{2}$ months, the pig weighs around 130 kg.

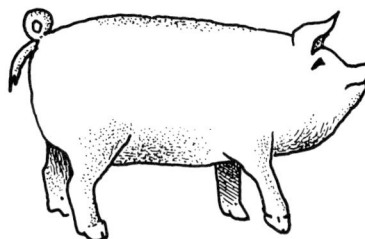

A mature pig aged 1 year weighs around 170 kg.

ENGLISH ACTIVITIES

C9

1 Ask the children to complete the chart on **copymaster 9** (Animal names) showing the names given to male and female animals at various stages in their growth. Explain to the children that castrated males have had an operation which prevents them reproducing.

2 Organise a class debate on controversial issues such as battery farming, hunting, and the use of chemicals in fertilisers and pesticides. Children can present arguments for and against such key issues, backed up by opinions gained from talking to friends, farmers, and their parents.

Good ar bad use of farmland?

3 Teach the Country Code, discussing the importance of each rule. This has useful cross-links with Citizenship and Personal and Social Education.

When out in the countryside, always follow the rules below.

The country code
1. Enjoy the countryside and respect its life and worth.
2. Guard against all risk of fire.
3. Fasten all gates.
4. Keep your dogs under close control.
5. Keep to public paths across farmland.
6. Use gates and stiles to cross fences, hedges and walls.
7. Leave livestock, crops and machinery alone.
8. Take your litter home.
9. Help to keep all water clean.
10. Protect wildlife, plants and trees.
11. Take special care on country roads.
12. Make no unnecessary noise.

4 Ask the children to do creative writing based on the farmer's year, for example on going out to feed the sheep by torchlight in the dark depths of a winter night-time blizzard.

Ask the children to tell a story from an animal's point of view, for example 'My life as a duck', 'Thoughts while chewing the cud', and 'Home in a stable'.

A wide range of stories and poems about farm animals and farm life is available to read.

HISTORY ACTIVITIES

1 Find out about and discuss the origins of farm animals and their breeds. Over hundreds of years farm animals have changed shape and colour through breeding. This will link into studies of present day breeds.

2 **Copymaster 10** (The old and the new) is a matching exercise to reinforce the basic historical concept of change through time. Children can link the drawings of modern farm animals with those from which they have developed. With the help of books and reference material, pictures can be coloured accurately as an aid to identification and classification.

Sheep and cattle were first tamed thousands of years ago. Hunters would follow grazing herds, gradually coming to be in control of them.

As animals were tamed, the larger ones were used for herdsmen to ride on. Help the children find out about the most common present day breeds of farm animals.

3 Investigate the possibility of visiting a farm museum. Find out how customs, equipment, machinery and clothing have changed over the years.

36

A shepherd's smock

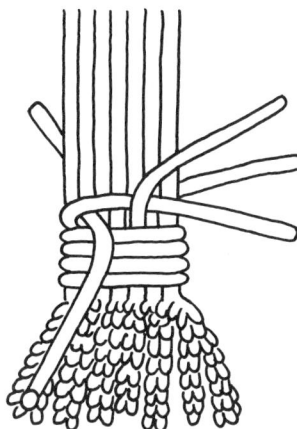

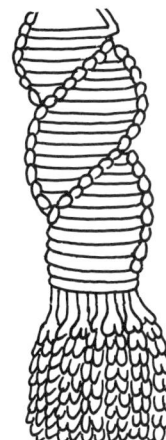

Regional variations led to a number of traditional designs of corn dollies: symbols of fertility.

SCIENCE ACTIVITIES

C11 –12

original leaf

after decomposition in soil

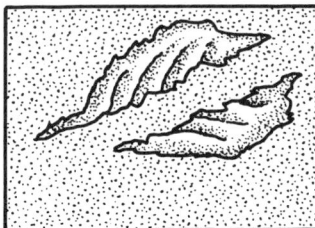

After decomposition in soil, what area is left?

1 Investigate the importance of soils. Key questions are: What is soil? Why does a farmer need to use fertilisers?

Collect soil samples from various locations. Let the children feel the texture, look at its contents both with the naked eye and under a microscope.

2 Do an experiment to illustrate the key concept of decomposition. Put a sample of damp soil in a plastic bag (each child can set up his/her own experiment, or the children can work in groups). They should take a

dead leaf, draw around it on graph paper and calculate its area. They should then bury the leaf in the soil in the bag, fasten it securely and leave it in a cool dark place for 4–6 weeks. After that time, they should open the bag and investigate what portion of the original leaf is left. In some cases, the leaf may have disappeared altogether, a vivid portrayal of the decomposition process. This can be related to natural cycles, the importance of soil nutrients and the varying quality of soils.

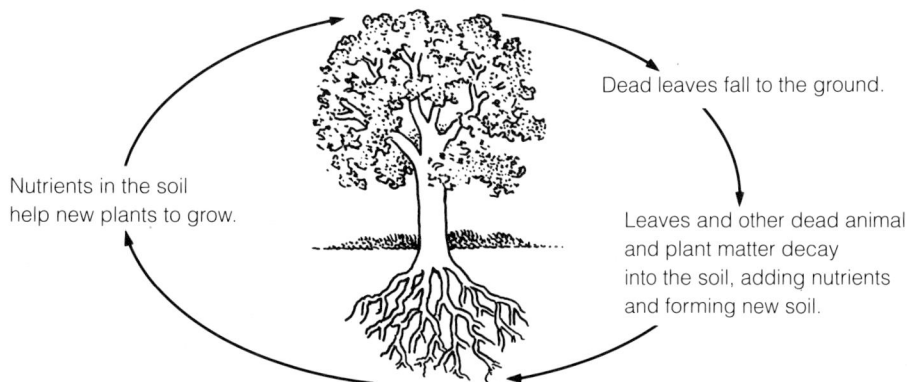

Dead leaves fall to the ground.

Nutrients in the soil help new plants to grow.

Leaves and other dead animal and plant matter decay into the soil, adding nutrients and forming new soil.

3 Introduce the concepts of acidity and alkalinity. Use pH testing papers or soil testing kits to test the acid content of soils from a variety of locations. At this level, it is sufficient for children to have an understanding that some plants prefer to grow in acid soils and others in alkaline soils. It is important for a farmer to know the chemical composition of the soil and how soils may be treated.

4 Germinate seeds, such as wheat. Set up classroom experiments to investigate optimum conditions for growth. How critical is light, temperature, space, water, etc?

5 The crossword on **copymaster 11** (Words from the soil) aims to reinforce key words associated with soil science and help the children make connections between soils and farming.

6 **Copymaster 12** (Food chains) is designed to develop an understanding of food chains and the classification of animals into herbivores, carnivores and omnivores. At a basic level, the children can link animals with the foods they eat. Animals or plants can then be drawn or cut out and arranged into food chains and more complex food webs. Creatures can also be arranged into sets depending on food preferences.

ART AND CRAFT ACTIVITIES

1 Help the children make food chain mobiles. Draw on card, paint and cut out farm animals and their food choices. Link them together and suspend them from the classroom ceiling.

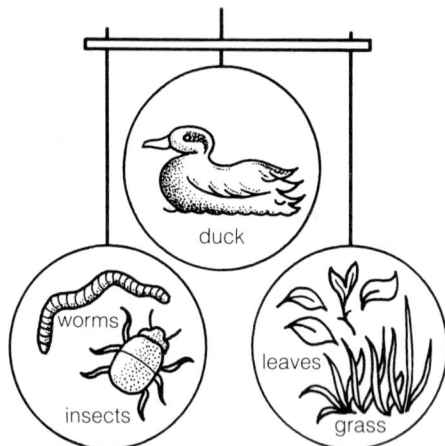

A simple food chain mobile

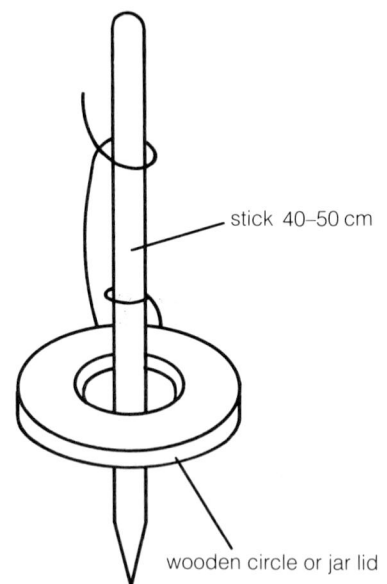

2 Collect some sheep's wool from the hedgerows. Perhaps the farmer will give you some at shearing time. Some farmers are willing to sell whole fleeces. Ask the children to write about the feel and texture of the wool. Clean it, spin it, weave it, experiment with natural plant dyes, investigate how wool is commercially processed in factories. All of these processes can be accomplished in the classroom.

A simple spindle can be made with a stick of wood 40–50 cm long, a circle of wood or jar lid with a hole in the centre and a piece of knitting wool. Tie the wool around the stick above the circle. Pass it under the

circle, around the stick and back up again. Tie a half-hitch three-quarters of the way up the stick. Raw sheep's wool is then twisted on to the end of the knitting wool.

Hold the ball of sheep's wool in one hand. Spin the stick. Let the stick go and allow it to spin slowly round. Gradually ease out more sheep's wool from the ball.

3 Ask the children to print some footprints. They can draw the shape of footprints of various animals onto polystyrene, then cut them out and print on to paper or material to show imaginary trails across fields.

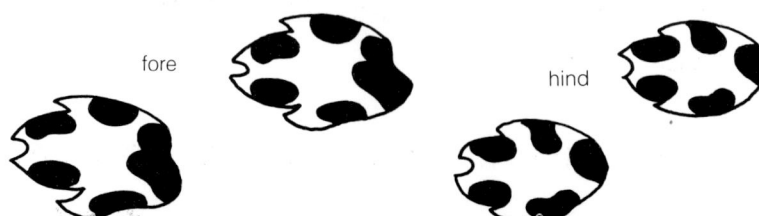

Footprints of a fox

What goes in must come out

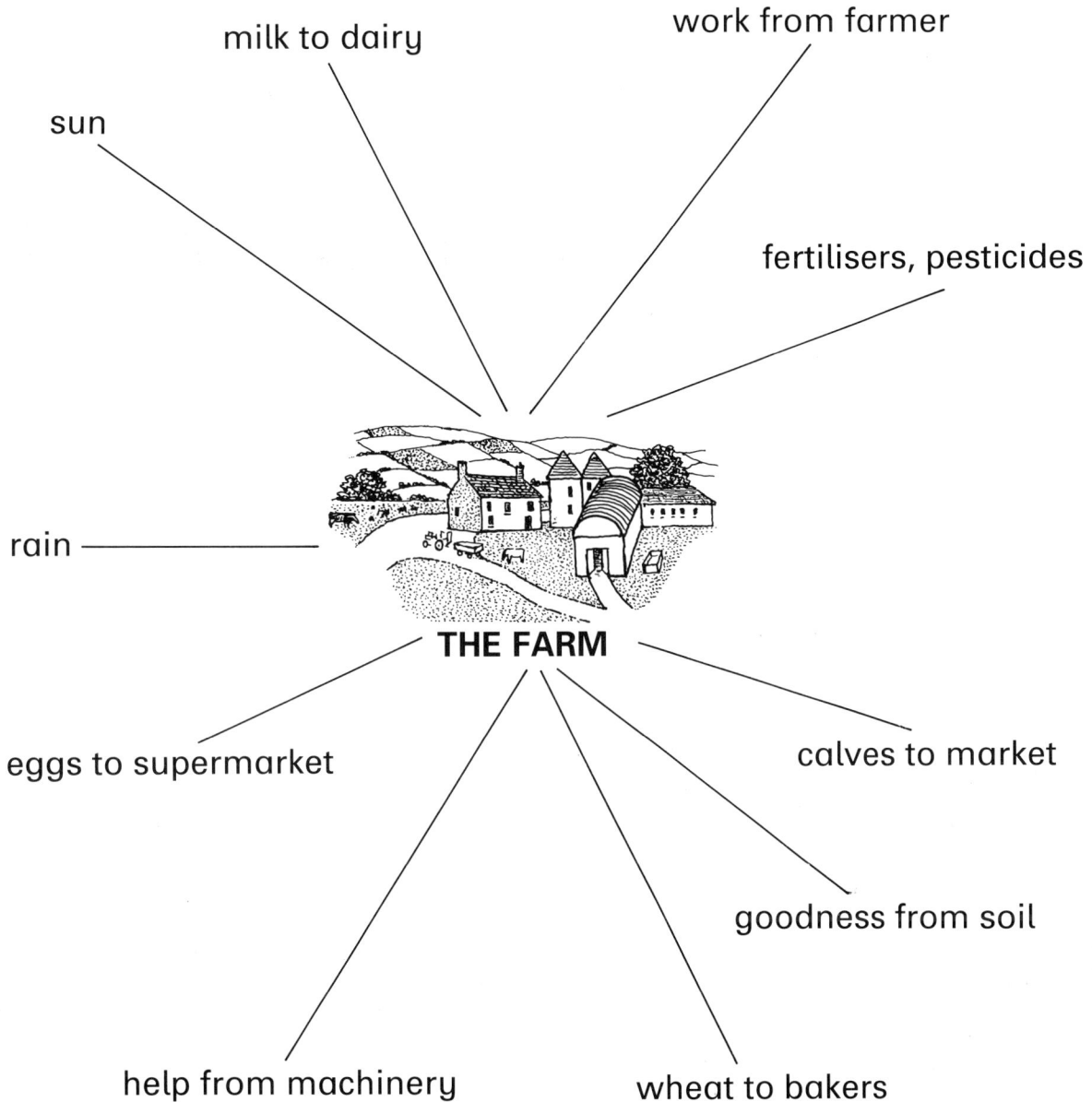

milk to dairy

work from farmer

sun

fertilisers, pesticides

rain ————————

THE FARM

eggs to supermarket

calves to market

goodness from soil

help from machinery

wheat to bakers

What goes **in** to the farm to help animals and crops to grow?
(Colour these words in green.)

What comes **out** of the farm for people and animals to eat?
(Colour these words in red.)

Turn the lines into arrows to show what is going in and what is coming out.

A year in the life of a farmer

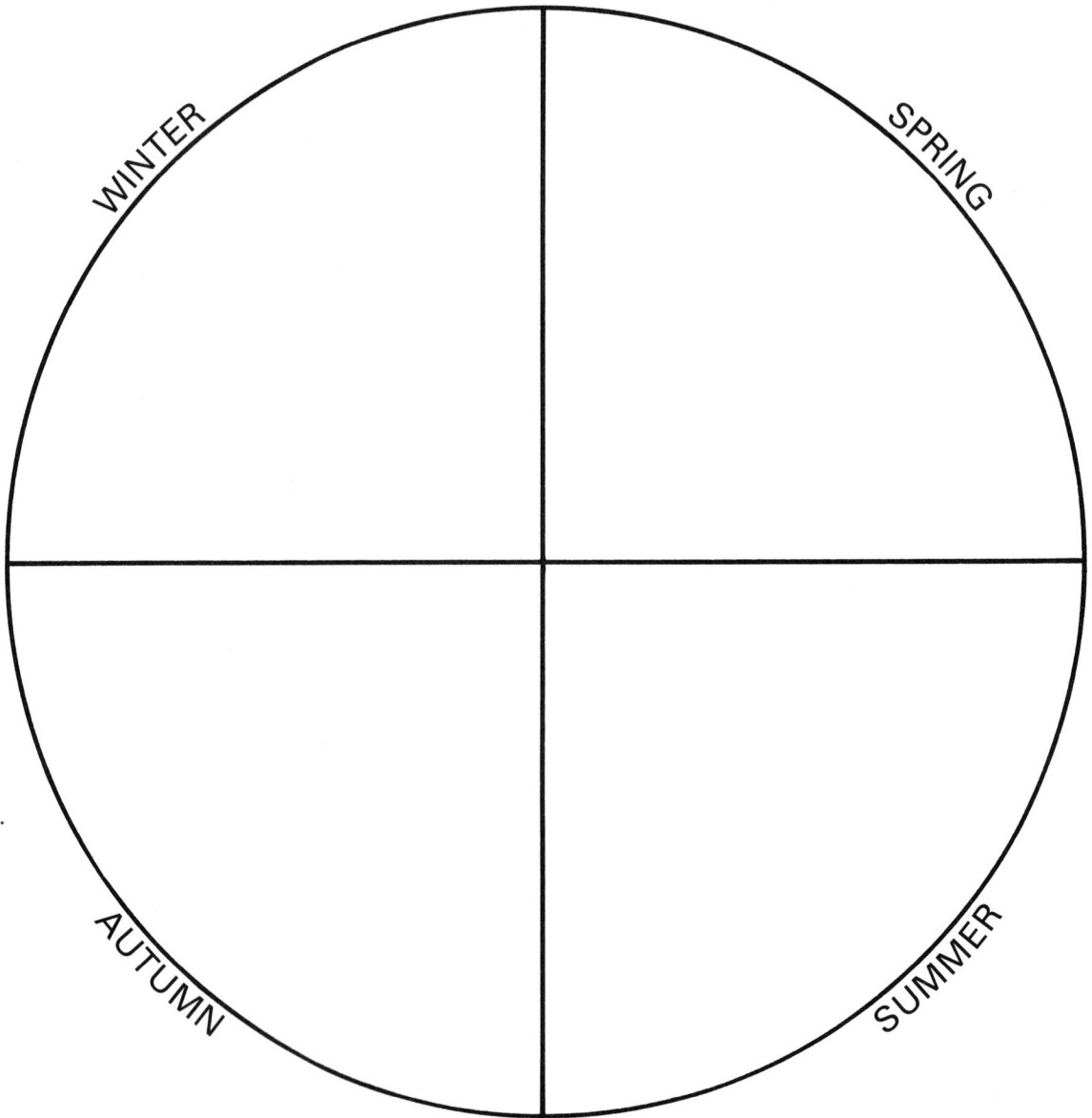

WINTER

SPRING

AUTUMN

SUMMER

Animal names

	Baby	Young female	Castrated male	Adult male	Adult female
Chickens					
Sheep					
Pigs					
Cattle					

Write these words in the correct space to complete the chart:

Bull   Teg   Cockerel

Ewe   Sow   Capon   Cow

Piglet

Pullet   Wether   Hog   Chick

Hen   Gilt

Bullock   Boar

Heifer

Lamb   Calf

Ram

41

The old and the new

Draw a line to link the animals of today with those of yesterday.

ON THE FARM TODAY   WILD CREATURES OF DAYS GONE BY

wild auroch

wild mountain sheep

wild jungle fowl

wild boar

wild mallard duck

Colour your drawings accurately. Over thousands of years, farm animals have changed shape and colour.

Words from the soil

CLUES

Across
1   Family of toadstool decomposers
3   Breakdown of dead matter into the soil
6   pH 8
8   Neither acid nor alkaline

Down
1   Unit of farmer's land
2   Useful invertebrate decomposer
4   Valuable farm plants
5   In search of prey to eat
7   Added to fields to increase alkalinity

Food chains

Who eats what?   Who eats whom?

Match the animals to the food they eat by linking them with arrows.
Who is a herbivore?   Who is a carnivore?
Who eats both plant and animal food?

worms

barley

grass

silage

hay

MILK POWDER

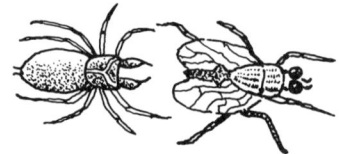
insects

potatoes

kale

sugar beet

oats

clover

PONDS

National curriculum links

Principal location in the National Curriculum

- Water • Plants and Animals

Other areas covered by topic

- Climate

Context of study

- Local issues • The aesthetic dimension

Suggested sub-topics and their location in areas of study of curriculum guidelines for Environmental Education

Sub-topic	Areas of Study in the National Curriculum						
	Climate	Soils, Rocks, Minerals	Water	Materials, Resources, Energy	Plants and Animals	People and Communities	Buildings, Industrialis-ation, Waste
Pollution		○	●	○	○	●	●
Fresh water supplies	○		●	○	●	●	○
Conservation		○	●	●	●	○	
Change			●	○	○	●	○

Key ● Principal location ○ Part coverage

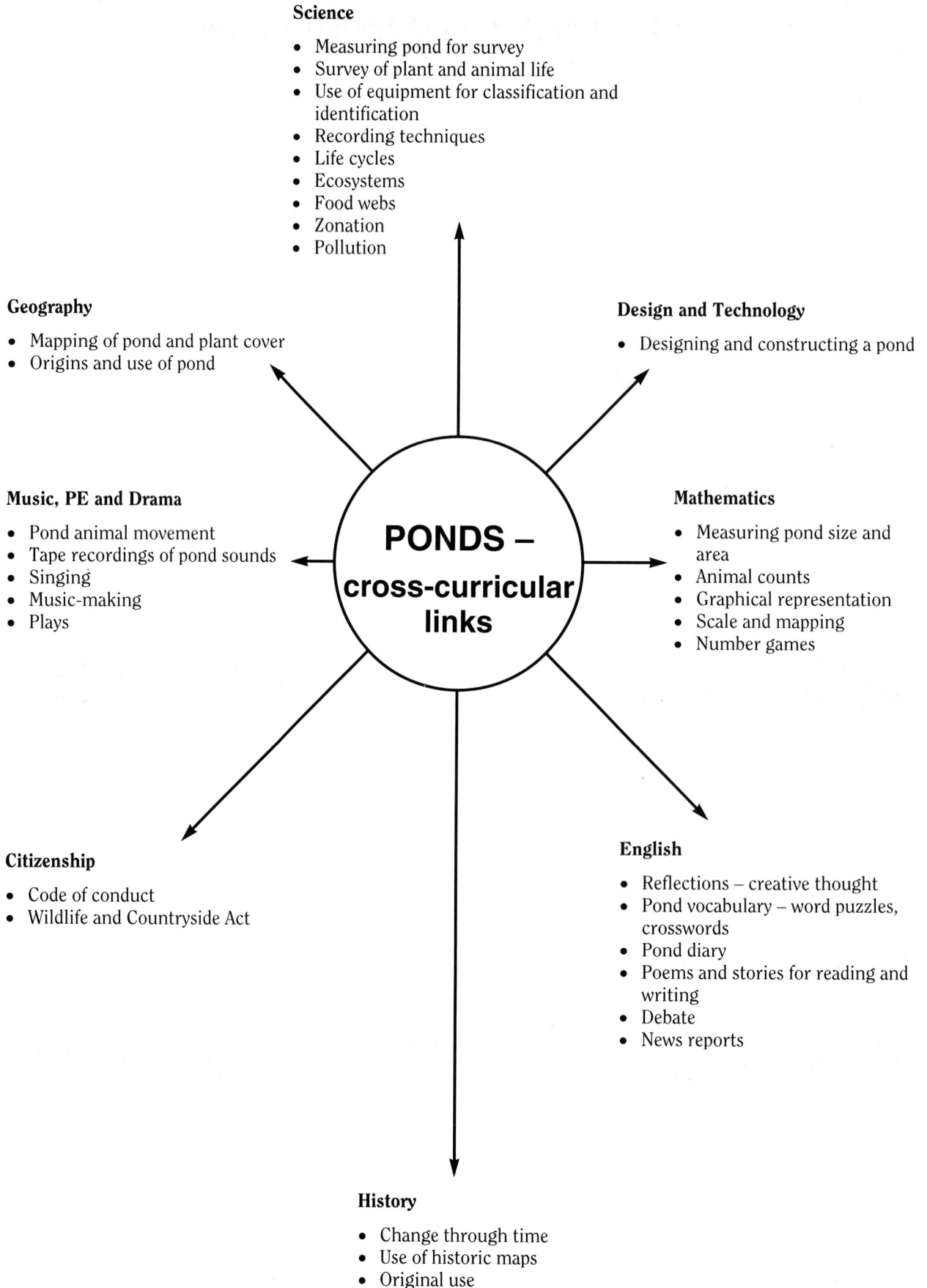

Science

- Measuring pond for survey
- Survey of plant and animal life
- Use of equipment for classification and identification
- Recording techniques
- Life cycles
- Ecosystems
- Food webs
- Zonation
- Pollution

Geography

- Mapping of pond and plant cover
- Origins and use of pond

Design and Technology

- Designing and constructing a pond

Music, PE and Drama

- Pond animal movement
- Tape recordings of pond sounds
- Singing
- Music-making
- Plays

PONDS – cross-curricular links

Mathematics

- Measuring pond size and area
- Animal counts
- Graphical representation
- Scale and mapping
- Number games

Citizenship

- Code of conduct
- Wildlife and Countryside Act

English

- Reflections – creative thought
- Pond vocabulary – word puzzles, crosswords
- Pond diary
- Poems and stories for reading and writing
- Debate
- News reports

History

- Change through time
- Use of historic maps
- Original use

Basics to be developed throughout the topic

Concepts

- The importance of fresh water in sustaining all life
- Inter-dependence and inter-relationships of animal and plant life in a freshwater environment
- Importance of ponds and pond life in the overall balance of nature and to planet Earth generally
- A pond as an ecosystem

Attitudes

- Appreciation of, and care and concern for, the environment and all living things
- Care and respect for our Earth and its resources
- Tolerance of other people's points of view about controversial issues

Environmental issues

- Water conservation
- Problems of water supply
- Causes of water pollution
- Resource limitation
- Destruction of natural habitats

STARTING POINTS

- Construct a pond in the school grounds. This can be a long-term project with a discernible core of study in Science and Design and Technology (see pages 48–51 and 53). Study the colonisation and development of the pond over a period of time.

- Visit a pond in a local park, woodland or farm. Obtain permission if necessary and undertake pond dipping activities to investigate water life.

- Observe life on the surface and around a pond in different seasons of the year.

- If possible, compare and contrast life in two or more ponds of different sizes and locations.

- Make a collection of reference books, films, stories, posters and information packs about ponds and pond life.

- Gather the equipment necessary for pond work, including collection, observation, identification and recording equipment.

- Check safety aspects. It is essential to ensure the safety of children working in or near water.

ENGLISH ACTIVITIES

C13
–14

1 Begin with a visit to a pond. It is essential that time is spent in quiet reflection and thought before practical activities are undertaken. Give the children an opportunity to appreciate the total environment of the pond, its aesthetic qualities as well as the practical scientific aspects. This is an important phase which allows the children time and personal space for imagination. It encourages them to take the whole exercise seriously, rather than viewing it as a time to 'play in water'. Furthermore, once a practical survey is begun, animals will be disturbed and will inevitably disappear into the depths. Observe surface life while the pond is tranquil.

Ask the children to sit in silence around the edge of the pond for five to ten minutes and to look, listen and think. They can use **copymaster 13** (Reflections) for recording thoughts, and key words that come to mind, perhaps sounds, shapes and colours. If the weather is good and a whole visit can be used for reflection, children can write poems and work on creative writing whilst at the pond side. If, however, this is a preliminary to practical investigation, words and sketches can be taken back to the classroom for development later.

2 As preparation for the field work, introduce and reinforce basic pond vocabulary. Design word puzzles,

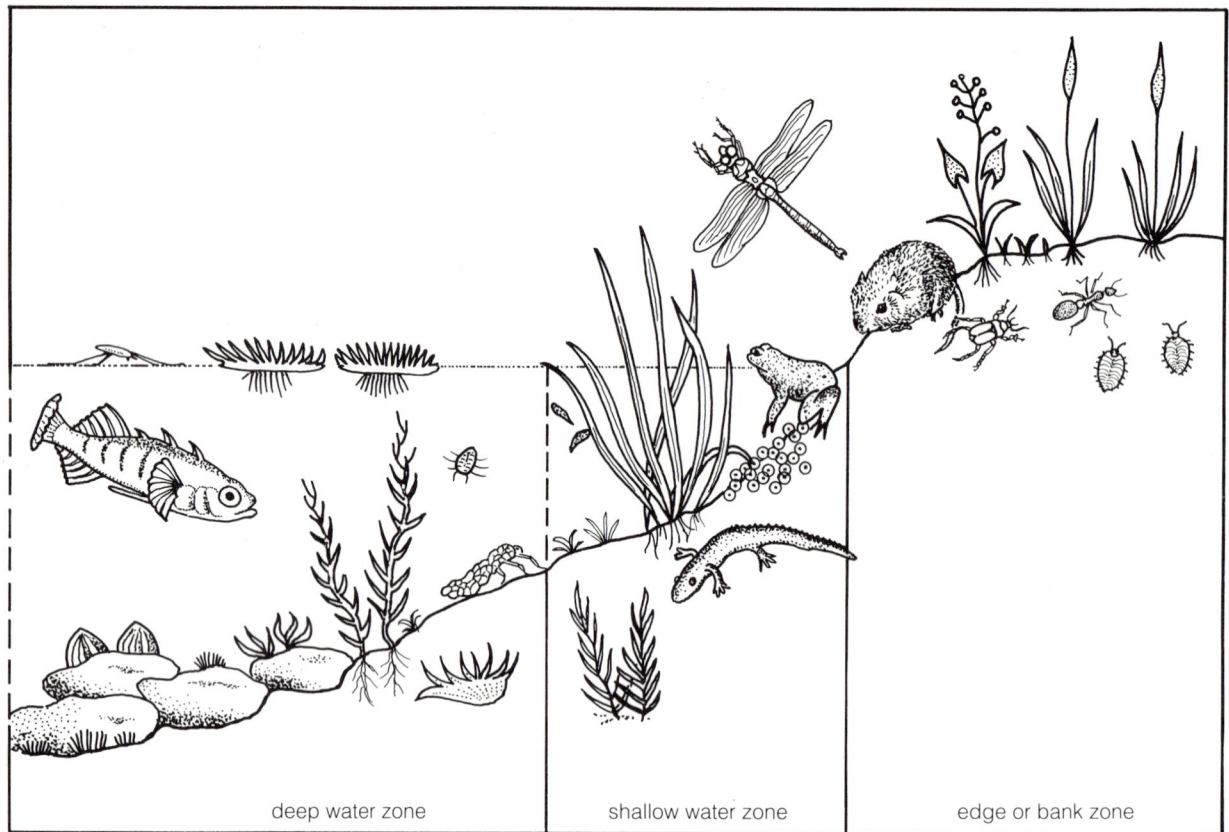

Cross-section of a pond

crosswords, activities of matching words to drawings. Relevant words may include physical aspects of the pond, for example surface, edge, depth, perimeter, bottom, together with the names of common animals and plants which are likely to be found.

3 Ask the children to draw a cross-section of a pond and to label appropriate zones.

Copymaster 14 (Word puzzle) can be used to reinforce some basic vocabulary that will be needed throughout the topic. Explain to the children that the letters of the words they are looking for may be arranged vertically or horizontally. They should draw a box around the missing words as they identify them.

4 If regular visits can be made to a pond, ask the children to keep a diary. This could be done as a personal record of observations by individual children, or they could make a class journal with collective accounts. Ideally, visit a pond in each month of the year, when very significant seasonal changes will be seen. If the topic is to last only a term and the pond is nearby, make weekly visits. The diary could contain a mixture of

factual writing, and imaginative or creative contributions and suitable illustrations or photographs.

5 Ask the children to read and write poems and stories about pond science and water life. For example, say to them: 'Imagine you are a dragonfly, tell what you see as you hover above the water'; or 'Imagine you live on the bottom of the pond and describe your life of hiding in the mud'; or 'Imagine you are a duck in search of food: describe your hunt, its dangers and rewards'.

6 Organise a class debate. Ask the children to imagine a situation where a farmer wishes to fill in a pond to gain more space for animals to graze. Have panels of children speaking in favour of arguments on either side of this controversial situation. Reach a majority decision and discuss the outcome.

7 Ask the children to write a news report based on the above debate. They can imagine they are journalists and write an account of the situation. Help them to be aware of bias when presenting a controversial issue in the press.

SCIENCE ACTIVITIES
C15 –17

1 Undertake a pond survey. Collect together appropriate equipment.

You will need
- Measuring equipment

- Long-handled pond nets for sweeping in the water and on the surface
- Short-handled nets for transferring creatures for close observation
- Paint brushes for picking up very small animals

- Buckets in which to keep specimens
- White trays for close observation
- Magnifying equipment
- Recording equipment (paper, pencils, record sheets, identification keys, reference books).

2 Help the children make an underwater viewer.

A home-made underwater viewer

You will need
- A large plastic jar (such as an empty sweet jar)
- A sheet of clear polythene
- A strong elastic band.

What to do
- Remove both ends of the jar with the teacher's supervision (use a tin opener).
- Cover one end with polythene; secure it with the elastic band.
- Place the covered end into the water and look through the open end.

3 Help the children measure the pond in preparation for drawing a plan. Measure length, width, perimeter and depth, if possible (see Geography activities, page 51).

4 Divide the class into groups to survey pond life. Each group should have a bucket, a white tray, large and small nets, brushes and a range of magnifying, identification and recording equipment. Show the children how to fill the buckets and white trays with pond water. Each member of the group should take turns with the large net. They should sweep it in a figure-of-eight motion across the surface, being careful not to drag weeds and other plants out of the pond. They should take samples from different water depths and different areas of the pond so that comparisons can be made. They should empty the net into the bucket and pass it on to the next person. While waiting for their turn, other children in the group can use small nets and brushes to transfer creatures from the bucket to the observation tray, where they can be closely examined with the aid of magnifying equipment, identified, sketched and recorded.

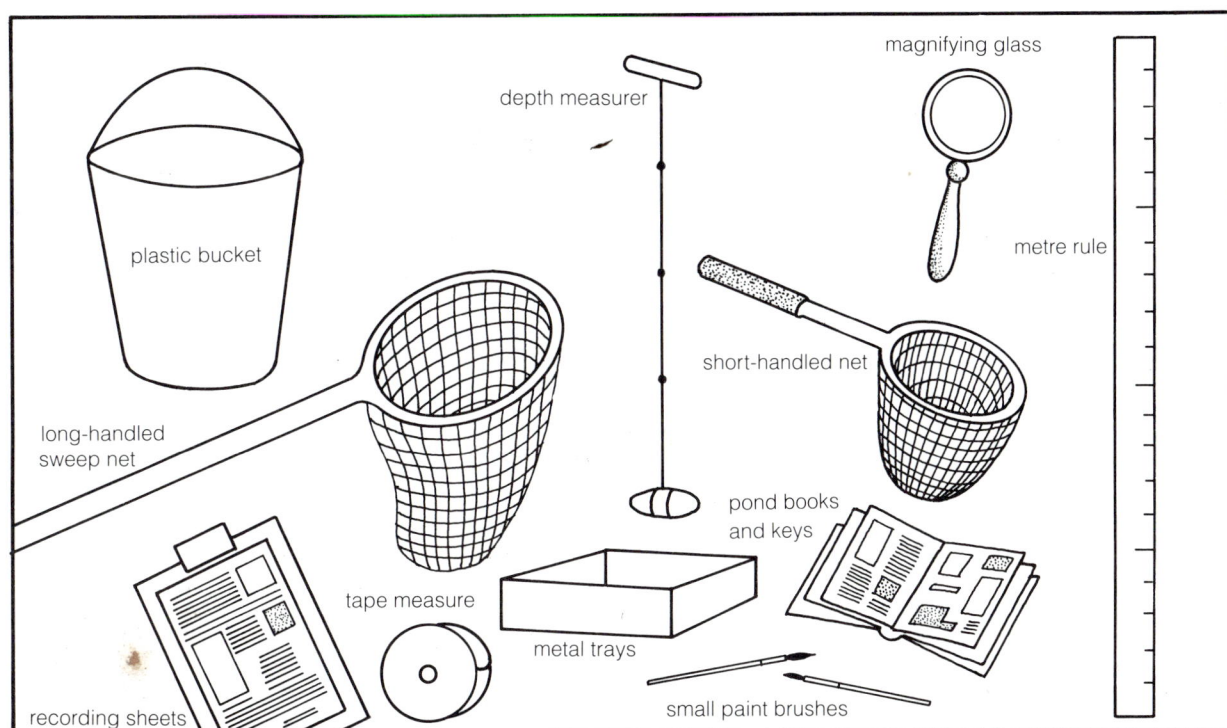

Useful pondwork equipment

Consult books and freshwater keys for aids to identification. Methods of recording will depend on the purpose of the visit. If a series of visits can be made, some of these may be for a general survey, others for detailed study of individual creatures.

Always return creatures to the pond after completing field work.

5 **Copymaster 15** (Pond survey recording sheet) is a suggested recording sheet for an initial general survey of a pond. It focuses attention on physical aspects such as water quality, size of pond and the nature of the bottom of the pond, as well as on the range of both plant and animal life. This copymaster is useful for a first visit or preliminary survey, after which more specific details can be observed, measured and recorded.

6 **Copymaster 16** (Survey of a pond animal) is designed for the more specific recording of characteristics of individual animals found. Do preliminary work on classification so that the children understand that 'animal' is a collective term which includes vertebrates and invertebrates as shown below.

7 Collect pictures of a wide variety of freshwater animals and ask the children to sort them into two basic sets of vertebrates and invertebrates, and then into family sub-sets within each.

8 Investigate the concept of change through a study of animal life cycles. Observation of pond life at different times of the year is necessary. Encourage the children to note the presence of eggs, young and adult forms. Key vocabulary will include nymph, larva and adult. Focus on growth and development by pointing out changes in colour, shape, size and body parts, presence and number of legs, wings, etc.

9 Analyse the pond as a complex ecosystem. Study who eats what or whom. Ask the children to build up food chains and food webs in pictorial and diagrammatic forms. Divide creatures into those which eat only plant life (herbivores), those which eat only animal life (carnivores) and those which eat both (omnivores).

10 Play a food web game. Children can prepare cards with drawings of pond creatures and arrange them like dominoes in order of who eats whom as illustrated on page 51.

VERTEBRATES

(animals with backbones)
mammals, birds, amphibians, reptiles, fish

INVERTEBRATES

(animals without backbones)
snails, insects, worms, spiders, fleas, mites

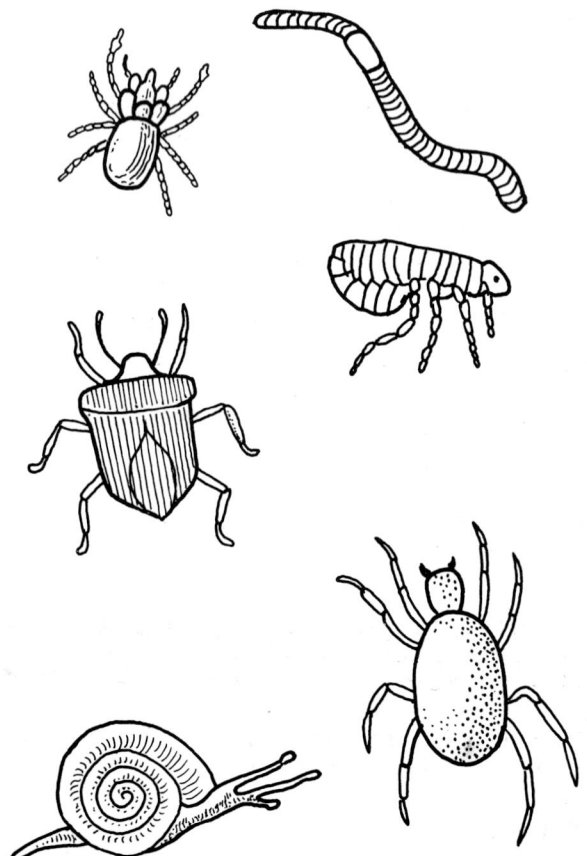

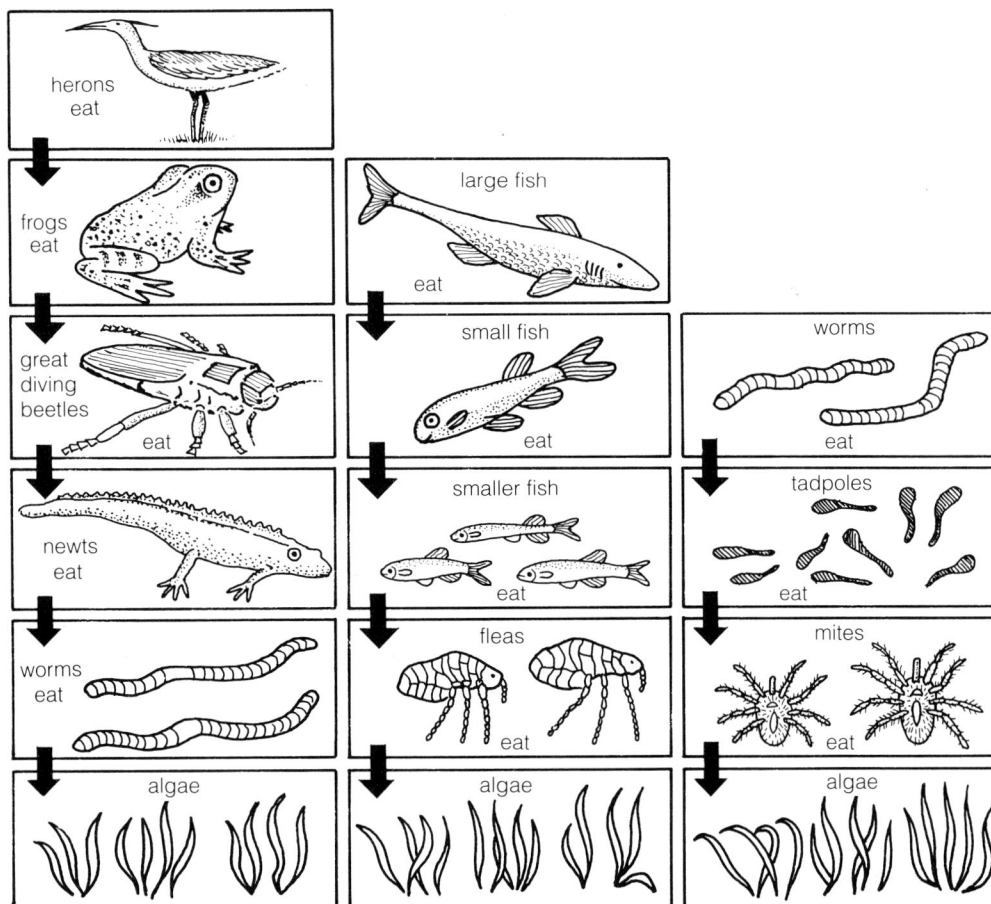

Consider numbers involved in the above pattern, and the fact that there are many more herbivores in the ecosystem than large carnivores. Data can be derived from pond surveys.

11 Ask the children to draw a diagram to show zones of the pond. In field work, take samples of animals from various water depths ranging from the surface to the bottom. They should draw a cross-section and record the presence of animals in the edge or bank zone, shallow water zone and deep water zone. This can be done individually or recorded in the form of artwork (painting or collage) on a large classroom wall frieze.

12 Encourage the children to consider problems and issues that affect a pond habitat, notably pollution and habitat destruction. On the visit, look for evidence of litter, or other forms of water pollution. Pollution may not be evident to the naked eye, and indicators will be necessary. The presence of certain forms of animal life is a very good indicator of the level of water pollution.

Mayfly nymphs, for example, will only be found in pure fresh water.

13 **Copymaster 17** (Pollution key) can be used to carry out various tasks. Ask the children to colour the drawings, identify the creatures and write their names. Hopefully this copymaster will be used in association with field work, in which case it can be used as an I-spy activity, with ticks to record creatures found. To draw attention to pollution levels indicated, children can colour the left-hand column in traffic light colours: the top band in green, the middle band in amber and the lower band in red.

14 Discuss potential origins of fresh water pollution. Develop a sub-topic on this theme. Help the children make a large collage frieze to draw attention to potential sources of pollution of fresh water supplies, including poisons from industry, mining wastes, sewage waste, agricultural 'run-off' (insecticides and fertilisers) and dumped rubbish. Ask the children to write about the consequences for animal, plant and human life.

GEOGRAPHY ACTIVITIES ▶

1 Make a plan of the pond you are studying and map the plant cover using the following technique.

What to do
● Take two lengths of string, longer than the length and width of the pond.

● Tie short pieces of coloured string along them at regular intervals of 1 metre.
● Stretch the long strings along the length and breadth of the pond, at right angles to each other.
● Tie them securely to stakes in the ground.
● Draw a map on a large sheet of graph paper, using a

Measuring the length and breadth of the pond

grid and an appropriate scale, for example 1 cm square to represent 1 square metre of pond area.
● Work your way along the boundary strings, noting plants at 1 metre intervals. Record findings on the pond map.
2 Find out if your pond is a natural one or if it was made by people. With the children, interview the farmer or landowner if it is on private property. Find out how long it has existed. Has it changed in any way through time? What is the significance of the pond today? (See also History activities, page 54.)

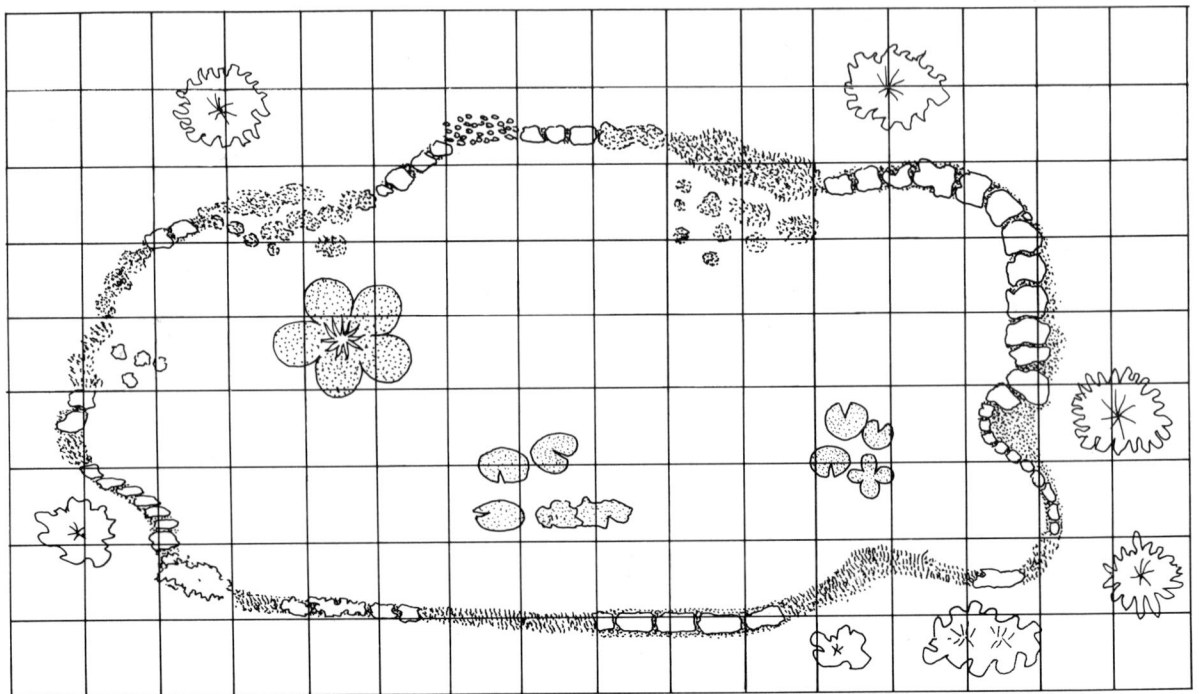

scale: 1 cm square represents 1 m square.

Recording findings on the pond map

DESIGN AND TECHNOLOGY ACTIVITIES

1 Design and organise the construction of a pond in your school grounds. A number of useful practical guides are available for consultation (for example, *Developing a School Nature Reserve*, published by the National Association for Environmental Education). Involve the children at all stages in the design process. Consider the following:

- Size, depth, position
- Lining (fibreglass, concrete or flexible)

- Excavation of hole (who will dig?)
- Stocking the pond (when and with what)
- Maintenance (your pond should become a balanced ecosystem, requiring little attention)
- Costing
- Legal aspects (safety, boundaries, etc.)

Consult the Governing Body and parents for help and practical support.

MATHEMATICS ACTIVITIES C18

1 Help the children measure the width, area, depth, perimeter and water temperature of the pond.

2 Ask the children to count the number of animals found in various zones. They can then draw graphs of the data obtained.

3 Ask the children to calculate the surface area covered by plants.

4 Carry out scale and mapping activities (see Geography activities, page 51).

5 Centre everyday mathematics (for example, number work) around a pond theme. **Copymaster 18** (Mathematics in the pond) involves simple numerical calculations to match each creature with its home. Sums could be simplified or made more complex according to the ability of the children.

CITIZENSHIP ACTIVITIES

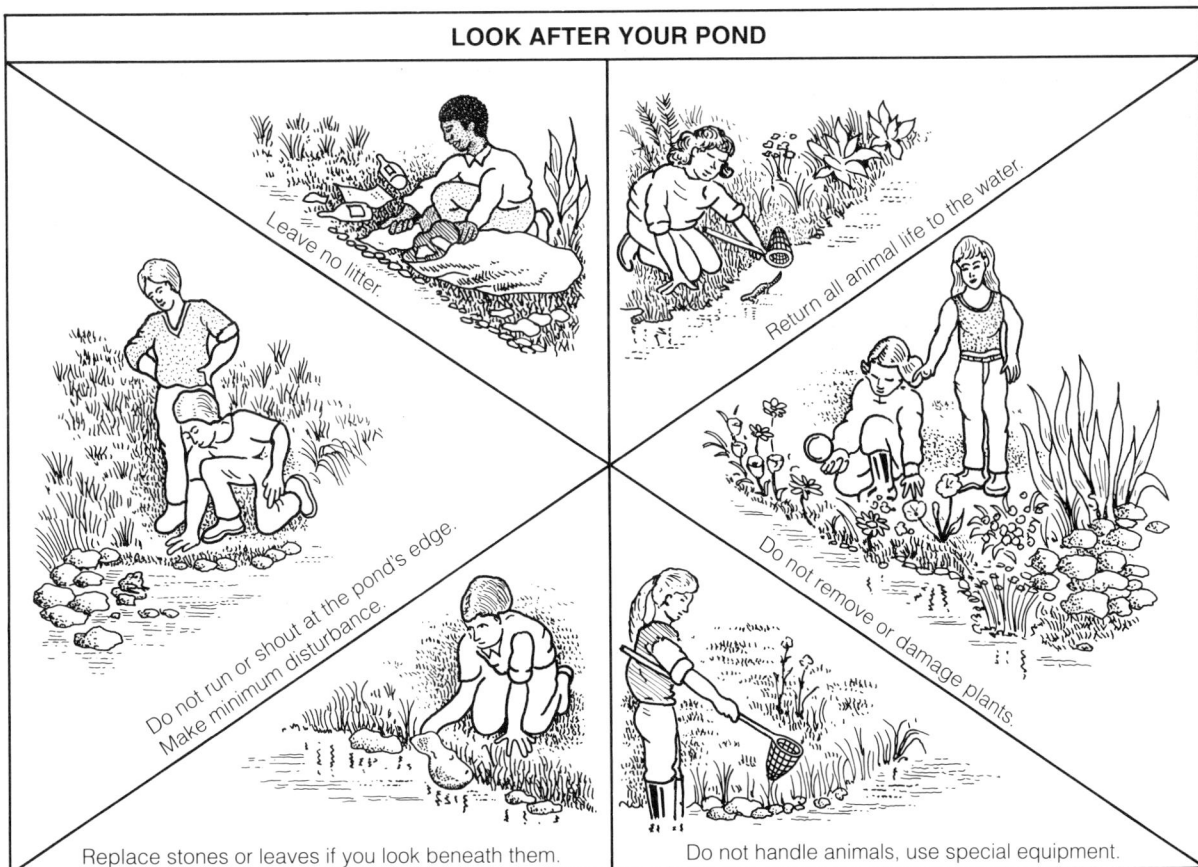

LOOK AFTER YOUR POND

A code of conduct for pond studies

1 Encourage the children to design a code of conduct for pond studies. Present this in poster, collage or written form so that basic information is readily understood by all who consult it.

2 Teach the children the basic facts of the Wildlife and Countryside Act. It is against the law of this country to remove certain wild animals and plants from their habitats. Explain that there are good reasons for this. Investigate species that are protected. Relate this knowledge to the importance of conservation of wildlife habitats including areas of fresh water.

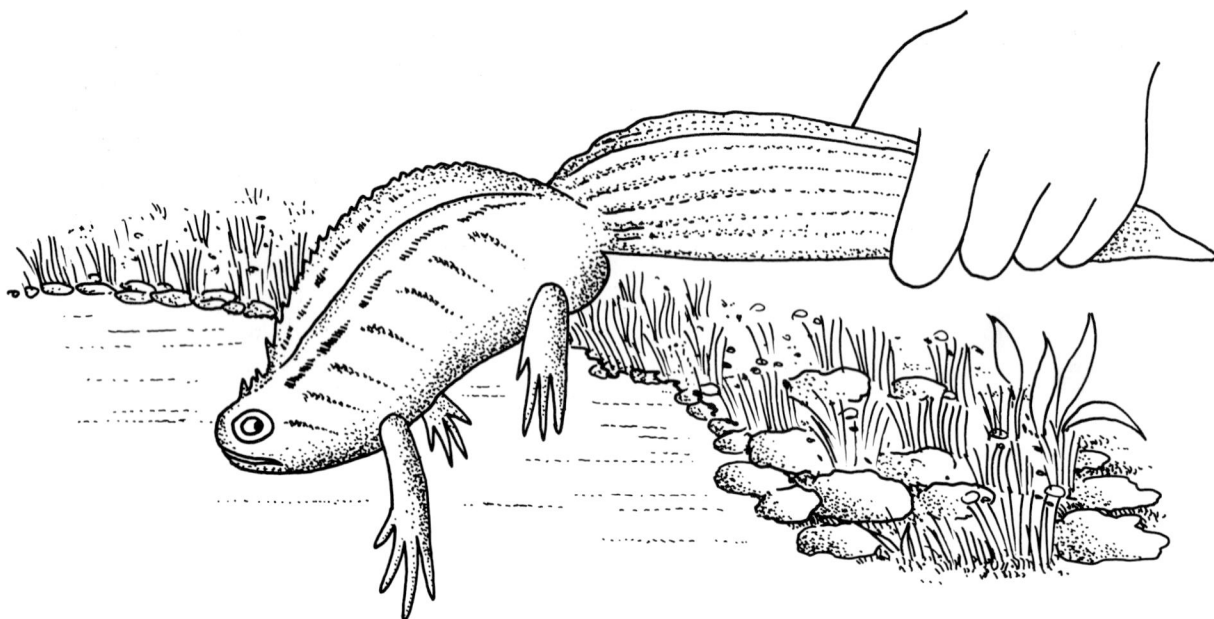

Moving certain wild creatures from their habitats is against the law.

HISTORY ACTIVITIES ▶

1 If your adopted pond has an owner, try to find out whether there have been any significant changes to its size and/or boundaries. Help the children find out if it has always been there. To assist this investigation, visit the local studies department of your local public library and study historic maps of the locality.

2 Discover whether the pond is natural or if it was made be people. If people made it, try to find out why it was created. Was it for rearing fish, for supplying water for humans or livestock, or for ornamental purposes or recreation?

3 Ask the children to write stories and draw pictures of people who may have used the pond in days gone by.

MUSIC, PE AND DRAMA ACTIVITIES ▶

1 Ask the children to act out the movement of various pond animals, accompanied by appropriate music for swift running, smooth gliding and swimming, erratic hopping, graceful flying, hovering, etc.

2 Listen to tape-recorded sounds of the pond: ducks quacking, frogs croaking, etc. Ask the children to write stories and poems to accompany these sounds.

3 Encourage the children to sing songs about water and pond life, and accompany them with sounds made on percussion instruments.

4 Help the children write and act out plays with pond animals as central characters. This activity allows great scope for movement, sound effects and music-making.

Reflections

Sit quietly by a pond for 10 minutes.

Look, listen and think.

Sounds

Shapes

Colours

Word puzzle

Can you find these words in the pond puzzle?

INSECT	PONDSKATER	SNAIL	WATER
DUCK	WORM	NEWT	EGG
FISH	MOORHEN	FROG	TOAD

E F W L M C F K
V T O A D D I L
U P R Z E F S P
J H M Y H G H Q
A B F S N A I L
P I N S E C T R
O Z N E W T J S
N X M Q D U V T
D O O B U C A W
S P O M C G B X
K T R N K K E Y
A V H O D L G Z
T W E F R O G H
E E N E F N M I
R F W A T E R J

Pond survey recording sheet

C15

Does the pond have a name? Where is it?	How big is the pond? How long? How wide? Estimate how deep it is.
Look at the water and tick the appropriate boxes. The water is ☐ clear ☐ still ☐ cloudy ☐ moving ☐ muddy ☐ full of rubbish ☐ smelly ☐ oily on the surface	Can you see the bottom of the pond? If so, tick what it is like ☐ stony ☐ muddy ☐ covered with leaves ☐ covered with rubbish ☐ other
Look for evidence of creatures. Tick if you see the following. Name them if you can or sketch them to identify later. ☐ fish in the water ☐ insects on the surface ☐ birds on the surface ☐ birds on the edge ☐ creatures clinging to plant ☐ other animals in the water ☐ other animals on the surface Names of creatures found	Look for evidence of plants. Tick if you see the following. Name them if you can or sketch them to identify later. ☐ plants floating ☐ plants growing up from the bottom of the pond ☐ plants beneath the surface ☐ plants in the soil on the edge of the pond Names of plants found

Survey of a pond animal

Choose one pond creature to investigate.

Sketch the creature you have chosen.	Where did you see it? (On a plant, near the edge, swimming on the surface?)	
	How many legs does it have?	Does it have wings?
How big is it?	How does it breathe? (Does it come to the surface for air?)	
What colour is it?	How does it move?	
What do you think it eats?	Identify and name your creature.	

Pollution key

Pollution level	Name the creature	Tick if seen
No pollution		
Medium pollution		
Heavy pollution		
	No life at all	

Mathematics in the pond

Can you take each creature to its home in the pond? Draw a path to the correct answer.

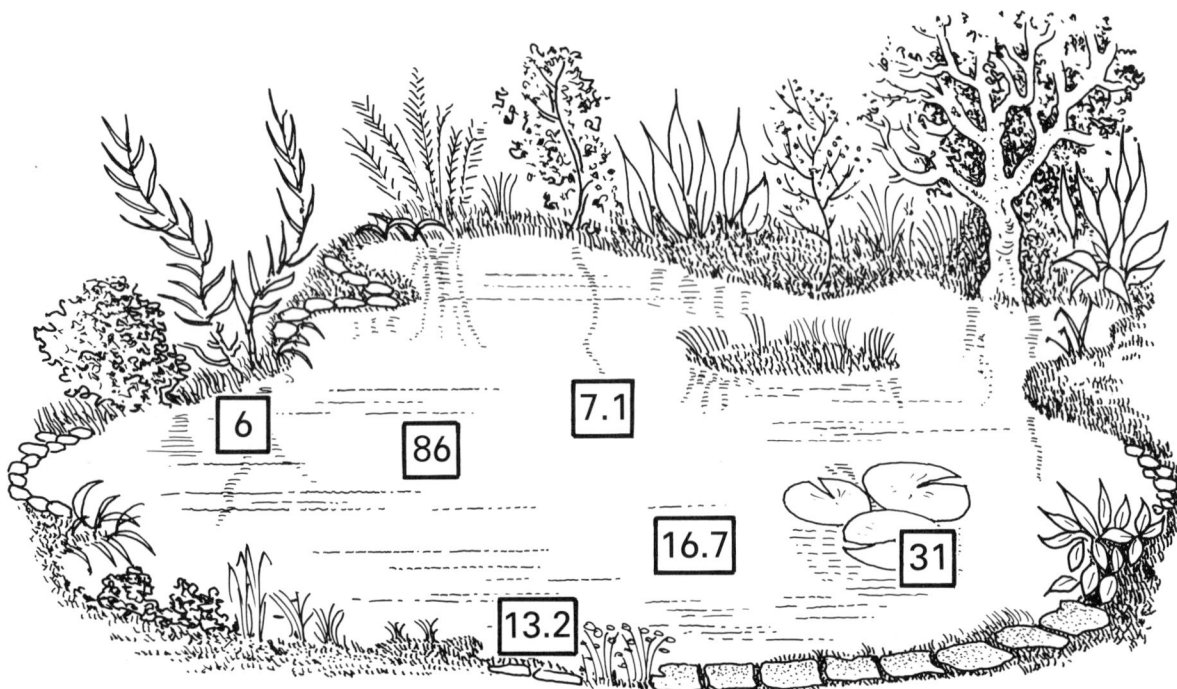

6   86   7.1   16.7   31   13.2

11 + 9 + 18 − 7 = ?

8 × 3 − 18 = ?

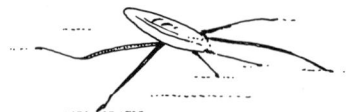

3.6 + 7.2 + 5.9 = ?

18.7 − 3.2 − 2.3 = ?

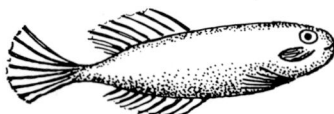

9 × 11 − 13 = ?

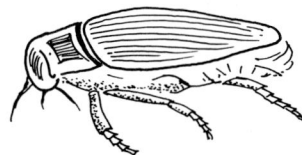

3.8 + 10.2 − 6.9 = ?

ENERGY

National curriculum links

Principal location in the National Curriculum

- Materials, Resources, Energy

Other areas covered by topic

- Water ● People and Communities ● Buildings, Industrialisation, Waste ● Plants and Animals
- Soils, Rocks, Minerals

Context of study

- Local to global concerns

Suggested sub-topics and their location in areas of study of curriculum guidelines for Environmental Education

Sub-topic	Areas of Study in the National Curriculum						
	Climate	Soils, Rocks, Minerals	Water	Materials, Resources, Energy	Plants and Animals	People and Communities	Buildings, Industrialis-ation, Waste
Nuclear power				●		●	○
Pollution	○	○	○	●	○	○	●
Fossil fuels		●		●		○	●
Heat	○		○	●	○	●	○

Key   ● Principal location   ○ Part coverage

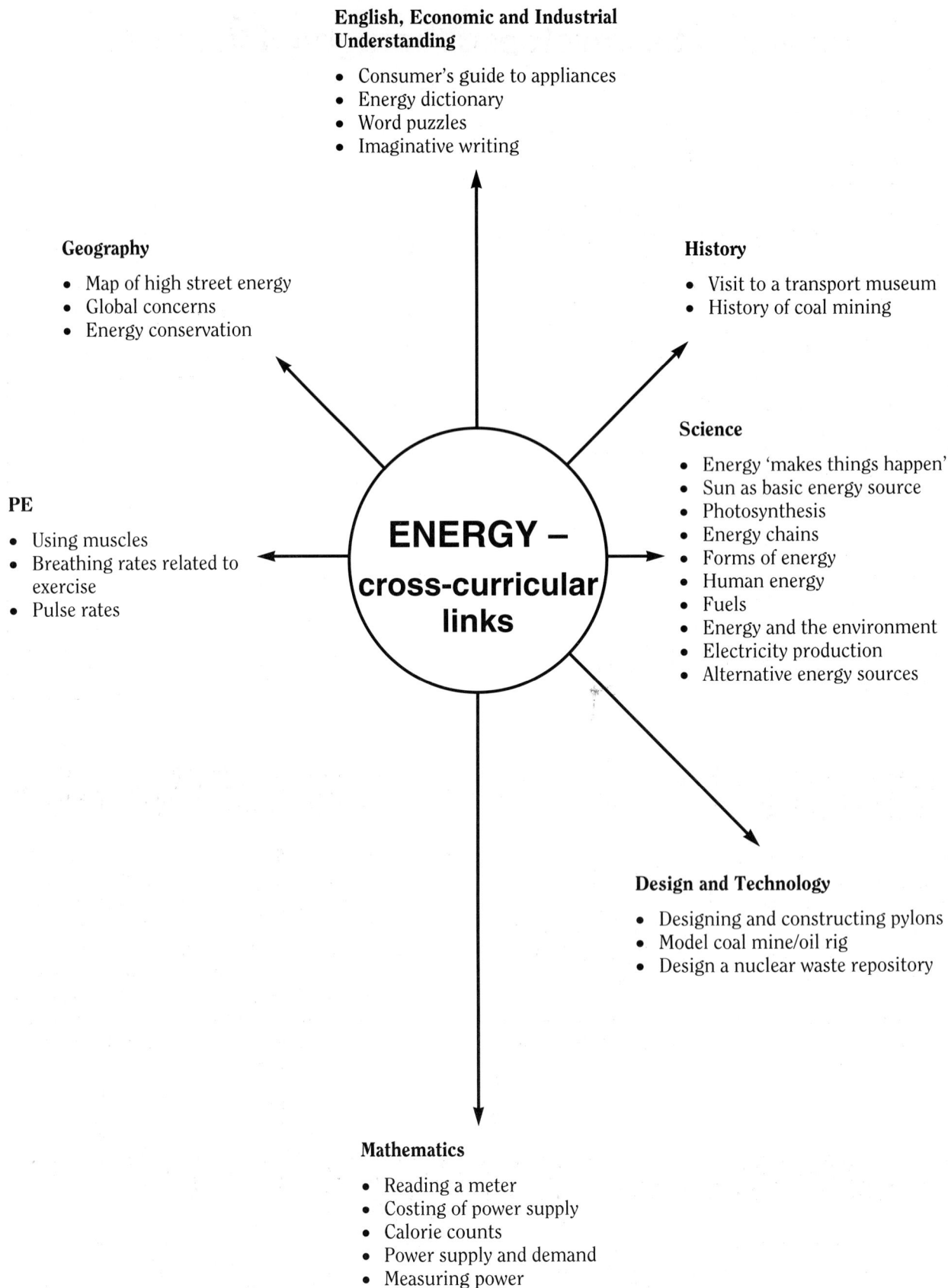

English, Economic and Industrial Understanding

- Consumer's guide to appliances
- Energy dictionary
- Word puzzles
- Imaginative writing

Geography

- Map of high street energy
- Global concerns
- Energy conservation

History

- Visit to a transport museum
- History of coal mining

Science

- Energy 'makes things happen'
- Sun as basic energy source
- Photosynthesis
- Energy chains
- Forms of energy
- Human energy
- Fuels
- Energy and the environment
- Electricity production
- Alternative energy sources

PE

- Using muscles
- Breathing rates related to exercise
- Pulse rates

ENERGY – cross-curricular links

Design and Technology

- Designing and constructing pylons
- Model coal mine/oil rig
- Design a nuclear waste repository

Mathematics

- Reading a meter
- Costing of power supply
- Calorie counts
- Power supply and demand
- Measuring power

Basics to be developed throughout the topic

Concepts

- It takes energy to make things move
- We use energy all the time
- The Sun is a basic source of energy
- We can make energy available in various ways
- Energy can be stored
- Energy must be conserved

Attitudes

- Appreciation of, and care and concern for, the environment and its resources
- Independence of thought on environmental issues
- Respect for the beliefs and opinions of others
- Respect for scientific evidence

Environmental issues

- Energy conservation
- Pollution effects of energy use
- Fossil fuels as limited resources
- Management of resources

STARTING POINTS

- Energy is a difficult concept to grasp because of its abstract nature. Make it as real as possible by visits and field work for first-hand experiences. For example, visit a power station, a transport museum, an airport or railway station, or simply walk down the high street looking for 'energy in action'.

- Seek the services of visiting speakers, for example from the Gas or Electricity Board, or from a museum education service.

- Collect a wide range of background materials, including books on energy sources and conservation pictures, films and other visual material, and information packs from organisations such as British Nuclear Fuels, the United Kingdom Atomic Energy Authority, Gas and Electricity Boards and Greenpeace or the Alternative Energy Centre (in Wales). Domestic appliance showrooms in retail stores are good sources of advertising material which can be used in a variety of ways.

SCIENCE ACTIVITIES

C19
–21

1 Use **copymaster 19** (Energy on the move) as an introductory discussion sheet to begin the topic. Children can colour it in and use it as a cover for their topic workbooks. Talk about the things that are happening in the picture and the fact that they are all linked by the concept of energy. The key message of the illustration is that energy is all around us and makes things happen. Nothing could move without energy in some form or other, and there are many different kinds of energy.

2 Introduce the fact that the Sun's energy is the basis of life on Earth. Without sunlight, there would be no plant life. Without plants there would be no animals and, without plants and animals, no people.

3 With the children, investigate photosynthesis. This is the process by which plants use energy from the Sun to make carbohydrates from carbon dioxide in the air and water. (In this process, light energy is changed to chemical energy.)

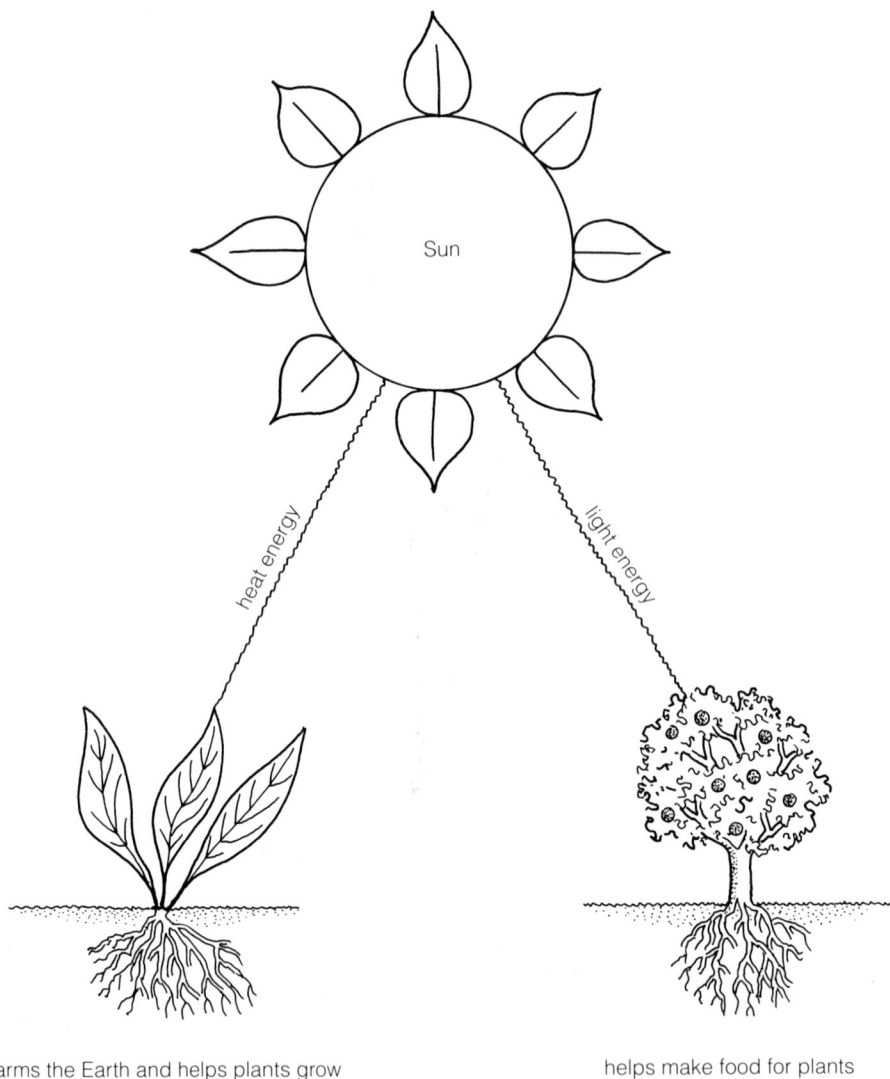

Sun

heat energy

light energy

warms the Earth and helps plants grow

helps make food for plants

The Sun's energy is the basis of life on Earth.

What to do
- Take two shallow dishes and line them with damp kitchen towel.
- Sprinkle cress seeds on both of them, then place them in a dark cupboard for two days.
- After this time, remove one of the dishes and place it on a sunny window sill. Leave the other in the dark.
- Observe both dishes at daily intervals and record observations. Look at growth and at the colour of the young cress leaves.
- Help the children to write conclusions about the critical role of light energy in developing chlorophyll in plants.

4 **Copymaster 20** (Energy chains from the Sun) helps children to build on their understanding of the Sun's energy by introducing the key concepts of energy chains and energy changes. It reinforces the fundamental importance of the Sun's energy and links this to plant production, food production and the forms and changes of energy involved.

The key facts to discuss with the use of this copymaster are:

- We cannot create or destroy energy.
- When one form of energy is used, it changes into one or more other forms.
- When energy changes, some may be 'lost', that is changed into forms that may not be wanted. For example, with electric light some energy is lost as heat.

5 **Copymaster 21** (Forms of energy) can be used to consolidate discussion or as an introduction to the many forms of energy in the world around us. Children are asked to match the labels at the bottom with the pictures. Link this to work on copymaster 20, which has already introduced the idea of nuclear energy (nuclear reactions inside the Sun release huge amounts of energy, some of which travels as light), light energy and chemical energy (when we eat plants, we make a store of chemical energy in our bodies). The topic could then be developed by examining one form of energy in greater depth or by continuing with a general theme of energy.

High-energy use	Low-energy use
Running to school	Sleeping all night
Playing games in the playground	Taking a shower and cleaning teeth
Doing PE lesson	Sitting and eating meals
Riding a bicycle	Sitting at desk in classroom
Going swimming	Watching TV

*An 'Energy diary' of high-
and low-energy use*

Explain that kinetic energy is another term for movement energy and that thermal energy is heat.

6 Ask the children to write a diary for one day, noting down everything that they do. They could call it 'My energy diary'. Explain that we use energy all of the time, even when we are sitting still or asleep. Consider the day's activities and divide them into high-energy use and low-energy use.

This activity helps the children begin to understand about energy in our bodies, and how we 'burn up' energy at different rates, depending on what we are doing. Explain that we get our energy from food. (See also activity 7.)

7 Keep another diary (see activity 6), this time of food eaten in a day. It would be useful to select a day and keep the two parallel records on the activities undertaken and the foods consumed. Explain that ideally the quantity and variety of food eaten should balance the amount of energy we use.

8 Do a sub-topic on food (see Food topic, page 93). We need to take in enough energy stored in food to keep us healthy and active. If we eat too little for our energy needs, we lose weight and become ill. If we eat too much for our energy needs, we put on weight which is also bad for our health.

Help the children investigate the calorie content of various foods, and the calorie expenditure of certain activities. Books on slimming and diet are useful sources of information (see also Mathematics activities, page 68).

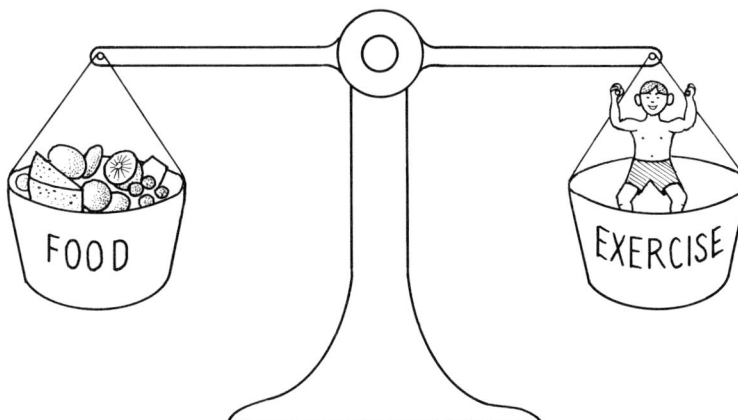

*We need a careful balance between
food and exercise.*

Wood has stored energy. Burning changes some of this chemical energy to heat energy.

Chemical energy stored in food is released and 'burnt' by our muscles.

9 Investigate ways in which energy can be stored. Food is a form of energy store; so too are fuels, for example gas, coal, oil and wood. Help the children make energy chain diagrams to show the release of stored energy, as in the example above.

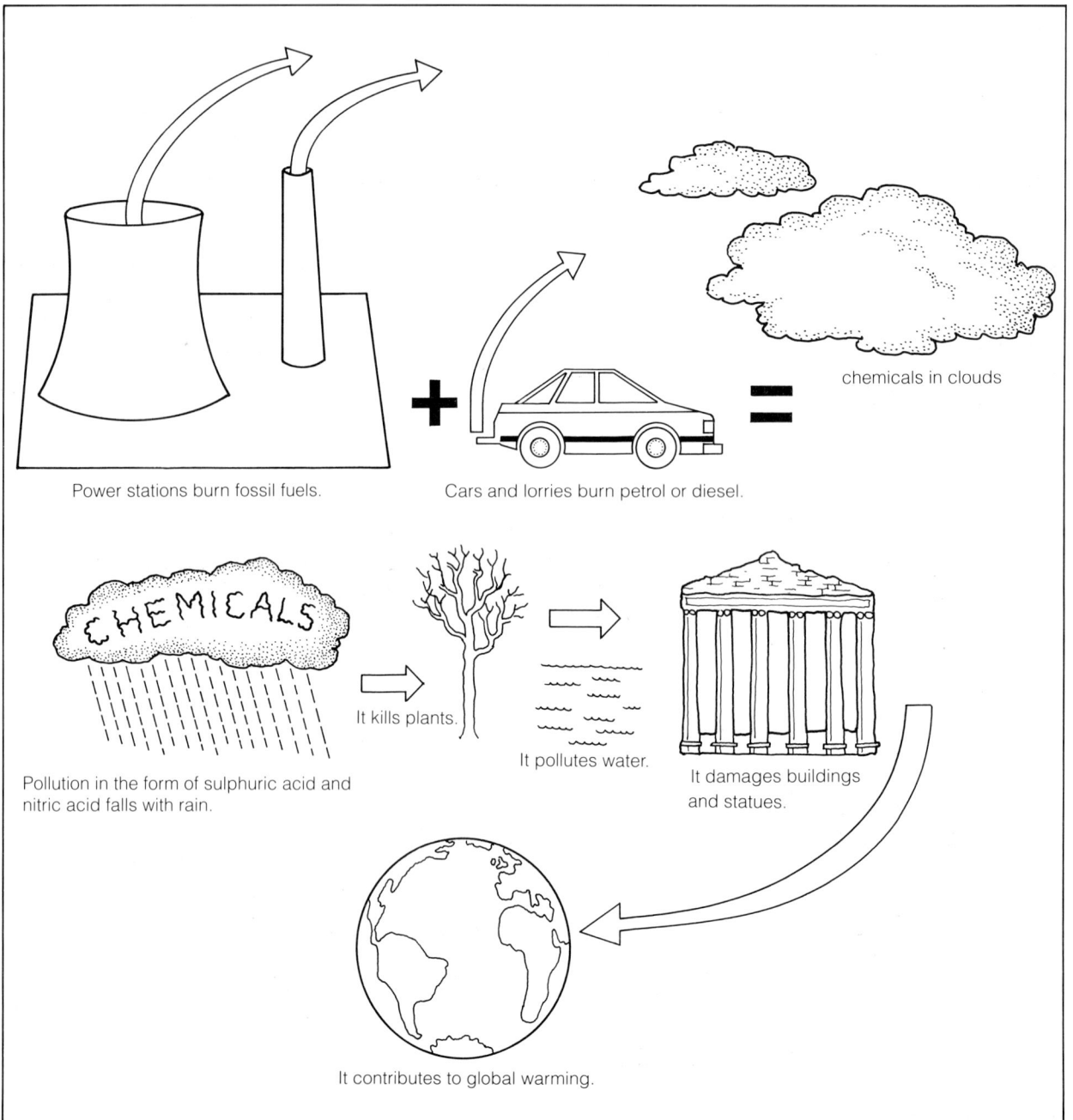

Power stations burn fossil fuels.

Cars and lorries burn petrol or diesel.

chemicals in clouds

Pollution in the form of sulphuric acid and nitric acid falls with rain.

It kills plants.

It pollutes water.

It damages buildings and statues.

It contributes to global warming.

10 Do sub-topics on the various common fuels in use – perhaps the class could be divided into groups, each to research the origins of a fuel. If possible start with something tangible: take a piece of coal, for example, inspect it under a microscope or a magnifying glass, look for fossils, trace its journey from the earth to the fireplace. Also take a look at oil, feel its texture, try mixing it with water, find out how it is extracted.

11 Make a 'black book' of energy and the environment. Write a class account with suitable illustrations of the problems of burning fossil fuels. Help the children to understand that these are finite resources and that we need to conserve them. Also, point out that the use of fossil fuels is causing great damage and pollution to the environment. Investigate the problems of acid rain, the greenhouse effect and oil spills. Measure the acidity of rain water (see Weather topic, page 12) and design posters to explain these problems as illustrated on page 66.

12 With the children, make an 'oil spill' in a metal tray, and do experiments to investigate its properties. Fill the tray almost to the top with water, then add two tablespoons of cooking oil. Ask the children if it sinks or floats. Can it be absorbed with paper or a dishcloth? Devise experiments to find the most effective way of removing it. For example, use drops of washing up liquid to break it up (how many drops are needed?). Can they design ways of controlling it, that is stopping it from spreading?

13 Contact the Royal Society for the Protection of Birds to ask for information on how oil kills sea birds. Do fund-raising activities to support RSPB bird rescues. (Each regional area of RSPB has an education officer who will give talks in schools.)

14 Make a special study of or do a sub-topic on nuclear fuel and the nuclear power debate. Encourage the children to write about the advantages and disadvantages of nuclear power. Collect pictures and information from British Nuclear Fuels and/or the United Kingdom Atomic Energy Authority, Greenpeace and the Alternative Energy Centre (in Wales). Ask the children to do a survey of parents or teachers in the school to find out their views on nuclear power. Discuss why this issue is so controversial and be prepared to accept and respect the opinions of people who hold different views from your own. Organise and display illustrated arguments on a wall frieze.

15 Ask each child to make an inventory of things which use energy in his/her home. They should do this room by room and classify the results into sets; for example electrical energy, gas, oil, etc. Ask the children to tabulate and make graphs of the results, and consider the following types of questions: Which is the most popular energy source? Which items require more than one source of energy? Which items involve heat, light, sound or movement?

16 With the children, draw or collect pictures of all of the items in the home which are powered by electricity. Make a large wall display of these pictures, surrounding a painting of the source of the electricity. Ask the children to write about how and where the electricity is produced.

17 Help the children find out how much electricity each item uses. The rate of use is measured in units called watts (1000 watts equals 1 kilowatt). Draw a line from each item to the power station and write on it the rate of use.

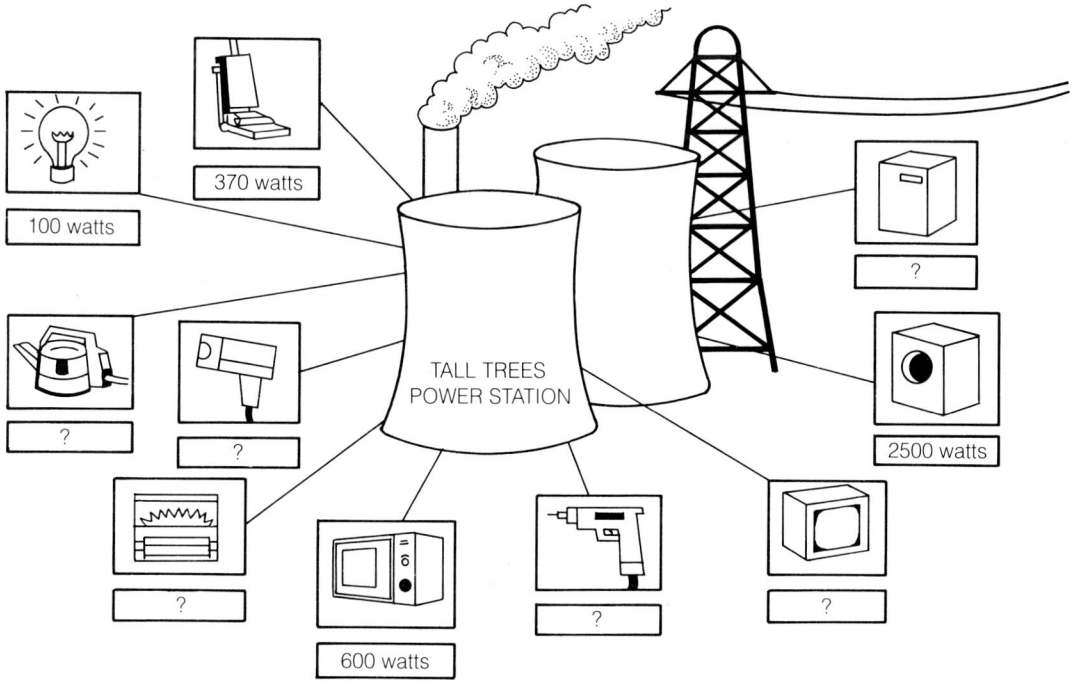

100 watts

370 watts

TALL TREES POWER STATION

?

?

?

?

?

600 watts

?

?

2500 watts

Rates of use of electricity

18 With the children, write a list of all the ways in which electricity is produced that you can think of (for example, coal-fired power station, oil-fired station, gas-fired station, nuclear power, hydro-electric power). Read more about them. Discuss the advantages and disadvantages of each, particularly in relation to their impact on the environment (pollution) and their use of finite resources.

19 Make a special study of new ways of getting energy, often called alternative energy sources. Find out about the advantages and disadvantages of each, and locations in the world where they are being developed and used. Alternative sources include those illustrated below.

20 Investigate engines – machines which work when heat causes pushes and pulls. Ask the children to draw modes of transport which depend on engines to make them move. Find out what fuels they burn.

21 Demonstrate magnetic energy.

You will need
● A magnet
● Some paperclips
● A piece of card
● Small samples of fabric, wood, paper, plastic, rubber and glass.

What to do
● Let the children test all of the samples to see which materials are magnetic.
● Place the paperclips on the card.
● Place the magnet beneath the card, in contact with it, and move it about.
● Ask the children to observe what happens to the paper clips.
● Test to see whether the other materials will allow magnetic energy to pass through. Does the thickness of the material make any difference to the results?

windmills

solar panels

biomass energy (from living or dead organic matter)

tidal and wave energy

geothermal energy (heat from the Earth itself)

Alternative energy sources

MATHEMATICS ACTIVITIES

1 Teach the children how to read an electricity meter. If the children do not have one at home, use demonstration materials obtained from the Electricity Board. Use real data obtained from homes which have an electricity meter. Ask the children to do calculations on the amount of electricity used per day. If possible, do this activity in both cold weather and warm weather to see if there is a difference.

2 Help the children to find out how much electricity costs. Bills will provide this information; bring in a set of bills to use for mathematical calculations. Ask the children to see if they are correct! If parents are happy to co-operate, ask them to supply details of gas and electricity bills. Which is the most expensive fuel? Note variables, for example some bills may include central heating, others may not.

3 Ask the children to collect data and draw bar graphs of energy-related topics in the children's lives, for example:

● How we heat our homes
● Energy by which we cook
● Fuel we use in the car
● Favourite high-energy foods.

All of these will lead to discussion and raise awareness of key environmental issues such as the conservation of energy.

To use up 300 calories I need to:

sleep for _____ minutes.

jog for_____ minutes.

swim for _____ minutes.

walk for_____ minutes.

cycle for_____ minutes.

Make up a plate of food containing 300 calories.

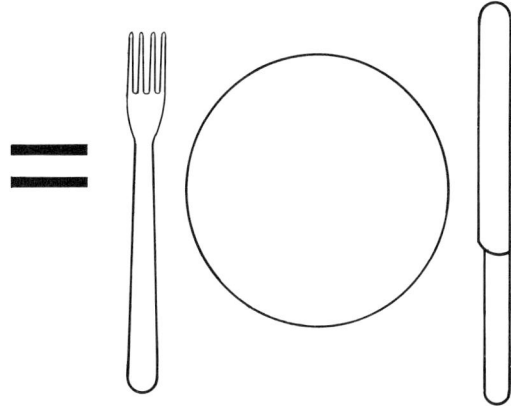

A calorie equation

4 Ask the children to do calculations on the calorie content of foods, and the expenditure of calories in exercise. Consult books on diet and weight control which print such information. Do 'calorie equations' and make the scales balance.

Ask the children to read food packaging labels; there is an increasing trend to write calorific content on packaged foods.

5 Find out how far energy 'travels'. What is the distance of the school from its source of electricity? What is the extent of the area supplied by the power station? Discuss the concept of a national grid and distribution of power. Find out other interesting facts and figures, for example what is a station's maximum output? Has this ever been reached? What happens if demand exceeds supply?

6 Help the children to plot peak times of electricity demand on a diagram, perhaps in the form of a clock face. Discuss whether these times vary from season to season, and from country to country. (Whilst a peak demand time in England is early evening in the depths of winter, peak demand in California occurs in the summer when everyone is using air-conditioning.)

7 Make a table of power measurement (watts) of common items of household equipment. Ask the children to arrange these in rank order and represent the results on a graph.

PE ACTIVITIES

C22

1 Use PE lessons to investigate matters relating to body energy. It is in our muscles that oxygen is used to 'burn' our food fuel to release energy. Ask the children to practise using muscles. Ask them to hold a weight in one hand with an outstretched arm and raise it into the air. Can they see or feel muscles working in their arm? Use a timer to see for how long they can hold the weight. Time different children to see who is the 'strongest'. Make the test fair by ensuring that all weights used are the same.

2 Do experiments on breathing rates. You can use **copymaster 22** (How many breaths?) to record the number of breaths taken in one minute immediately after completing the named activities. Children should work in pairs and time each other. Use the data for discussion on the value of aerobic exercise, and the relationship between exercise and breathing rates. Compare results from individual children. Some will be fitter than others. Who has the lowest breathing rate after a five minute run? Does this person do a lot of active sport? *Note:* From a health and safety point of view, it is important to ensure that children do not over-exert or exhaust themselves during these activities, particularly those with any adverse medical history or condition.

3 Teach the children how to take pulse rates. Repeat the activities shown on copymaster 22 and make a chart to record pulse rates after exercising. Help the children find out what 'normal' resting pulse rate should be, and an accepted maximum pulse rate after exercise.

ENGLISH, ECONOMIC AND INDUSTRIAL UNDERSTANDING ACTIVITIES

C23

1 Compile a comprehensive 'Which?' guide to domestic appliances. Collect a wide range of pictures to illustrate the book. Ask the children to collect data from interviews with parents and friends. They should find out what makes are in use, whether their owners think they are good products, what are their advantages and disadvantages, and any strengths or weaknesses. Ask them to do a write-up for each item and arrange over-all results in table and graph form. Select a 'star buy' in each category.

In the first instance, do not take cost into account. A second phase of the project could involve comparing the costs and working out best value-for-money in each category. Consider the economics of producing inexpensive items, and the concept of built-in obsolescence.

2 Find out which is the longest-serving appliance owned by a class member's family. Speculate on why it has lasted so long: for example through careful use? Regular servicing? Was it an expensive make?

3 Help the children compile an 'Energy dictionary'. This will give excellent practice in skills of reading, writing and arranging words in alphabetical order, as well as helping them learn the meaning of energy-related words. Use this to clarify, for example, the difference between 'energy' and 'power' (terms which are often confused; power is the rate at which energy is produced or used).

4 Design word games on energy vocabulary. **Copymaster 23** (New ways of getting energy), for example, is a word puzzle which contains the names of alternative energy sources, and gives a conservation message. Ask the children to colour the pictures, untangle the words, and write sentences about the advantages and disadvantages of each source.

5 Ask the children to write imaginative stories on 'Energy of the future', 'The night of the power cuts' and 'A world beyond electricity'.

DESIGN AND TECHNOLOGY ACTIVITIES

1 Help the children design and construct electricity pylons in a classroom corner. Use string for cables. Suspend pictures of appliances which depend on electric power.

This would be a very effective model when placed in front of the power station wall frieze (see Science activities, page 67).

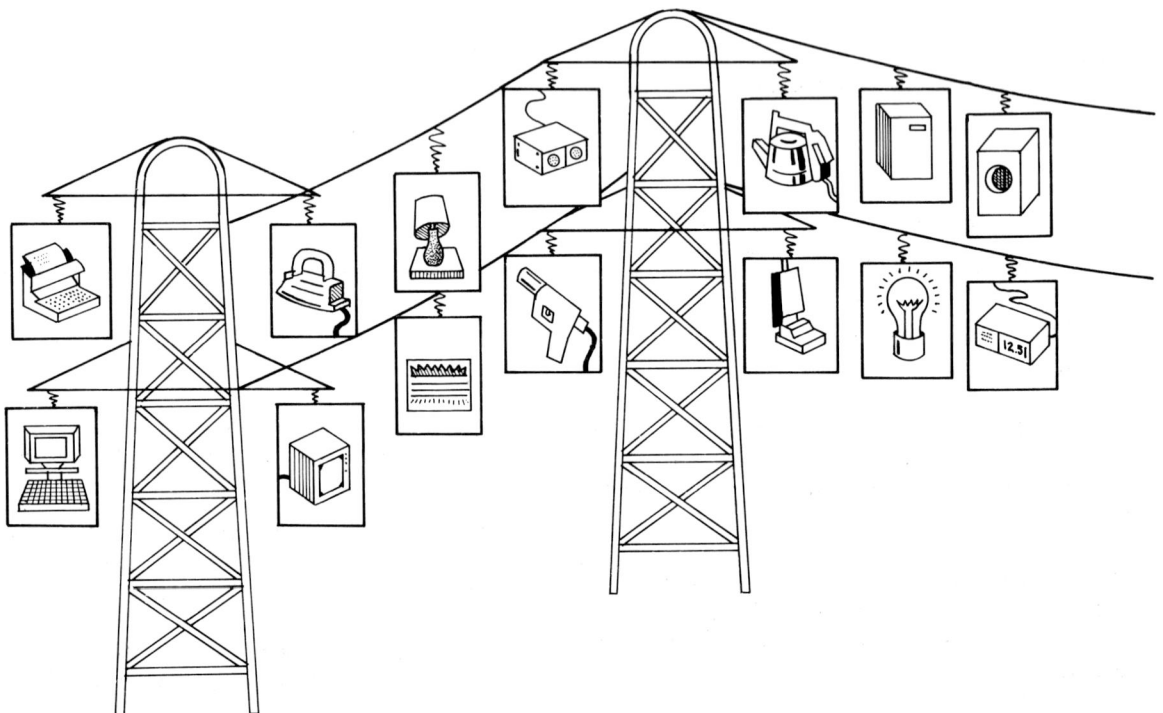

Appliances which depend on electric power

2 With the children, make a model of a section of a coal mine and/or an oil well. Layer clay or papier mâché to represent layers of rock in the earth. Construct buildings, rigs and mine shaft out of cardboard.

3 Help the children design a land repository for nuclear waste materials (intermediate level waste from a power station). The design should include details of where it will be sited, materials needed for its construction, depth in the ground, and so on. All these should be carefully researched beforehand. Ask the children to write an accompanying statement aimed at persuading citizens that the radioactive material will be safely buried.

GEOGRAPHY ACTIVITIES

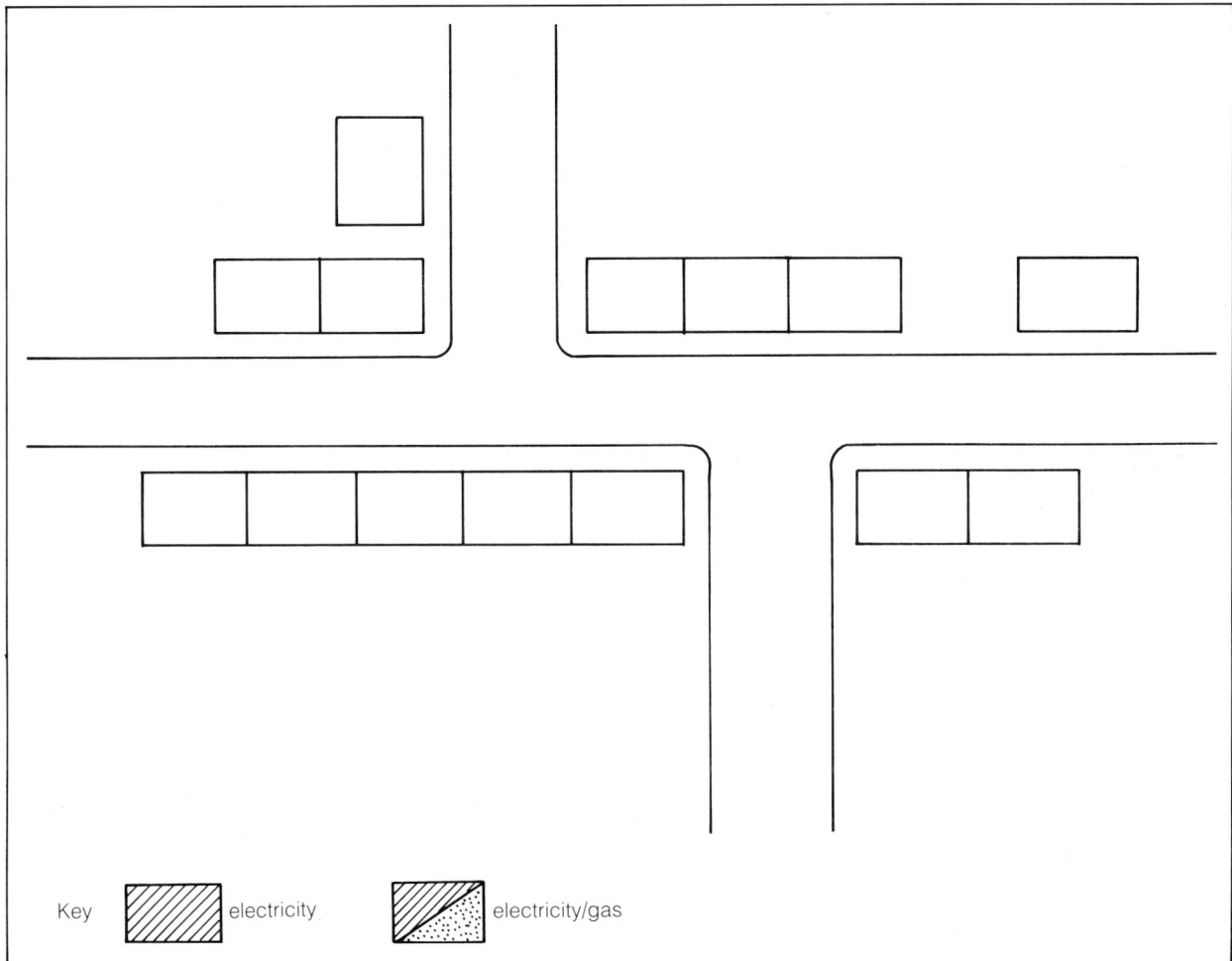

Key ▨ electricity ▨ electricity/gas

High street shops and the power sources they use

1 Take the children out to do 'energy field work' in the local shopping centre or high street. Talk to shopkeepers about their energy needs. Take a simple base map of shops and record the power sources they use.

No doubt all will use electricity, though some may have other power sources too. This activity will give practice in mapwork skills, including orientation and the use of keys.

2 Ask the children to do field sketches of 'street furniture' which is dependent on energy, for example street lights, traffic lights and escalators.

3 From local issues go on to consider energy sources and demand as global concerns. Introduce or reinforce key facts, including:

● The Earth's known reserves of fossil fuels are limited.
● Energy consumption on a worldwide basis continues to grow.
● Many countries depend on buying fuel from others, for example the USA consumes far more oil than it produces.
● Energy conservation is essential. This must involve reductions in energy use and the development of renewable sources such as sun, wind and water.

4 Help the children make posters and write sentences about energy conservation, demonstrating that every individual can contribute to the process.

5 Put the above ideas into practice in the school wherever possible. Write a 'School energy conservation policy'. Post a copy in every classroom and corridor.

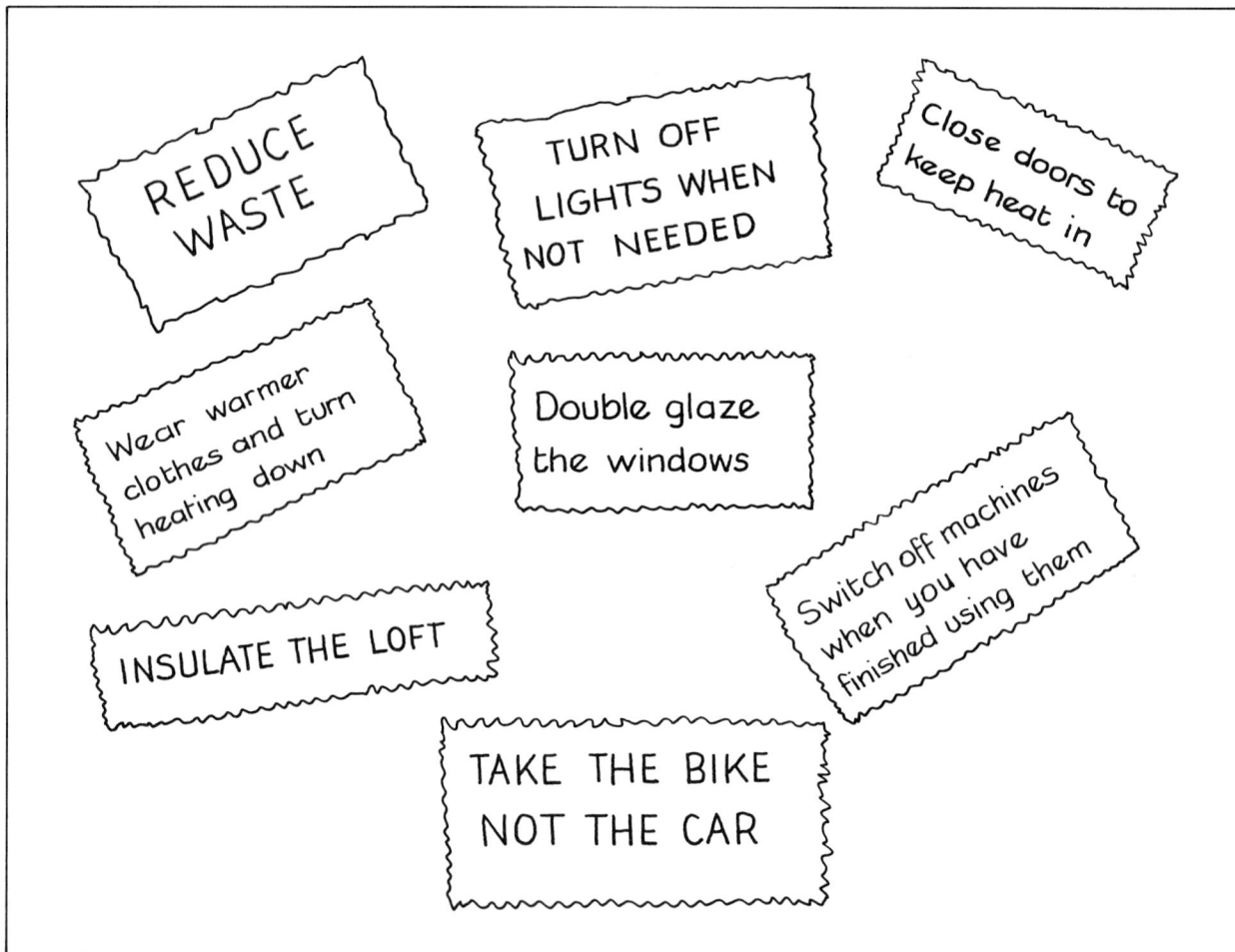

REDUCE WASTE

TURN OFF LIGHTS WHEN NOT NEEDED

Close doors to keep heat in

Wear warmer clothes and turn heating down

Double glaze the windows

Switch off machines when you have finished using them

INSULATE THE LOFT

TAKE THE BIKE NOT THE CAR

Energy conservation slogans

HISTORY ACTIVITIES
C24

1 Visit a transport museum. Ask the children to interview elderly friends and relatives to get information on how transport has changed in the past 40 years or so. Ask the children to paint pictures and write about steam railways, early cars, the use of horses and carts, etc. Make a frieze of a Victorian street, depicting energy in use: transport, street lamps, oil lamps in shops and so on.

2 Use **copymaster 24** (Life down the mine) as a basis for discussing the dramatic changes which have taken place in the coal industry. Ask the children to colour in the picture and imagine the life of a pit pony, spending almost its entire existence underground pulling trucks of coal. Find out about bell pits, the earliest British mines of the twelfth century, and about mining hazards such as floods and cave-ins. If possible, listen to the powerful folk songs of Ewan MacColl and Peggy Seeger, for example *The Big Hewer, Down In The Coalmine,* and

The Gresford Disaster. MacColl's LP entitled 'Steam Whistle Ballads' (Topic Records 12T104, first published in 1964) contains 16 industrial songs, many of which involve mining or steam engines. The LP 'Something To Sing About' by the Ian Campbell Folk Group (Pye Records, PKL 5506, first published in 1972) contains a moving song entitled *The Testimony of Patience Kershaw*, describing working conditions in the mines for children 150 years ago, while the song *Leave Them A Flower* suggests a change in our treatment of the precious environment which we have in keeping for future generations.

This wealth of material will enable the children to write imaginative stories about historical mining and its harsh working conditions. These can then be compared and contrasted with factual accounts of how the industry has changed with technological advances.

Energy on the move

What do all of these things have in common?

Energy chains from the Sun

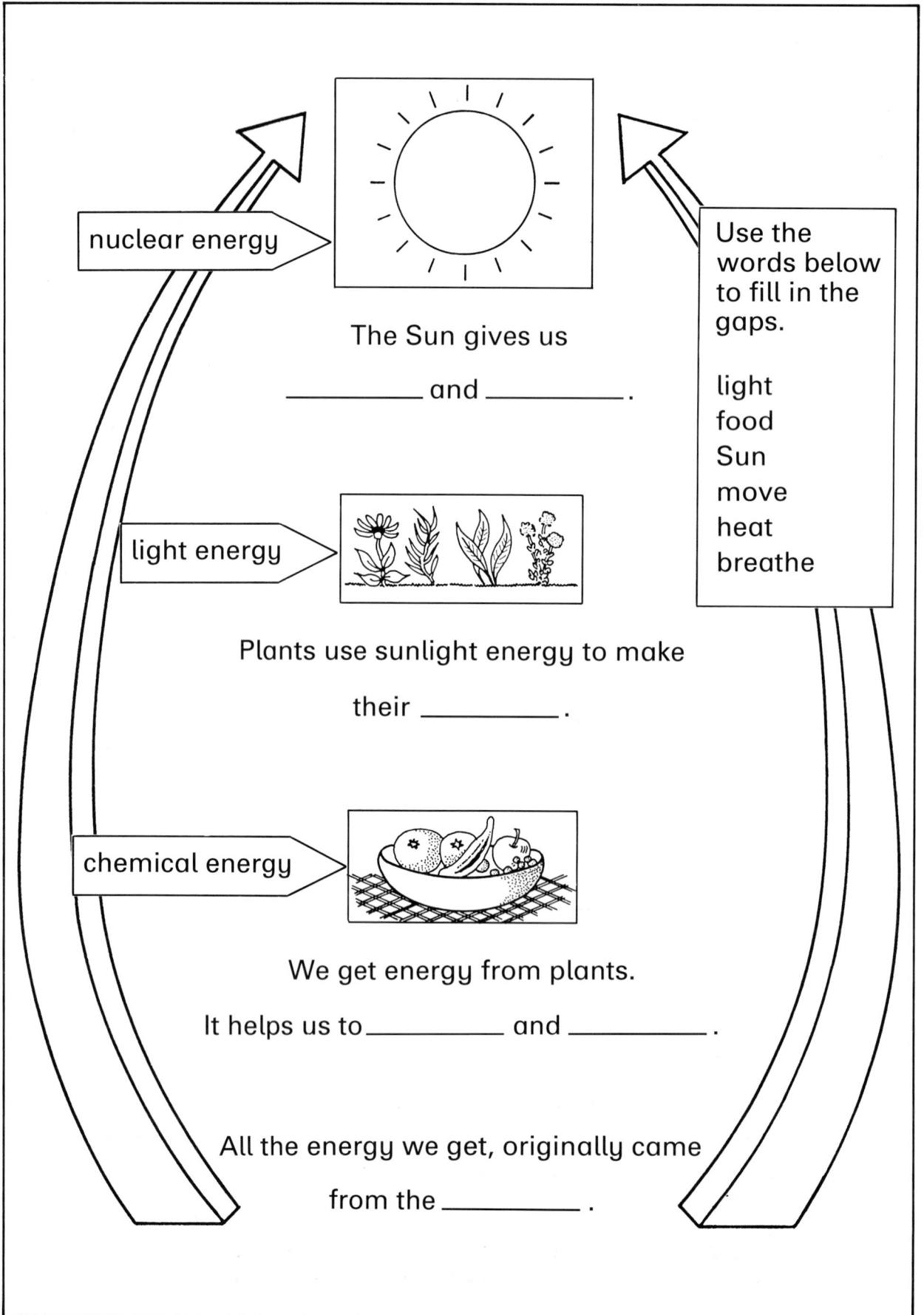

C20

nuclear energy

The Sun gives us

_____ and _____ .

Use the words below to fill in the gaps.

light
food
Sun
move
heat
breathe

light energy

Plants use sunlight energy to make

their _____ .

chemical energy

We get energy from plants.

It helps us to _____ and _____ .

All the energy we get, originally came

from the _____ .

Forms of energy

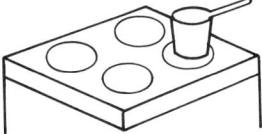 _____ energy

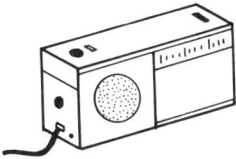 _____ energy

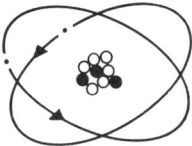 _____ energy

 _____ energy

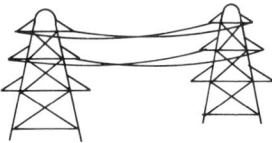 _____ energy

 _____ energy

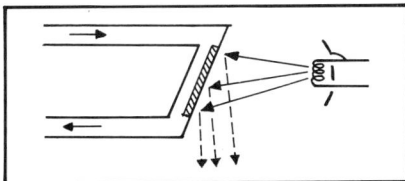 _____ energy

Match these words with the type of energy.

sound	chemical	nuclear	thermal

kinetic	electric	electro-magnetic

How many breaths?

How many breaths in 1 minute? Complete the chart.

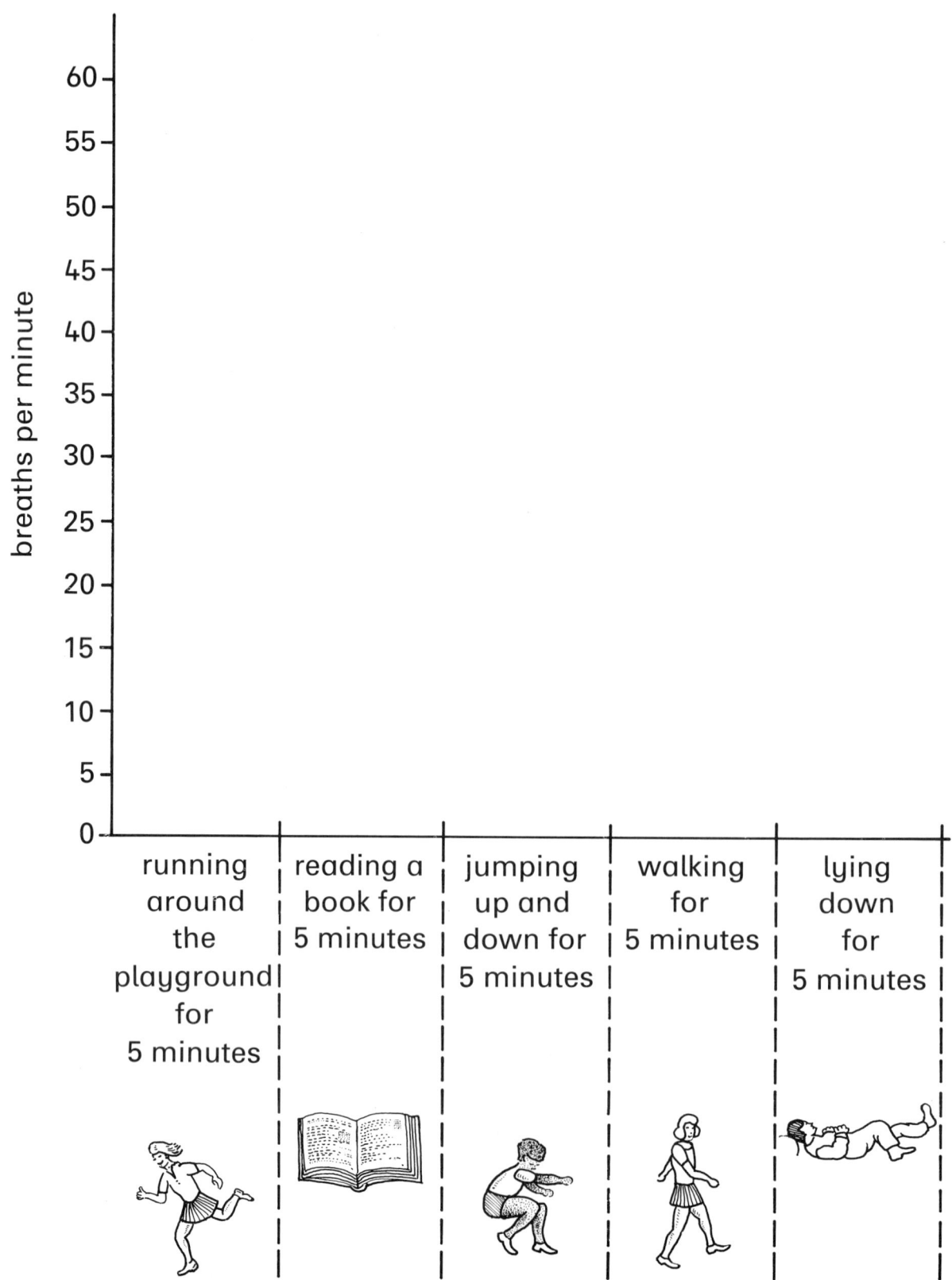

breaths per minute

60 –
55 –
50 –
45 –
40 –
35 –
30 –
25 –
20 –
15 –
10 –
5 –
0

running around the playground for 5 minutes	reading a book for 5 minutes	jumping up and down for 5 minutes	walking for 5 minutes	lying down for 5 minutes

New ways of getting energy

SAVE FOSSIL FUELS

Unscramble the letters to find the alternative sources of energy.

W   W
O
R   E
P   N
I
D

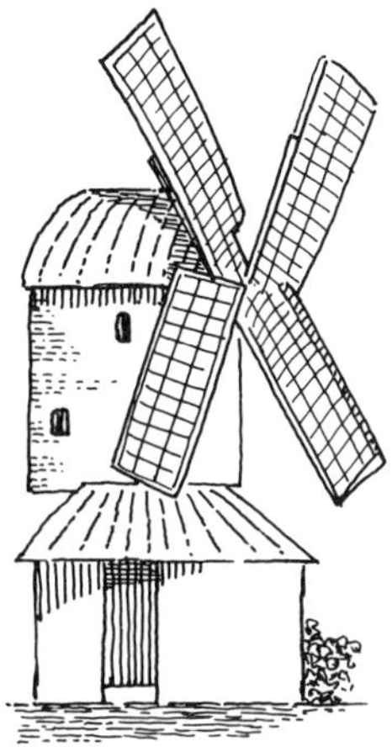

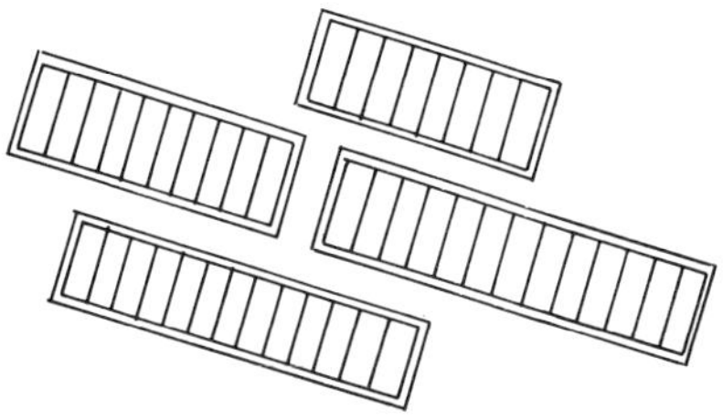

P   L   N   E   S
O   A   R   L   A   S

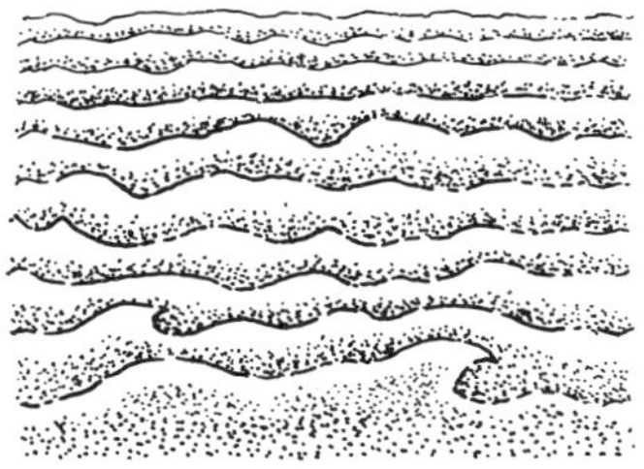

W   P   E   W
A   O   V   E   R

E   D   T
C   R   C
H   P   R
I   O   O
E   W   Y
L   E   R

TREES

National curriculum links

Principal location in the National Curriculum

- Plants and Animals

Other areas covered by topic

- Climate ● Water and Water Supplies ● Materials and Resources ● People and Communities
- Soils, Rocks, Minerals

Context of study

- Local to global concerns

Suggested sub-topics and their location in areas of study of curriculum guidelines for Environmental Education

Sub-topic	Areas of Study in the National Curriculum						
	Climate	Soils, Rocks, Minerals	Water	Materials, Resources, Energy	Plants and Animals	People and Communities	Buildings, Industrialis-ation, Waste
Tropical rain forests	●	○	○	○	●	●	
Wood/Timber	○			●	●	○	○
Woodland habitat	○	○	○		●		
Deforestation	○	○	○	○	●	●	

Key ● Principal location ○ Part coverage

79

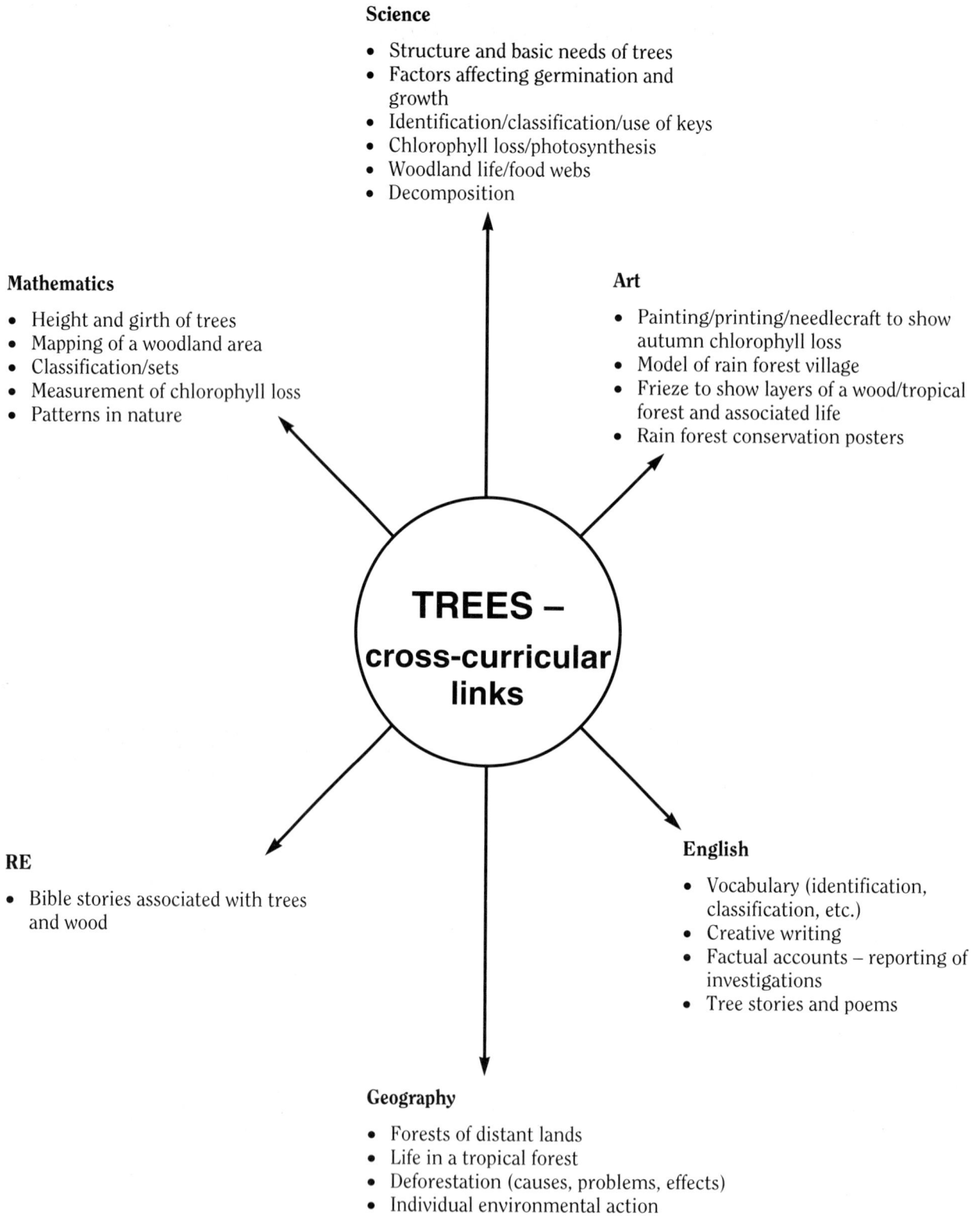

Science

- Structure and basic needs of trees
- Factors affecting germination and growth
- Identification/classification/use of keys
- Chlorophyll loss/photosynthesis
- Woodland life/food webs
- Decomposition

Mathematics

- Height and girth of trees
- Mapping of a woodland area
- Classification/sets
- Measurement of chlorophyll loss
- Patterns in nature

Art

- Painting/printing/needlecraft to show autumn chlorophyll loss
- Model of rain forest village
- Frieze to show layers of a wood/tropical forest and associated life
- Rain forest conservation posters

TREES – cross-curricular links

RE

- Bible stories associated with trees and wood

English

- Vocabulary (identification, classification, etc.)
- Creative writing
- Factual accounts – reporting of investigations
- Tree stories and poems

Geography

- Forests of distant lands
- Life in a tropical forest
- Deforestation (causes, problems, effects)
- Individual environmental action

Basics to be developed throughout the topic

Concepts

- Relationships between living things (plants and animals) and the Earth: the natural cycle, decomposition
- Dependence of human life on trees
- The importance of trees in our world

Attitudes

- Appreciation of and care for living things
- Care and respect for the Earth on which we depend
- Appreciation of the aesthetic qualities of trees as well as their practical use

Environmental issues

- Conservation
- Deforestation
- Management of the world's resources
- Effects of climate on plant and animal life
- Endangered species
- Destruction of natural habitats

STARTING POINTS

● Use the local environment to investigate trees from first-hand experience. Almost all schools will have one or more trees on the site, and the surrounding neighbourhood will provide ample scope for initial observations. This topic can be developed in any season of the year. More often than not, teachers undertake a study of trees in the autumn, yet all seasons provide worthwhile starting points. Look at tree flowers, the bark and visible roots, branches and twigs, opening buds, leaves and fruits.

● Wherever possible visit a park, woodland or forest habitat to enable the children to appreciate the complexity of an environment where many trees grow together, and inter-relationships that exist among trees, the natural world and other living things, including humans. Make a collection of books, posters and other illustrations to aid identification and the development of other knowledge and understanding about trees and forests.

SCIENCE ACTIVITIES

C25 –27

[1] **Copymaster 25** (What is a tree?) introduces children to the basic idea that a tree is a plant, and is made up of a number of parts in a similar way to other members of the plant world. Ask the children to colour each part, label it, then consider how a tree grows.

Numbers 1–6 can be put in the boxes underneath the drawings to show the order in which these parts of a tree grow, starting at ground level and working upwards. The sheet may be classroom-based in preparation for field work. Other words may be introduced and added to the children's own drawings of trees, for example crown, bark, branches and seeds.

[2] Discuss a tree's basic needs, including soil, water and sunlight.

[3] **Copymaster 26** (Good soil for healthy trees) is a practical activity to show how growth of trees is dependent on critical environmental factors. This leads on to an understanding of how soil type affects the growth of woodland and forest. Trees grow in many different soil types around the world, but some soils are better at promoting tree growth than others. In this experiment, the children will be able to compare the growth of two different tree seeds in three different soils.

You will need
- A plastic jar
- 6 small flower pots

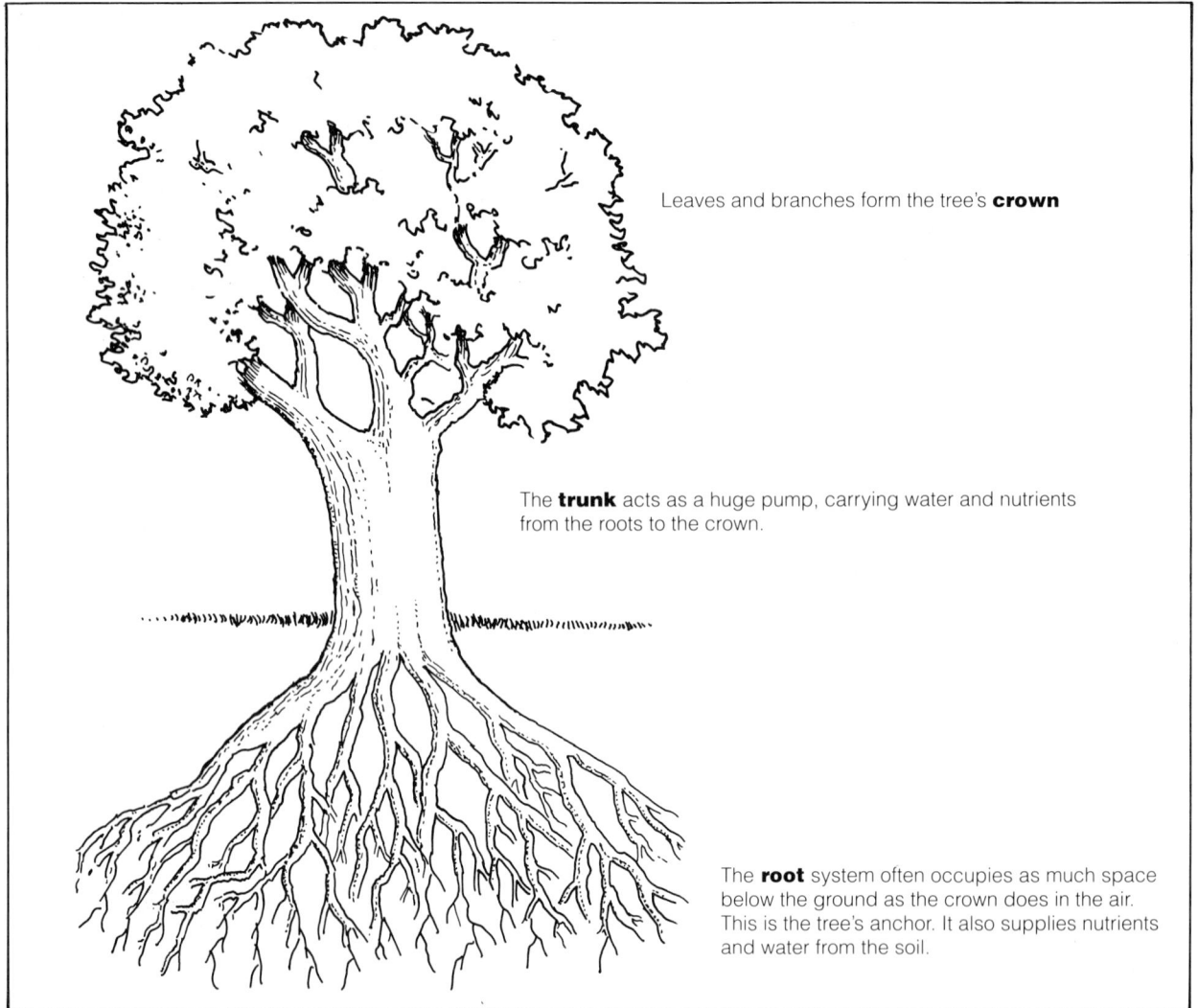

Leaves and branches form the tree's **crown**

The **trunk** acts as a huge pump, carrying water and nutrients from the roots to the crown.

The **root** system often occupies as much space below the ground as the crown does in the air. This is the tree's anchor. It also supplies nutrients and water from the soil.

- 3 acorns, 3 conkers
- Water
- Sand
- Clay
- Loam or potting compost.

What to do
- Fill the plastic jar with water and place the acorns and conkers in it for a few days. This encourages them to sprout.
- Place some sand in two of the pots, loam or potting compost in another two, and clay in the final two. All pots should be around three-quarters full.
- Carefully place the seeds in the pots, one acorn and one conker in each type of soil.
- Water each pot and place them all in a warm position.
- Observe them regularly. Water them every few days, or when the soil dries out. Keep the soil moist but not wet.
- As the seeds begin to grow, record observations on the chart. Growth can also be measured and recorded pictorially.

From this experiment, ask the children to answer the questions: Which soil seems best for the growth of tree seeds? Why?

Broadleaved trees have wide flat leaves. Their seeds are enclosed by fruits. The fruits vary from species to species. Some broadleaved trees have separate male and female flowers. Others have flowers with male and female parts. Most broadleaved trees are deciduous.

82

Coniferous trees have tiny leaves, either shaped like needles or like overlapping scales. They have both male and female flowers. Seeds of conifers are contained within cones, which open and release seeds when they are ripe. Most coniferous trees are evergreen.

4 Let the children observe trees growing in a variety of habitats: gardens, parks, school grounds and woodlands. When observation can be extended over the various seasons, a cyclical pattern of growth will be noted. The key skills and concepts to introduce and develop include identification of trees and tree parts, and classification into broadleaved/conifers and deciduous/evergreen varieties.

5 Ask the children to look carefully at leaves and other tree parts under a magnifying glass or microscope. Draw the pattern of veins. Discuss the difference in texture of broad leaves and coniferous leaves.

6 Ask the children to observe any interesting patterns of colour loss from broadleaved trees in the autumn.

The green colouring in leaves is chlorophyll, essential for the process of photosynthesis. Leaves are the tree's food-makers. In the process of photosynthesis, the chlorophyll absorbs sunlight. This light energy is used to make food from water and carbon dioxide in the air.

7 Trees affect the lives of many other living things. In any woodland or forest habitat, complex food chains and food webs exist. Take the children to visit a woodland and observe and record evidence of animals, birds and insects that live there permanently or are temporary visitors in search of food or shelter. Help the children to build up a knowledge of simple food chains in a woodland area.

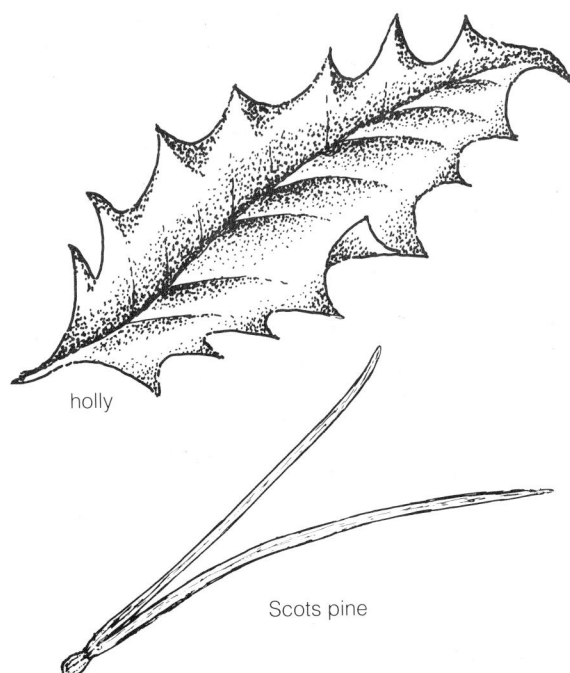

holly

Scots pine

Most evergreen leaves are either very small or else tough and waxy. This helps to stop them losing water into the atmosphere.

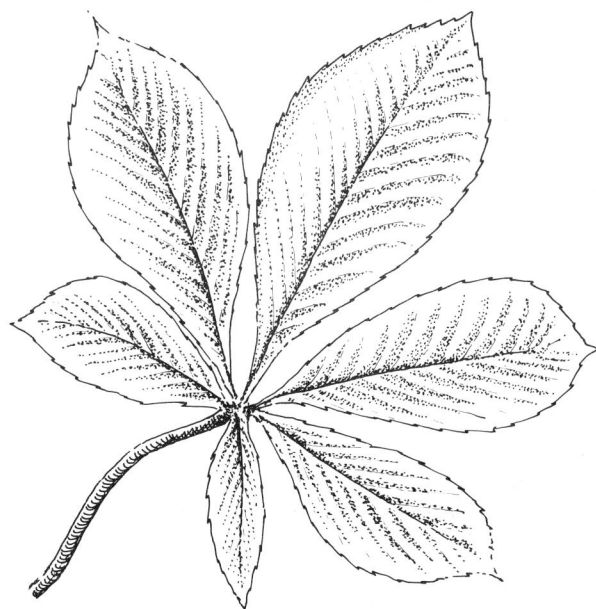

horse chestnut

Broadleaved trees have leaves that are softer and more delicate. They lose more water through their leaves.

83

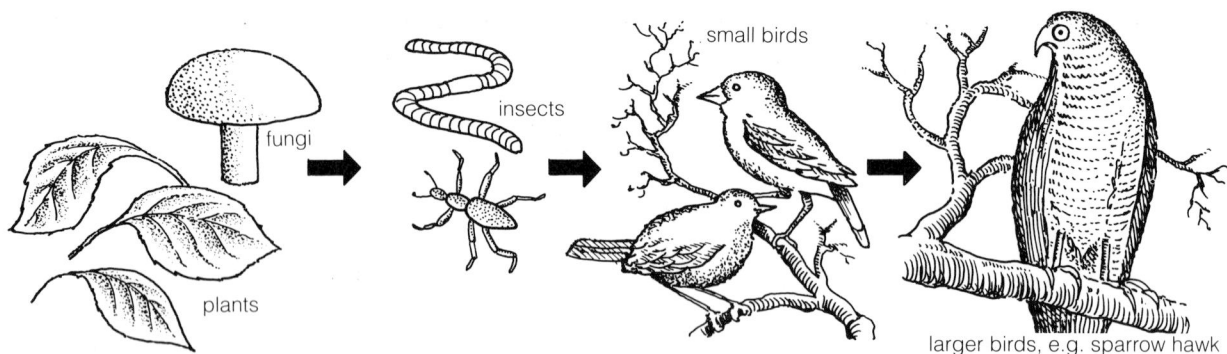

A simple woodland food chain

Use **copymaster 27** (Food web in a wood) to extend this into a more complex food web. Follow the food chains that make up the web. Draw arrows to show the direction of the food, linking the boxes.

8 Help the children investigate the key process of decomposition. Search on the woodland floor for evidence of rotting leaves. Collect some dead leaves and bury them in a bucket of damp soil. Ask the children to examine the remains after one month has passed, and again after two months. Discuss the role of trees in soil formation and in the natural cycle that exists. (See also Farms topic, Science activity 2, page 37.)

Investigate the role of decomposers: worms, bacteria, fungi, etc.

9 Use simple keys for identification of tree species.

10 Sub-topics with Science as a discernible core can be developed on a wide variety of themes: for example, plant life in woodlands, animal, bird or insect life, life in a coniferous wood, life in a broadleaved woodland, the woodland floor, the wood at night, uses of timber, and specific locations (such as tropical rain forests).

Leaves fall to the ground in autumn time.

Goodness from the soil returns to the tree.

decomposition of leaves and other dead material

The natural cycle of decomposition

MATHEMATICS ACTIVITIES

1 Do first-hand investigations to measure and compare the girth and heights of trees. Design and use a simple clinometer for measuring height.

2 Study the distribution of trees and/or plants on the woodland floor. Make a plan of a 5-metre-square area of woodland showing location of trees and other plants. A

wide area of woodland can be mapped in this way if children work in pairs, each pair covering one 5-metre-square area.

3 As a follow-on activity to identification, ask the children to organise trees seen in a wood into sets. This can be based on field work activities and the results of a

84

The background could be shaded to show the area covered by grass or other plants too small to be recorded individually.

Key

 tree (identify if possible)   ✳ bluebell   fern   fungus

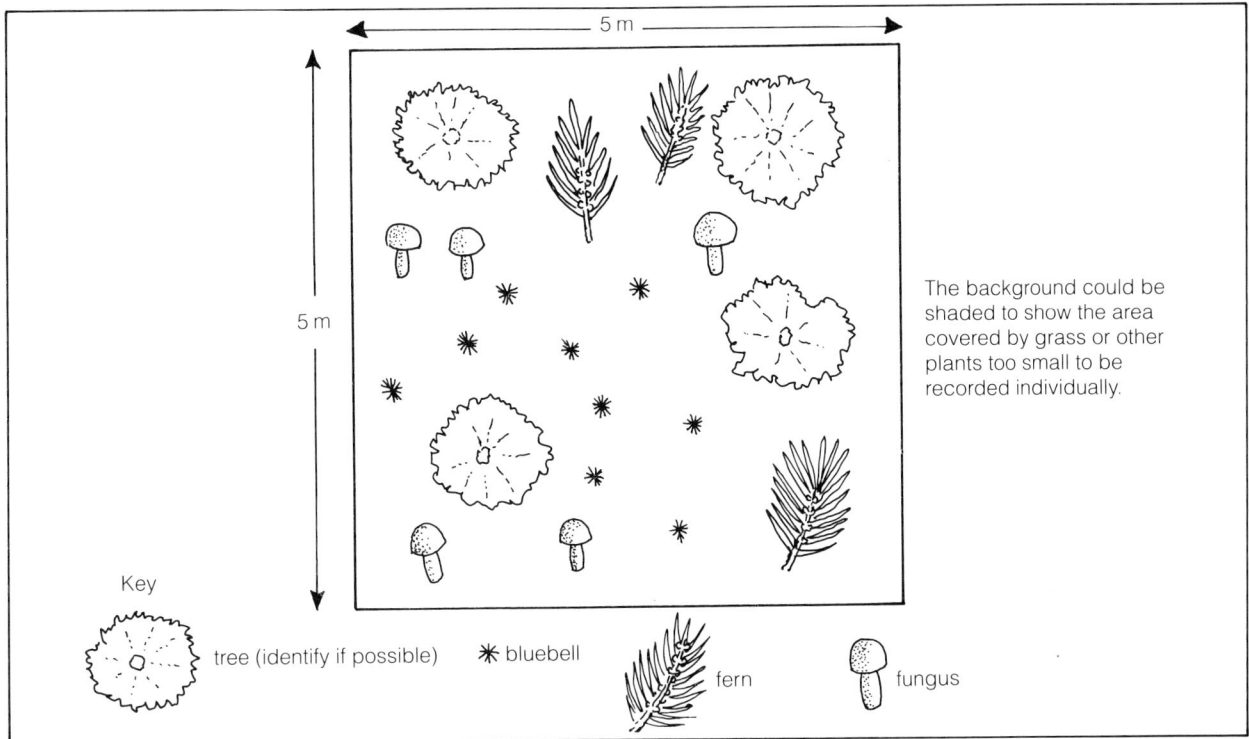

Distribution of trees and plants in a given area on the woodland floor

woodland survey. The four categories of deciduous, evergreen, broadleaved and conifers can be used for analysis of divisions and overlap.

4 Ask the children to draw graphs to show the number of trees identified in each of the above categories.

5 Ask the children to work in pairs to investigate the pattern and area of chlorophyll loss in autumn leaves. Each pair should collect six different horse chestnut leaves that have fallen from a tree and measure (using tracing paper and graph paper) the area of chlorophyll left in each.

Ask them to place the leaves in rank order from that with the greatest amount of chlorophyll left to that with the least (A–F), that is the 'greenest' to the 'brownest'.

Ask the children to observe the leaves closely. Does the chlorophyll remaining tend to be in a similar position on all leaves? Compare them with the other children's leaves to see if a pattern emerges in the class as a whole (chlorophyll often disappears from the edges of the leaves first, and from the area in and around the veins last). Consider why this happens.

Further investigatory work can be undertaken to consider whether this pattern is typical of *all* horse chestnut trees. Does a similar pattern exist in other tree species?

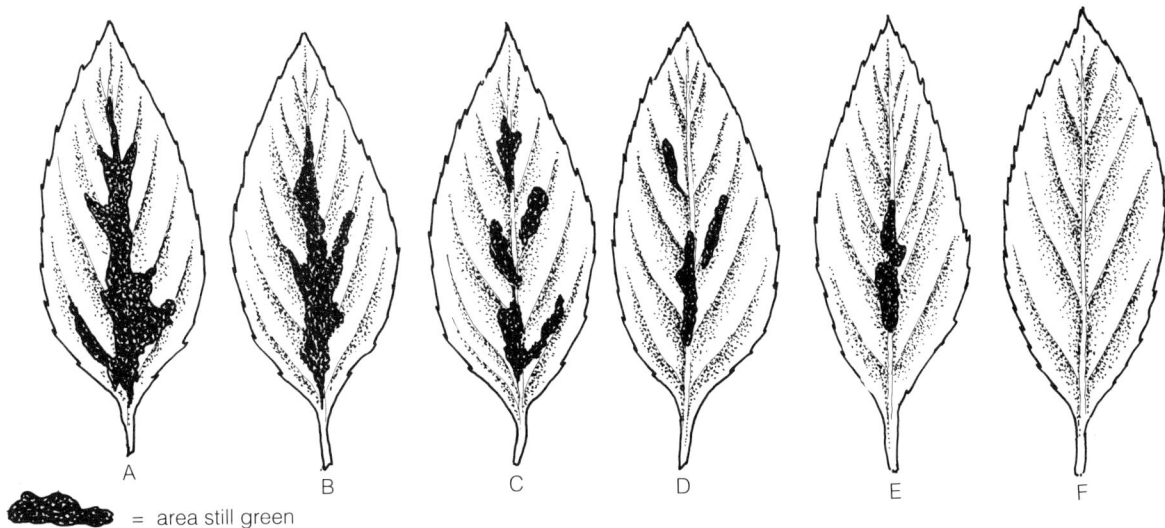

= area still green

Chlorophyll loss in autumn leaves

85

ENGLISH ACTIVITIES

C28 –29

1 Introduce and discuss vocabulary relevant to the identification and classification of trees. Key words to understand will be broadleaved, conifer, deciduous and evergreen.

Copymaster 28 (Woodland crossword) is designed to help children learn the vocabulary necessary to understand the life of trees and to reinforce key ideas associated with the growth pattern of trees and inter-relationships in a woodland.

2 Undertake creative writing activities based on tree and forest life. Story or poem titles may include 'The wood at night', 'My home on the woodland floor', 'In search of prey', 'Eyes at night', 'Creatures of the bark', 'Bird's eye view', etc.

3 Ask the children to do factual writing. Titles may include seasonal accounts, for example 'Woodland winter', 'Tracks and trails', 'Human impact on woodland' (cutting trees for timber, coppicing, pollarding trees), 'Temporary visitors', etc.

Copymaster 29 (Jumbled fruits and seeds) can be used to play a game. Write each of the jumbled words on a card and draw corresponding pictures on separate cards. The children can work in pairs to match the cards.

Alternatively, you can ask the children to work individually to unscramble the words, colour in the pictures and match them to the words.

4 Read stories and poems about trees and forest life.

GEOGRAPHY ACTIVITIES

C30

The topic of trees lends itself admirably to the study of distant places, notably tropical rain forests, which would make an ideal sub-topic with strong environmental content.

1 Discover the location of the world's rain forests, their importance and problems associated with them. Discuss the reasons for deforestation. These include:

- Providing timber for sale around the world
- Obtaining wood for fires and construction of homes for local people
- Providing land for cattle ranching
- Allowing space for other farming
- Clearing the way to construct roads, bridges, railways, etc.

2 Discuss the impact that deforestation has on the environment and all living things within it. What are the problems associated with deforestation? How do these problems affect local people, plant and animal life, climate and soils and our planet in general?

3 **Copymaster 30** (Layers in a tropical forest) can be used as a cover for the children's workbooks. Ask the children to colour in the picture, which shows the layers of a tropical forest. They can add their own drawings of forest animals, birds and insects in the appropriate places.

4 Discuss how people around the world may show concern for preserving these vital forest habitats. Emphasise the importance of taking individual action; people should appreciate the need for conserving and recycling paper and for not purchasing products derived from valuable hardwood trees.

5 Set up a paper recycling scheme in the school.

6 Investigate schemes in the local community.

RE ACTIVITIES

1 Tell stories from the Bible associated with trees and timber. Below are some examples:

- There is a legend that tells us that the wood of the dogwood tree was used for the crucifixion.

- The word Gethsemane means 'place of the oil press'. Olive trees grow there, which give us oil.
- Noah saved his animals in an ark built of wood.
- The Tree of Knowledge.

ART ACTIVITIES

1 Use paint or needlecraft to make accurate representations of chlorophyll loss in autumn leaves, related to Mathematics activity 5, page 85.

2 Help the children make a large collage frieze of woodland/forest layers, showing the canopy, sub-canopy and ground level plants. Add birds, animals and insects in the appropriate places.

3 Help the children make a model of a rain forest village.

4 Ask the children to design posters to tell others about the need for conservation of tropical trees.

Leaves and branches form the tree's **crown**

The **trunk** acts as a huge pump, carrying water and nutrients from the roots to the crown.

The **root** system often occupies as much space below the ground as the crown does in the air. This is the tree's anchor. It also supplies nutrients and water from the soil.

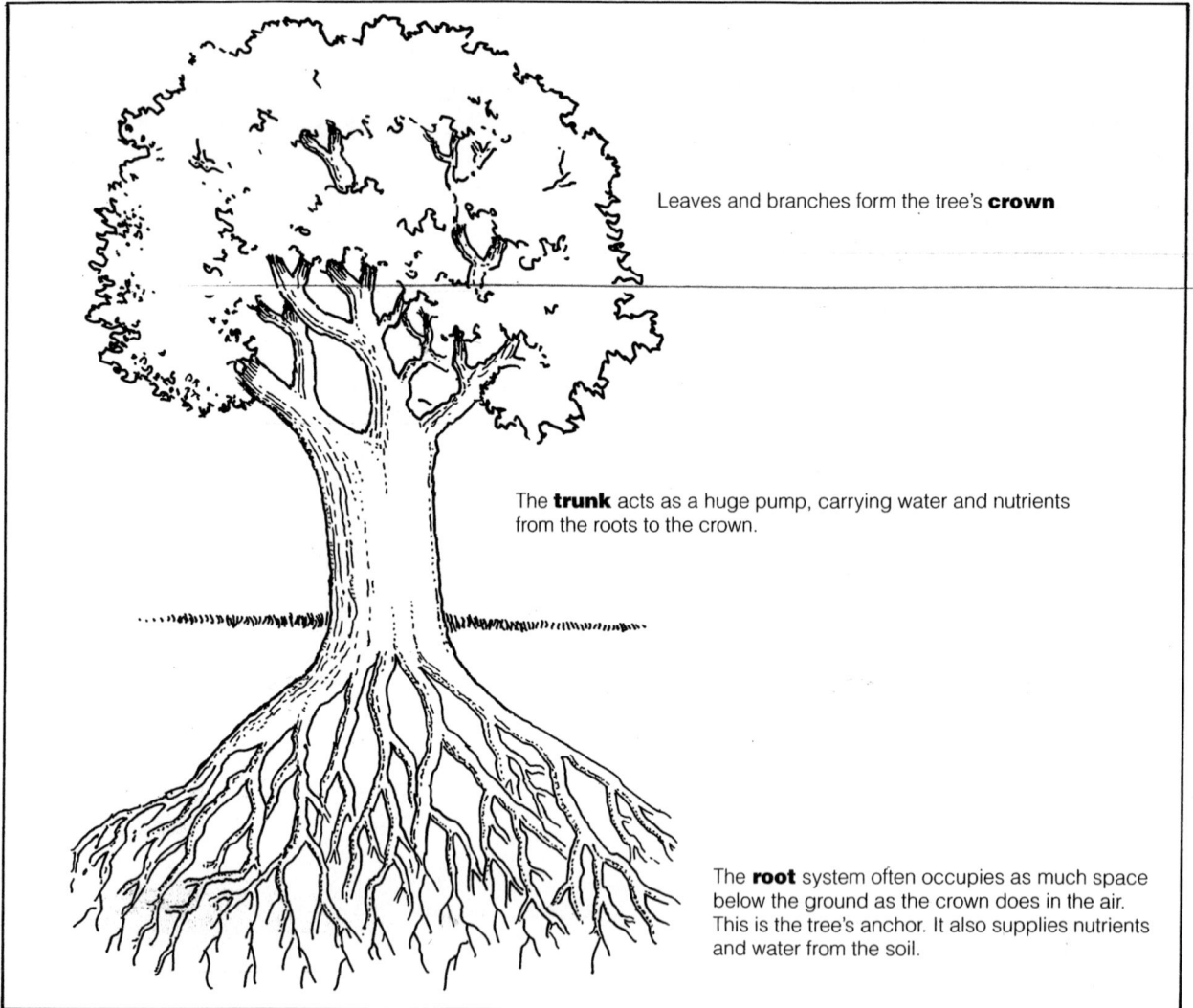

- 3 acorns, 3 conkers
- Water
- Sand
- Clay
- Loam or potting compost.

What to do

- Fill the plastic jar with water and place the acorns and conkers in it for a few days. This encourages them to sprout.
- Place some sand in two of the pots, loam or potting compost in another two, and clay in the final two. All pots should be around three-quarters full.
- Carefully place the seeds in the pots, one acorn and one conker in each type of soil.
- Water each pot and place them all in a warm position.
- Observe them regularly. Water them every few days, or when the soil dries out. Keep the soil moist but not wet.
- As the seeds begin to grow, record observations on the chart. Growth can also be measured and recorded pictorially.

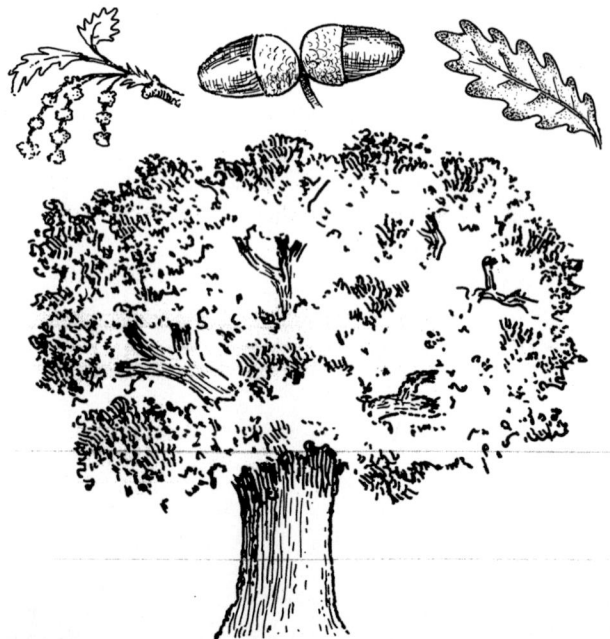

Broadleaved trees have wide flat leaves. Their seeds are enclosed by fruits. The fruits vary from species to species. Some broadleaved

What is a tree?

☐

☐

☐

☐

☐

☐

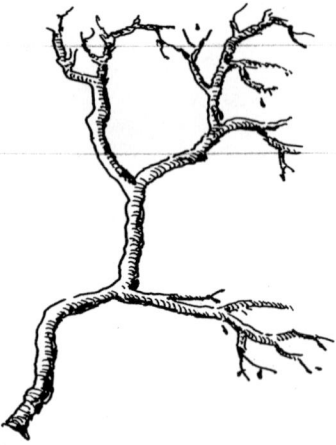

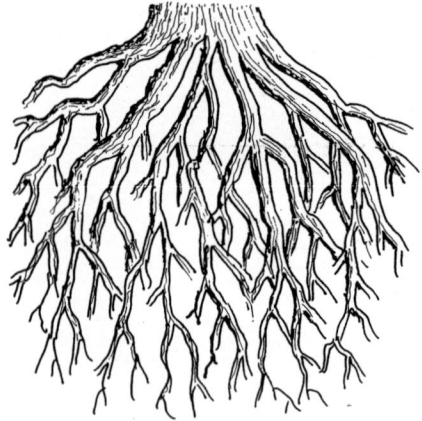

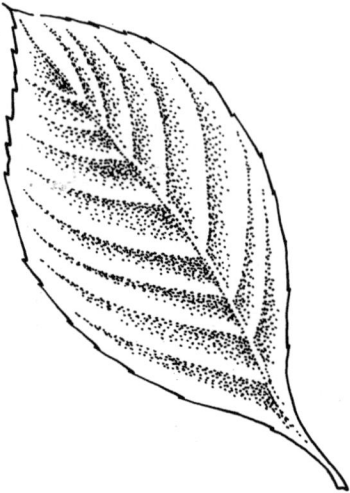

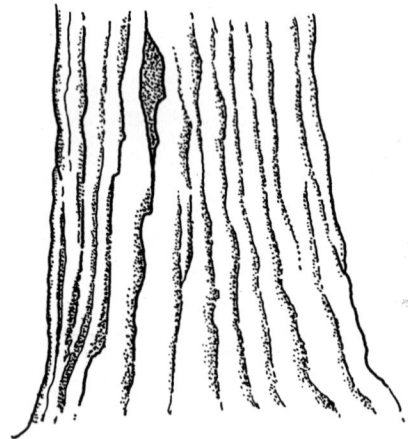

Label each part. Put a number from 1–6 in the boxes, to show the order in which the parts of a tree grow.

What is a tree?

☐

☐

☐

☐

☐

☐

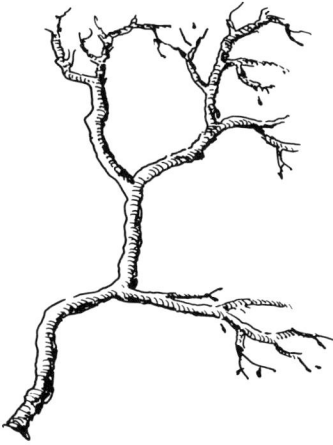

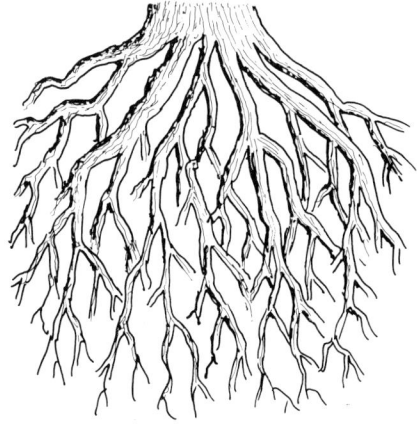

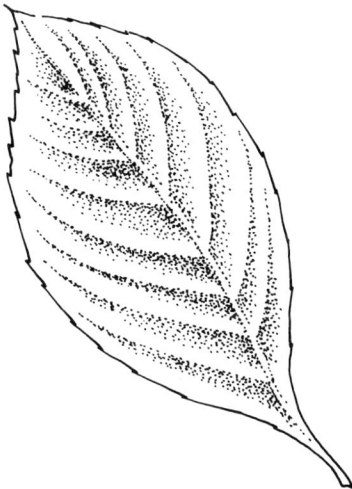

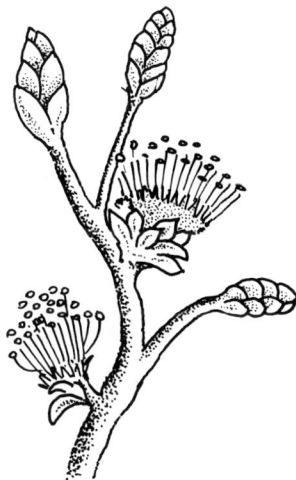

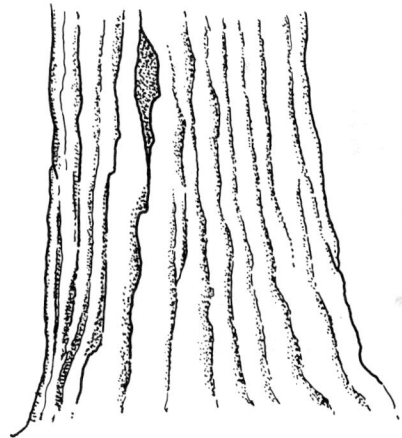

Label each part. Put a number from 1–6 in the boxes, to show the order in which the parts of a tree grow.

Good soil for healthy trees

Write and draw what happened.

acorn in sand	conker in sand
acorn in clay	conker in clay
acorn in loam/compost	conker in loam/compost

Food web in a wood

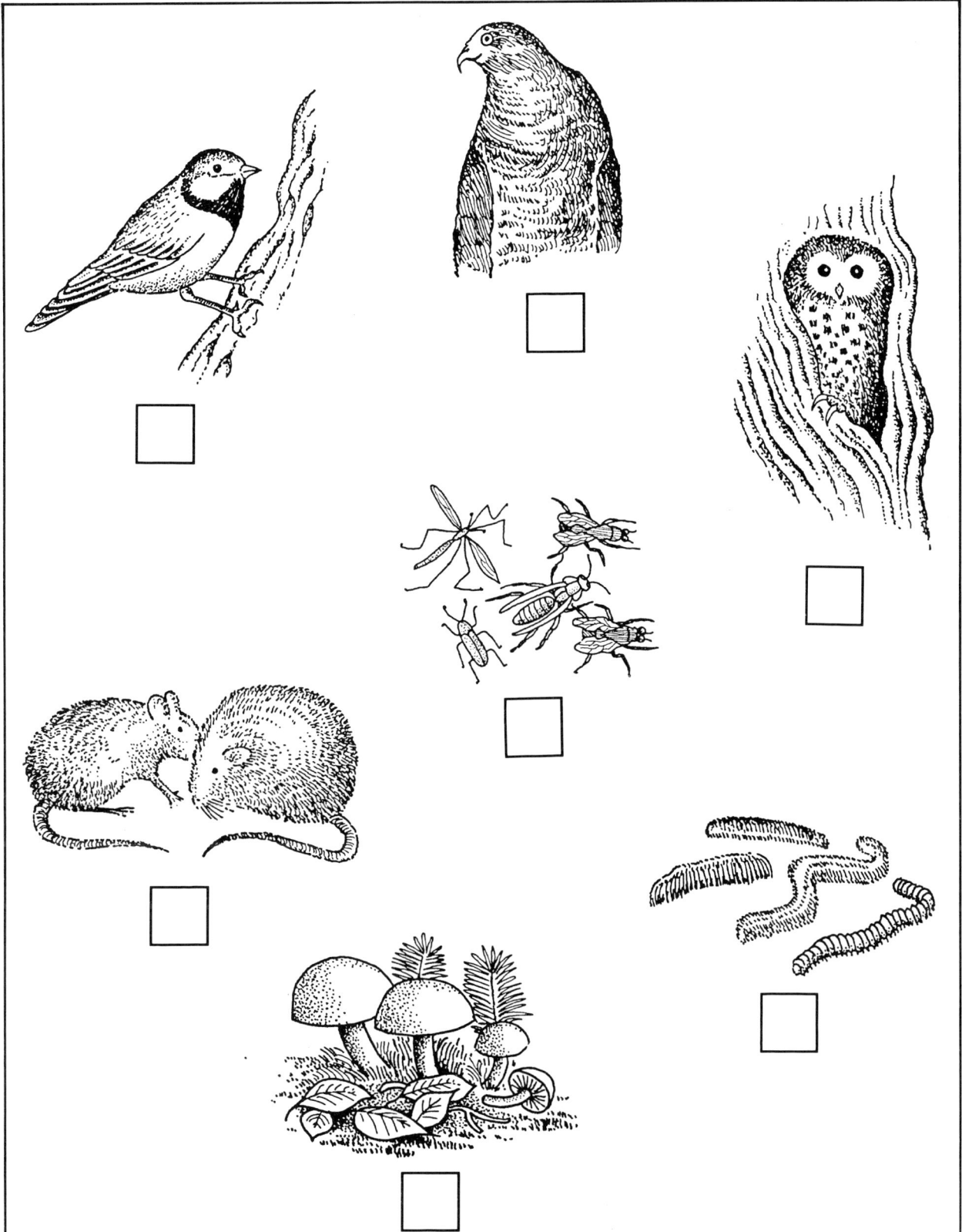

Draw arrows to link the boxes together to show the direction in which food goes.

Woodland crossword

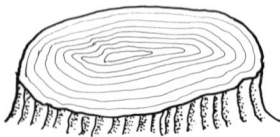

C28

CLUES

Across

2   Trees with wide, flat leaves
5   Seeds of these trees are born in cones
7   Added regularly to the trunk
8   Broadleaved, evergreen, well used at Christmas

Down

1   Top layer in a woodland
3   Have a habit of losing leaves
4   Many are found in the woodland habitat
6   Deciduous conifer

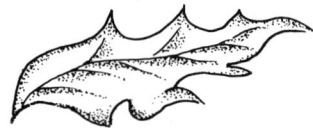

Jumbled fruits and seeds

Unscramble the words to discover the names of some well-known tree fruits and seeds.

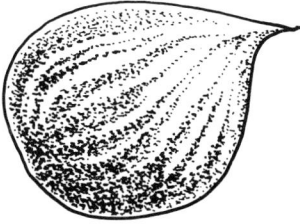  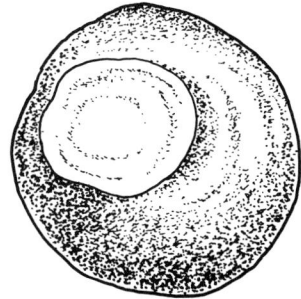

1 CRNOA

2 DEERL RESIEBR

3 EWTES HENTUSCT

4 ECRMYSAO NGWSI

5 ORCNEK

6 HCBEE UTN

 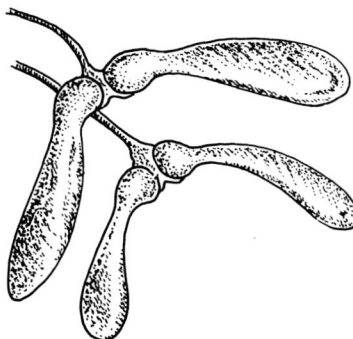 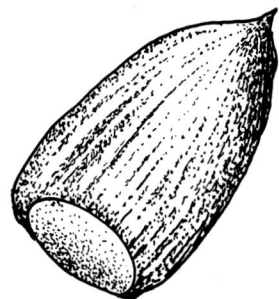

Layers in a tropical forest

CANOPY

SUB-CANOPY

GROUND COVER

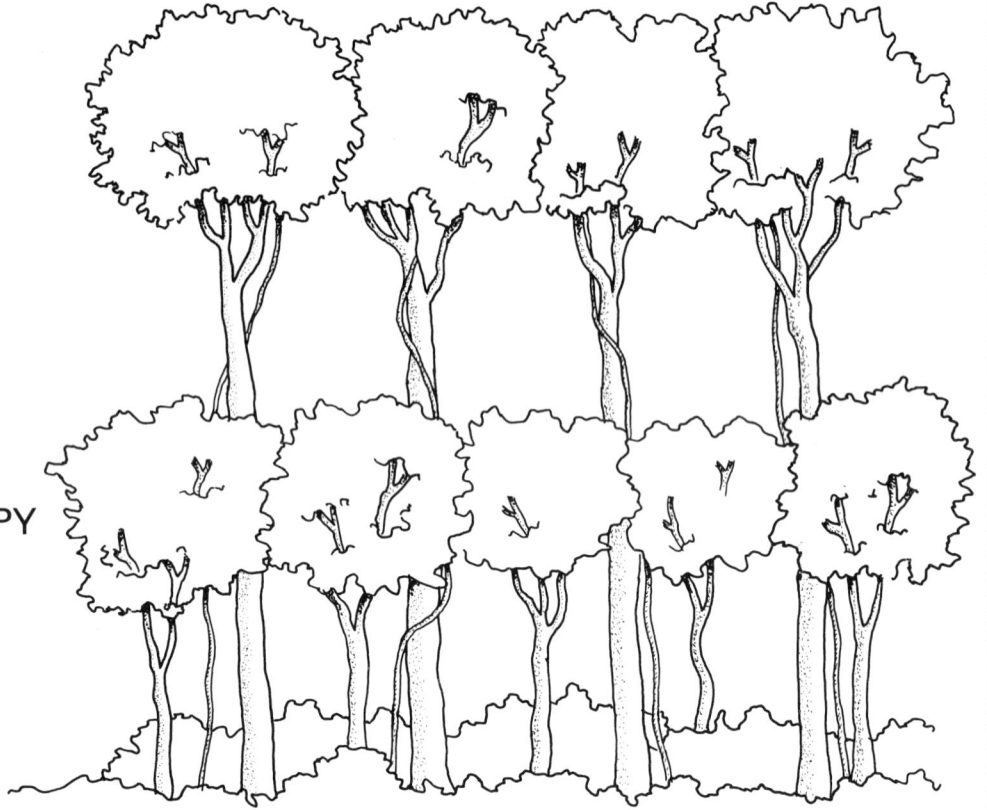

Where would you find: a gorilla, a tree frog, a humming bird, a spider monkey?

Add your own drawings of forest creatures.

FOOD

National curriculum links

Principal location in the National Curriculum

- Plants and Animals • People and Communities

Other areas covered by topic

- Soils, Rocks, Minerals • Materials, Resources, Energy • Water • Climate

Context of study

- Local to global concerns

Suggested sub-topics and their location in areas of study of curriculum guidelines for Environmental Education

Sub-topic	Areas of Study in the National Curriculum						
	Climate	Soils, Rocks, Minerals	Water	Materials, Resources, Energy	Plants and Animals	People and Communities	Buildings, Industrialis-ation, Waste
Farming	○	●	○		●	○	
Keeping healthy			○	○		●	
Food from other lands	●	○	●		●	○	
Running a restaurant				○	○	●	●

Key ● Principal location ○ Part coverage

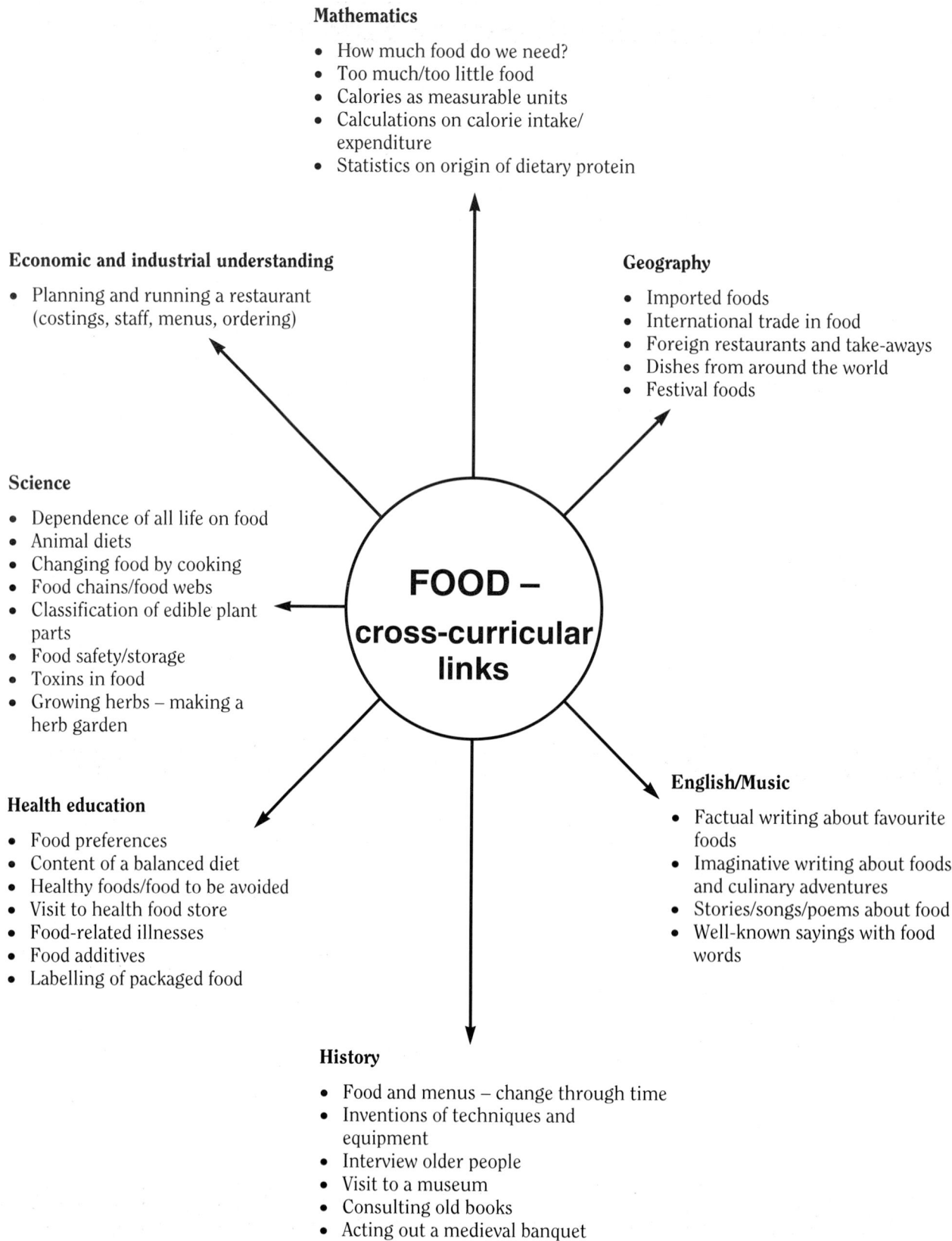

Mathematics

- How much food do we need?
- Too much/too little food
- Calories as measurable units
- Calculations on calorie intake/expenditure
- Statistics on origin of dietary protein

Economic and industrial understanding

- Planning and running a restaurant (costings, staff, menus, ordering)

Geography

- Imported foods
- International trade in food
- Foreign restaurants and take-aways
- Dishes from around the world
- Festival foods

Science

- Dependence of all life on food
- Animal diets
- Changing food by cooking
- Food chains/food webs
- Classification of edible plant parts
- Food safety/storage
- Toxins in food
- Growing herbs – making a herb garden

FOOD – cross-curricular links

English/Music

- Factual writing about favourite foods
- Imaginative writing about foods and culinary adventures
- Stories/songs/poems about food
- Well-known sayings with food words

Health education

- Food preferences
- Content of a balanced diet
- Healthy foods/food to be avoided
- Visit to health food store
- Food-related illnesses
- Food additives
- Labelling of packaged food

History

- Food and menus – change through time
- Inventions of techniques and equipment
- Interview older people
- Visit to a museum
- Consulting old books
- Acting out a medieval banquet

Basics to be developed throughout the topic

Concepts

- Inter-relationships of all living things
- Dependence of human life on plants and animals
- Essential nature of food in our own lives
- Relationships between living things and the Earth, soils, water and light

Attitudes

- Appreciation of and care for living things
- Care and respect for our Earth
- Tolerance of other people's customs, preferences and ways of life
- Concern for other people who are less fortunate than ourselves (those in lands of drought and famine, those who cannot afford food)

Environmental issues

- Importance of climate and soils
- Management of the world's resources
- Conservation
- Human populations and their needs
- Inequality between industrialised nations and the Developing World

STARTING POINTS

- Ask the children to write about or design their favourite meal. Discuss their menus. This will lead on to a wide range of questions and issues that can be developed in a cross-curricular way, and will include awareness of individual preferences, tastes, and tolerances of other people's likes and dislikes.

- Take a particular meal as a starting point, for example breakfast or the menu for school lunch. Analyse the ingredients and investigate such matters as where they were bought, where they originate from, how they were prepared, how much they cost, and why we eat these things.

- With the children, investigate menus from local restaurants and take-aways. Compare ingredients, costs and methods of cooking.

- Select a focus for development, perhaps deriving from one of the starting points above. This may be one commodity, for example bread, fish, potatoes, sugar or milk, or a more general theme such as farming for food, the supermarket, the Chinese take-away, school meals.

- Make a collection of books, posters, films, information sheets, etc. about the chosen focus and related sub-topics. National organisations such as the National Dairy Council and the Potato Marketing Board provide a wide range of materials for teachers and children.

MATHEMATICS ACTIVITIES

C31

1 Consider the basic questions of why we need food, and how much we need. Ask the children why they eat. Answers will no doubt include: 'Because food looks good'; 'Because food smells good'; 'Because it tastes good'; 'Because I am hungry'; 'Because our bodies need food'.
This leads on to the basic concept of energy, and that without food our bodies would not be able to move or survive. The question of 'how much food?' is clearly related to our basic needs. Ask the children to list, draw or write about the food they eat in a typical day. Ask them to consider whether some people eat more food than they need and whether others eat less food than they need. What is the correct amount of food that people should eat?
This can lead on to ideas and discussion about diets.

Why we eat food

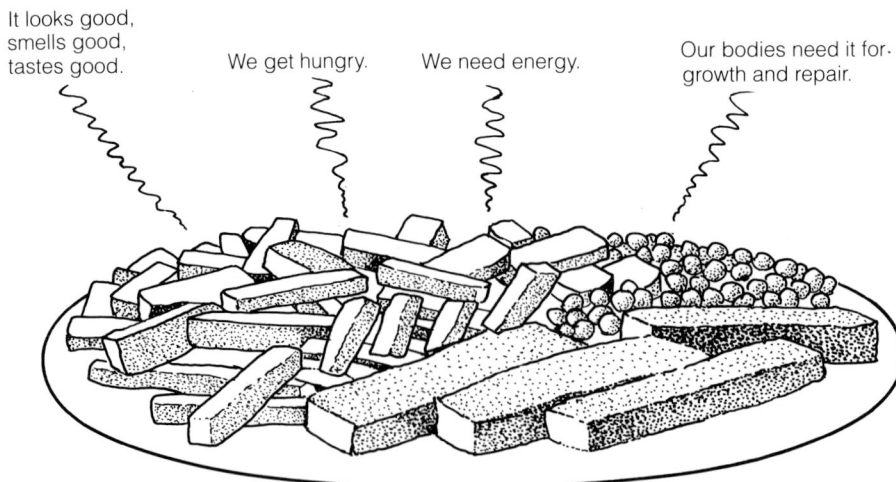

It looks good, smells good, tastes good.

We get hungry.

We need energy.

Our bodies need it for growth and repair.

Why we eat food

Weigh the children and ask them to represent the results in graph and table form. Find out what is an ideal weight for boys and girls of a certain age. *Note:* Handle this issue sensitively.

Discuss illnesses associated with too much and too little food. What is the correct amount? (See also Health Education activities, page 97.)

2 Help the children learn basic facts. For example:

● Food gives us energy, measured in units called calories.

● Almost all food gives us some energy. Different foods provide us with different amounts of energy.

● Main sources of energy are carbohydrates and fats.

● Energy also comes from proteins, which we need for building muscles, and growth and repair of our bodies.

● If we consume more calories than we need for energy and growth, then our bodies store them as fat.

● If we do not eat enough food to supply us with the energy we need, then our bodies use protein for energy instead of for growth and repair. We lose weight and may become very ill.

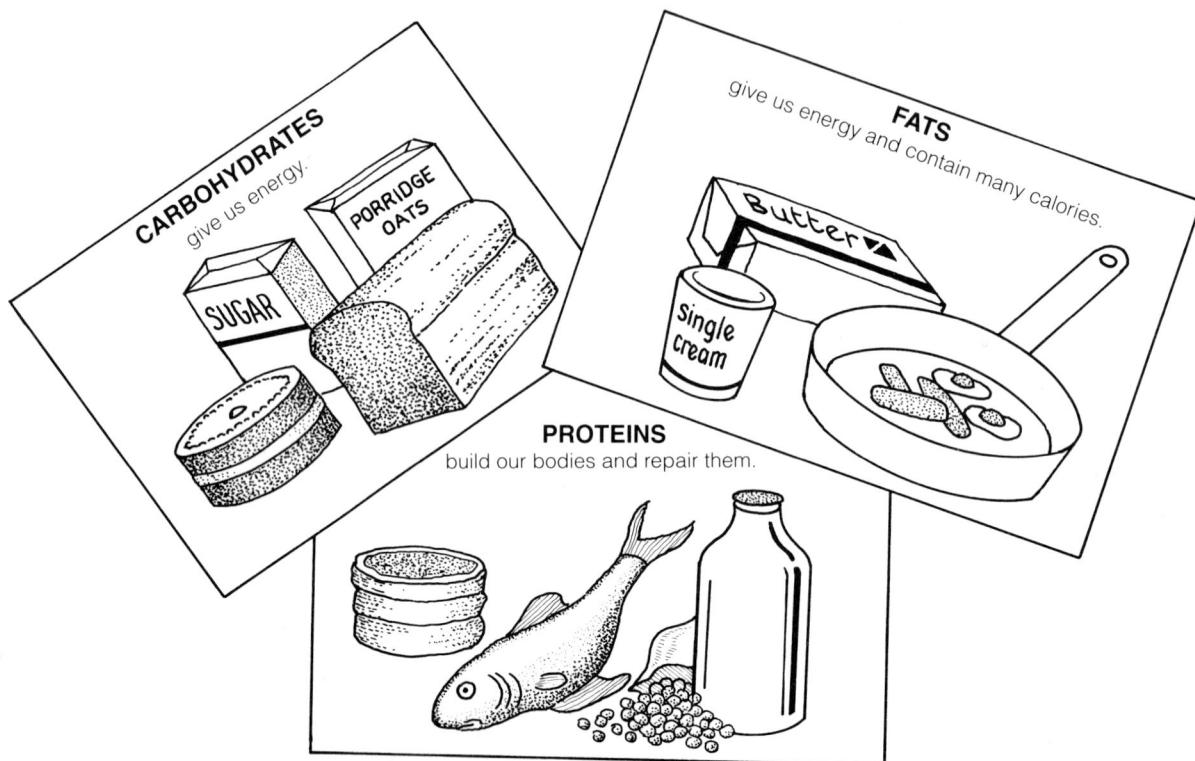

CARBOHYDRATES give us energy.

SUGAR

PORRIDGE OATS

FATS give us energy and contain many calories.

Butter

Single cream

PROTEINS build our bodies and repair them.

We take in . . .			We use up . . .		
	1 cup of tea with milk	15 calories		walking briskly for 1 minute	4 calories
	1 glass of milk	100 calories		swimming fast for 1 minute	10 calories
	1 slice of brown bread	70 calories		sitting in front of TV for 5 minutes	5 calories
	1 bar of chocolate	300 calories		Cycling for 5 minutes	35 calories
	1 egg sandwich	250 calories		dancing for 10 minutes	70 calories
	1 apple	50 calories		walking upstairs for 1 minute	5 calories
	1 banana	80 calories			

Calorie counts

3 Find out about the calorie content of a variety of foods. Ask the children to do calculations based on intake and expenditure of calories (see also Energy topic, Mathematics activity 4, page 69). For example:

● How many calories would you use in dancing for 20 minutes?
● How many calories would you use in swimming fast for 5 minutes?
● How many calories are there in a meal of an egg sandwich and a bar of chocolate?

● How long would you have to swim for in order to use up the energy from one bar of chocolate?

Copymaster 31 (Protein for growth) provides basic information and also scope for mathematical calculations. It reinforces the importance of protein in our lives, and good sources of protein. Sums are designed to help children appreciate that some sources are better than others, and that foods should be eaten selectively.

HEALTH EDUCATION ACTIVITIES `C32`

1 Plan a favourite meal. Ask each child to design their 'ideal food for the day'. Record the results written as a menu, drawn, or in the form of a photo montage of pictures collected from magazines. Suggest an imaginary scenario where food varieties are dramatically reduced. If the children had to live on one food for ever, what would it be? Discuss the pleasures and dangers of living for a whole week on, say, chocolate or chips.

2 Introduce basic facts about a balanced diet. For example:

● Carbohydrates and fats give us warmth and energy.
● Fibre helps clean out our bodies.

● Meat and fish give us body-building protein.
● Vitamins and minerals are also needed to keep us healthy and our bodies functioning efficiently.
● A balanced diet should contain all of these things, with an emphasis on 'healthy' foods.

3 **Copymaster 32** (Healthy eating) can be used by children to record their understanding of what constitutes healthy food, with a traffic-light symbol that can be coloured in red, amber and green sections. Ask them to draw appropriate foods in the three boxes. It may be necessary to give them a list of foods for thought and guidance, or to sort into the three sections as illustrated on page 98.

GREEN AMBER RED

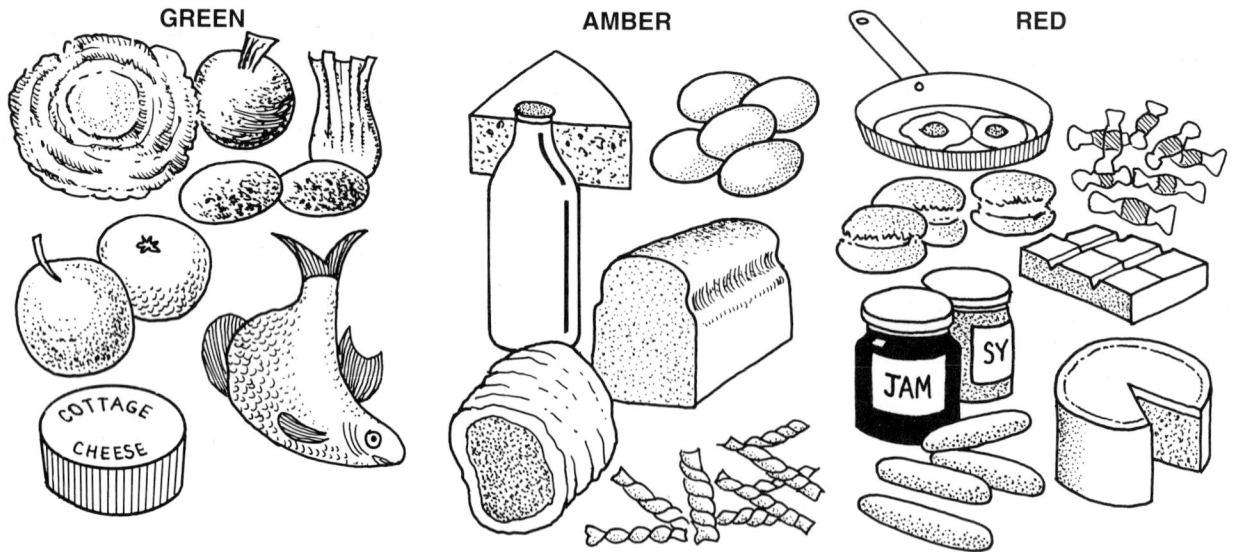

Healthy eating record sheet

4 Plan a day's food to give a balanced diet. Make sure it includes plenty of fibre, with some protein and carbohydrate and not too much fat.

5 Ask the children to calculate how many calories are consumed in the diet planned in activity 4.

6 Investigate good sources of vitamins and minerals. Help the children find out how our bodies use these.

7 Where's the fat? Do a simple experiment to tell if you are eating foods with a lot of fat.

You will need
• A brown bag
• Several different kinds of food (for example, meat, chips, milk, carrots, apples, orange juice, butter).

What to do
• Cut the bag into squares (7 cm approx). Label each square with one of the sorts of food that you have.
• Rub some of each food on the square with its name on. If it is a liquid, put a few drops on the square.
• Let the squares dry.
• When they are dry, hold each square up to the light. What effect did the different foods have on the paper?

8 Discuss what we mean by health foods. Visit a health food store and find out about the range of goods that are sold. Why do some people take special care to buy such things as wholemeal bread, wholemeal flour, wholegrain rice, free-range eggs, and untreated yoghurt? Discuss whether these foods are genuinely better and why.

The picture below can be adapted for use as a worksheet.

Health food biscuits and cakes are made with wholemeal flour, but still contain lots of fat and sugar.

Free-range eggs are from hens that wander freely rather than being kept in small cages. Some people believe that free-range eggs have a better flavour than other eggs.

Muesli bars contain less fat than chocolate bars, but still have a lot of sugar.

Health food jam has less sugar and more fruit than other varieties. It also has fewer preservatives.

Wholemeal pasta has more natural goodness and fibre than refined white varieties.

Health foods – good or bad?

9 Find out about food-related illnesses. Sub-topics could be developed on problems such as diabetes, coeliac disease, and food intolerance/allergies. Ask the children to write about how these affect people's lives, and what coping strategies are adopted by sufferers. Ask the school nurse or an informed parent or visitor to come and discuss the issue of living with a problem of this kind.

10 Ask the children to prepare special diets suitable for people with food-related illnesses. Discuss menus, ingredients, shopping and preparation of suitable food.

11 Ask the children to plan a balanced diet for someone who needs to lose weight for health reasons. How could you sensibly reduce the amount of calories consumed in a day? Make a diet sheet for a week that could be used over a period of three months. Remember that the person wants to enjoy the food as well as lose weight!

12 Find out about food additives. Introduce associated vocabulary such as flavourings, preservatives, colouring, sweeteners, emulsifiers and stabilisers. Consider key questions such as: Are additives necessary? Are they safe? How do we find out if food contains additives?

13 Make a collection of food labels. Read them and think about the additives to which they draw attention. Most countries have laws about food labelling. A manufacturer must identify the ingredients in packaged food. In EC countries, additives other than flavourings have an E number. Flavourings just have numbers. Consult books on nutrition to find out what these numbers stand for.

Ingredients

Carbonated water
Apple juice
Sugar
Flavouring
Preservative E211
Colouring E102

White sauce mix

Ingredients:
Wheatflour, skimmed milk powder, vegetable oil, salt, flavour enhancer, spices, emulsifier E471.

Read food labels.

SCIENCE ACTIVITIES C33

1 All living things need food. Investigate animal diets, perhaps beginning with an analysis of what the children's pets eat. Sort the results of these investigations into sets: those creatures which eat only meat (carnivores), those which eat only plants (herbivores) and those which consume both (omnivores). Ask the children which category we fit into, leading into discussion of individual and ethnic preferences, vegetarianism and veganism.

2 Consider why we cook food. What changes occur during cooking (in taste, smell, texture, appearance, state – solid or liquid)? Cook a variety of foods (for example, potatoes, tomatoes, eggs, jelly) to investigate changes brought about by heating and cooling. Does all food have to be cooked? Collect pictures of foods we like to eat raw. Ask the children to compare human likes with animal likes. Do animals cook food?

3 Investigate food chains. All life depends on soil. Without soil there would be no plants, without plants no animals, and without plants and animals, no people. Build simple food chains into more complex food webs relating to a particular habitat or ecosystem, such as a woodland or pond (see Ponds and Trees topics, pages 45–60 and 79–92). Relate this to the key concept of the balance of nature and inter-dependence of all forms of life. A species may become extinct if key members of a food chain are missing. Find out about animals in danger of extinction. What other creatures depend on them for food? (You could link this with a sub-topic on world habitats, especially one on tropical rain forests.)

4 Collect pictures of plant foods. Ask the children to sort them into sets according to the part we eat as illustrated on page 100. Of which plants do we eat more than one part? An example might be broccoli (stems and flowers).

5 We need food, but there are certain things that are *not* good to eat. Investigate topics such as food safety, poisonous plants, bacteria on food, salmonella in eggs, etc.

Salmonella are microscopic creatures or bacteria. They live inside most animals and are normally killed by cooking food. If they are not killed, they can cause food poisoning, which makes us very sick.

roots (turnip, carrot, potato)

leaves (cabbage, lettuce, spinach)

stems (rhubarb, celery)

flowers (broccoli, cauliflower)

fruits (tomatoes, cucumber)

seeds (wheat, barley)

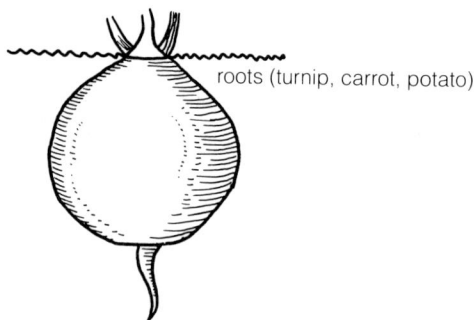

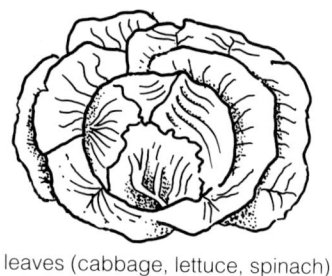

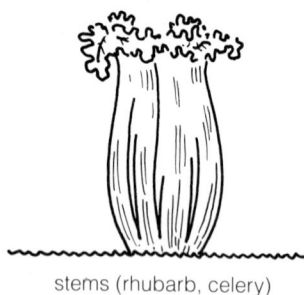

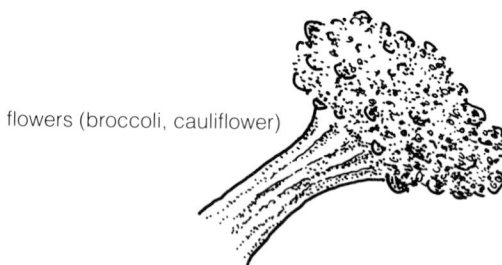

Which part(s) of the plant do we eat?

Staphylococci are another variety of bacteria which exist in our nose, throat and ears, and cause no problems. They can also exist in food, and produce a toxin which causes food poisoning.

Avoid food poisoning.

6 Ask the children to design posters on food safety. These can be displayed in the classroom or taken home. Encourage the children to include and illustrate instructions such as:

- Wash dishcloths regularly.
- Always wash hands before preparing food.
- Use the kitchen sink only for preparing food and washing up (not washing the dog!).
- Always cover meat and fish in the refrigerator.
- Keep pets away from food.
- Store raw and cooked foods separately.
- Eat meat within two or three days of buying it.
- Do not reheat leftover meat pies and stews.

7 Consider appropriate ways to store and prepare food. Ask the children to match food items with the most appropriate method of storage. Discuss the reasons for chilling, freezing and covering food and storing it in sealed containers.

8 Do experiments to investigate storage. If you have access to a refrigerator, observe that bananas go brown in there, so are best kept in a cool, dark place. Potatoes go green in the light. See whether salads keep better in the refrigerator or the vegetable rack. See whether milk keeps longer in a warm or cool place.

100

Can you design a poster on food safety?

Good ways of storing food

9 Let the children visit the school kitchen and interview the cook about food storage. Ask them to write down the safety rules observed there. Find out what happens to stale food.

10 Grow mould as an example of how food changes into something we would not wish to eat. *Note:* Ensure the children do not eat any stale food.

You will need
- A clean plate
- A piece of paper towel
- A slice of bread
- Plastic wrap.

What to do
- Wet the paper towel and lay it on the plate.
- Place a slice of bread on it.
- Cover it with plastic wrap and put it in a dark place.
- Leave it for a few days, then look at it.
- Ask the children to try looking at it through a magnifying glass or with a microscope. They should see clusters of microscopic plant organisms called moulds.

11 Help the children find out about the positive properties of moulds, for example the association with the discovery of penicillin and related medical uses.

12 Point out that quite often in food there are ingredients that we cannot see, for example flavour derived from herbs and spices. Ask the children to unscramble the words on **copymaster 33** (Herbs and spices: the hidden ingredient) to find the names of some well-known herbs and spices. The pictures will be of help: they can be coloured and used as an aid to identification from books and charts.

13 Consult cookery books to find recipes that use herbs and spices. Are certain herbs and spices associated with particular foods or particular ethnic dishes?

14 Grow some herb plants. Seeds are readily available from nurseries and garden centres. Many varieties are easy to grow and germinate readily in seed trays filled with a good seed compost. Make a herb garden in the school grounds. A traditional chequerboard garden is ideal, where a variety of herb plants are grown in squares of soil alongside paved squares where the children can stand, observe and sketch. A garden of this kind is easy to maintain. A group of children can be responsible for a particular square, so that no great weeding or maintenance work is involved.

A traditional chequerboard garden

ECONOMIC AND INDUSTRIAL UNDERSTANDING ACTIVITIES

C34

1 Design a restaurant. Divide the children into groups. Each group may work on one aspect of the class project (fixtures and fittings, menus, staff, costing, etc.) or each group may plan its own restaurant in its entirety. Clearly this could be a major sub-topic in its own right, if all aspects of detail are to be considered. Where possible, invite a local restaurant owner to come and talk to the children about the job. If this is not feasible, perhaps someone associated with restaurant work will agree to visit the school and be interviewed by the children. Perhaps one of the children has a parent who is a chef, waiter or waitress or hotel worker.

2 Turn the classroom into a restaurant for a day. Perhaps the children could cook lunch and take it in turns to prepare food, wait on tables, eat and wash up.

3 **Copymaster 34** (Menu) can be used in association with activity 2 above, or it could be used by individual children or groups for imagining business enterprises. It can be used to record the name of the restaurant, foods on the menu and prices. A great deal of mathematics will inevitably result as individual meals are costed.

Elaborate on this by having a blackboard with the message 'House specialities of the day' and a drinks menu.

Depending on age and ability, it may be possible to incorporate the mathematics of VAT. Most children will understand tips, even if they are unaware of a fixed percentage service charge.

ENGLISH AND MUSIC ACTIVITIES

1 Ask the children to write about favourite foods and about strong dislikes. Why do certain foods appeal so much? What are the aesthetic qualities that make certain foods so attractive? A suitable starting point could be the song *Food, Glorious Food* from the score of Lionel Bart's 'Oliver!'. Do creative writing on themes such as 'My most mouth-wateringest menu', 'Food for a space flight', 'Food for fun', 'The day I turned into a chip' and 'The purple breakfast cereal'.

2 Read stories and poems, and sing songs about food and eating. The scope is enormous. Roald Dahl's stories of 'Charlie and the Chocolate Factory' and 'James and the Giant Peach' are always good starting points for writing about new confections and culinary adventures.

3 **Copymaster 35** (Sayings with food words) contains some of the many well-known sayings associated with food. Ask the children to fill in the gaps, using the pictures to help them. Much discussion should ensue about the origin of such sayings. Are they logical? Can the children think of others?

HISTORY ACTIVITIES

1 Involve the class in research into ways in which food and menus have changed through time.

2 Discover when such things as refrigerators, freezers and microwave ovens came into common use.

3 Ask the children to interview grandparents to find out how foods and cooking have changed in their lifetimes. What were meals like during the war? Discuss rationing and food shortages.

4 Take the children to visit a local museum and observe historic cooking utensils and kitchen equipment. Set up a Victorian kitchen in the classroom if suitable artefacts can be obtained.

5 Look at cookery books of days gone by. Have menus and ingredients changed significantly?

6 Find out about medieval banquets and cooking in Roman times. The historic dimension has obvious cross-curricular links with Art and Drama. For example children can act out medieval feasting scenes and make a large wall collage of the colourful event. Associated vocabulary includes dagger, mead, venison, platter, boar.

A medieval banquet

GEOGRAPHY ACTIVITIES

1 Take the children to visit a local greengrocery store or supermarket. Investigate and record foods that have been imported from foreign lands. A wide range of exotic fruits and vegetables are now available in this country all through the year.

Help the children to locate the countries of origin of these items on a globe or world map. Find out about climatic and other conditions necessary for their growth. Who grows them? How are they harvested? At what time of the year are they picked? How are they packaged for international export? How are they transported?

2 Ask the children to map the routes of imported foods from their country of origin to the UK. How long does the journey take? What happens to them on arrival?

3 Discuss the importance of international trade and our dependence on the climate and food industry of other countries. What are the implications of our membership of the European Community?

4 Explore the neighbourhood and record or map the location of restaurants and take-aways that offer dishes native to other lands. Ask the children to analyse sample

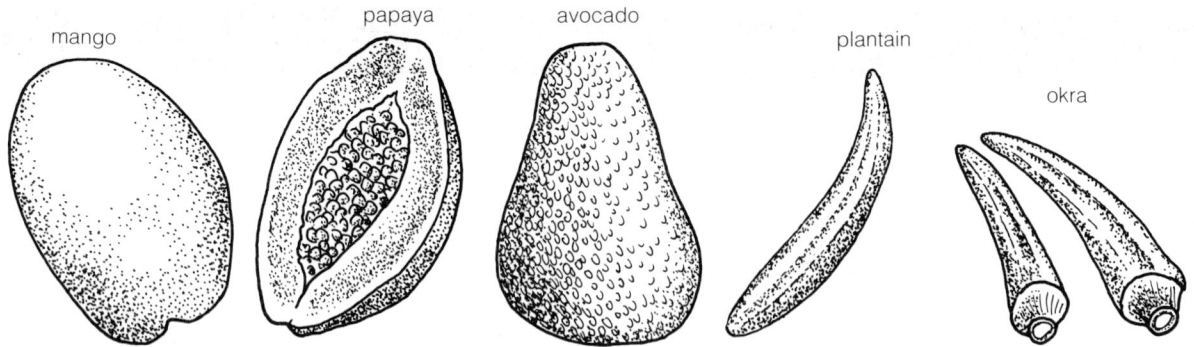

Exotic fruits and vegetables

menus and use these as a starting point for learning about distant lands and ingredients not native to our own country. Consider what makes such cuisine 'different'. Is it related to basic ingredients, subtle flavourings, cooking methods, presentation?

5 The children can use **copymaster 36** (Dishes from around the world) to match the dish with the country of origin. Study of restaurants and menus will aid research, as will consultation of cookery books containing international recipes. The copymaster can be used as an end in itself, or as a starting point for a study of the lands depicted. The class could be divided into groups, each group to study one of the countries mentioned, finding out about climate, customs, festivals, and general way of life.

6 Organise a 'food from distant lands' party. Countries on copymaster 36 would make excellent starting points. Prepare a food dish from each, sing songs or tell stories of that country, learn dances, share knowledge of local festivals and national costumes.

7 Prepare festival food from our own country. You could make it a sub-topic on Christmas. Discuss typical Christmas fare. You could make mincemeat for pies.

You will need
- 350 g (12 oz) raisins (chopped)
- 225 g (8 oz) chopped peel
- 225 g (8 oz) sultanas
- 225 g (8 oz) currants
- 250 g ($8\frac{1}{2}$ oz) suet (or suet substitute)
- 350 g (12 oz) soft brown sugar

- The grated rind and juice of 1 orange
- The grated rind and juice of $\frac{1}{2}$ lemon
- 450 g (1 lb) cooking apples
- 2 level teaspoons mixed spice
- $\frac{1}{4}$ teaspoon grated nutmeg

Method
- Place the raisins in a bowl with sultanas, currants, peel and sugar.
- Peel and grate the apples. Add to the bowl.

- Add the juice, rind, spice and nutmeg. Mix it all thoroughly.
- Leave covered for 24 hours, stirring regularly.
- Place in clean jars and leave for about 1 week before using to make pies.

8 Find out about the origins of other traditional Christmas foods: turkey, sprouts, sauces, stuffings, dried fruit and nuts.

9 Tell stories and legends of international Christmas foods and customs, for example the origin of the Christmas tree and the tradition of chocolate decorations. Find out how Christmas is celebrated in other lands.

An old Christmas tradition

10 Celebrate with fruit punch.

You will need
- 1000 ml (2 pints) of hot tea
- 1 orange
- 1 banana (sliced)
- 1 carton pineapple juice
- 3 lemons
- 100 g (4 oz) lump sugar
- 3 cloves

Method
- Rub the lumps of sugar on oranges and lemons.
- Place sugar in bowl.
- Add the tea, fruit juices and cloves. Stir well until the sugar is dissolved.
- Add banana and slices of orange.

Protein for growth

100 g beef → 25 g protein

100 g milk → 3 g protein

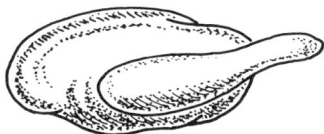

100 g chicken → 25 g protein

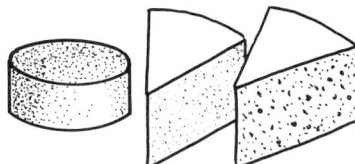

100 g cheese → 25 g protein

100 g eggs → 12 g protein

100 g baked beans → 5 g protein

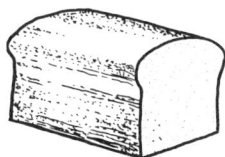

100 g white bread → 8 g protein

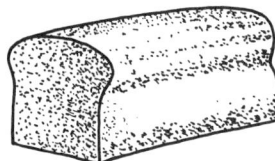

100 g wholemeal bread → 10 g of protein

100 g peanuts → 28 g protein

1   To have 20 g of protein I need to eat ☐ g of baked beans.
2   200 g of chicken gives me ☐ g of protein.
3   100 g of peanuts + 100 g of milk gives me ☐ g of protein.
4   400 g of wholemeal bread gives me ☐ g of protein.
5   For 12 kg of protein I need to drink ☐ g of milk.
6   100 g of beef + 100 g of cheese gives me ☐ g of protein.
7   200 g of white bread + 400 g of eggs gives me ☐ g of protein.
8   For 1000 g of protein I need to eat ☐ g of peanuts.
9   50 g of white bread gives me ☐ g of protein.
10 For 4 g of protein I need to eat ☐ g of baked beans and drink 100 g of milk.

Healthy eating

I can eat as much as I like.

colour
green

GO
for
these

I should eat these in moderation.

colour
amber

WAIT
and
think
about
these

I should eat only a little.

colour
red

STOP
after
a
little
of
these

Herbs and spices – the hidden ingredient

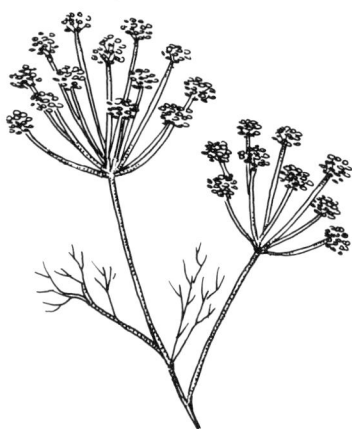

1 OSMYARRE

2 TMNGEU

3 GSEA

4 LHCILI

5 IKAPARP

6 YHETM

7 ILDL

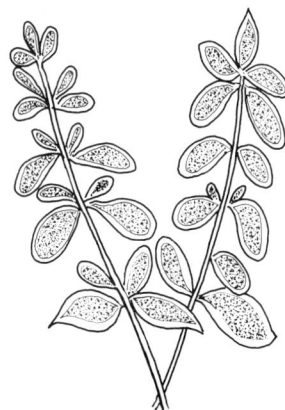

Menu

Enter the name of your restaurant in the space at the top of the menu.

STARTERS	PRICE £
MAIN COURSE	
DESSERTS	

PRICES INCLUDE VAT AT ___ %

SERVICE CHARGE NOT INCLUDED

Sayings with food words

There are many well-known sayings that include food words.
Fill in the gaps. The pictures will help you.

a. Like chalk and _____.

b. As cool as a _____.

c. _____ wouldn't melt in her mouth.

d. Worth his _____.

e. The proof of the _____ is in the eating.

f. As red as a _____.

g. Have your _____ and eat it.

Dishes from around the world

Match the dish with its country of origin.

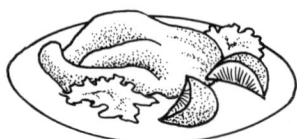

Tandoori chicken

tabouleh

paella

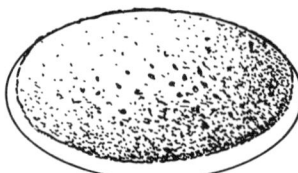

pizza

Pavlova

chilli beef tacos

sweet and sour pork

Spain

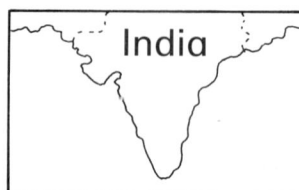

India

Mexico

Australia

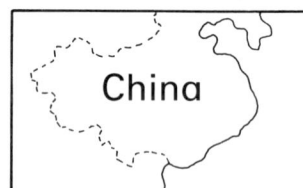

China

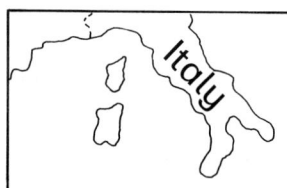

Italy

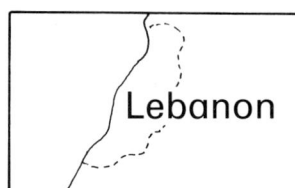

Lebanon

WASTE

National curriculum links

Principal location in the National Curriculum

- Buildings, Industrialisation, Waste

Other areas covered by topic

- People and Communities ● Materials, Resources, Energy ● Plants and Animals ● Water
- Soils, Rocks, Minerals

Context of study

- Local to global concerns

Suggested sub-topics and their location in areas of study of curriculum guidelines for Environmental Education

Sub-topic	Areas of Study in the National Curriculum						
	Climate	Soils, Rocks, Minerals	Water	Materials, Resources, Energy	Plants and Animals	People and Communities	Buildings, Industrialisation, Waste
Recycling		O	O	O		●	●
Water	O	O	●	O	O	●	●
Soil		●	O	O	O	O	●
Nuclear power		O	O	●	O	●	●

Key   ● Principal location   O Part coverage

Design and Technology

- Packaging design
- Design of recycling systems
- Construction of recycling facilities
- Evaluation of existing recycling systems
- Modern technology in disposal facilities
- Integrated management of waste disposal

English

- Environmental quality – 'the good, bad, ugly' – poems and creative thoughts
- Vocabulary of waste
- What we throw away – factual recording
- Debates of controversial issues
- Writing a classroom newspaper
- Letter writing

Mathematics

- Application of basic numerical skills to everyday 'waste'
- Distances travelled for the purpose of recycling
- Dustbin awards game
- Waste code

Geography

- Neighbourhood recycling survey
- Conservation of resources
- Reasons for recycling

WASTE – cross-curricular links

Science

- Litter/pollution survey
- Analysis of household waste
- Waste disposal techniques
- Physical properties of waste
- Energy consumption
- Recycling processes
- Decomposition of organic material
- Building a compost heap
- Landfill sites
- Gas from waste
- Disposal of nuclear waste

Art

- Photography – aesthetic qualities of the environment
- Design posters
- Impressions of pollution (slides, videos, photographs)
- Collage friezes
- Papier mâché
- Waste materials in collage/design

History

- Stories, interviews to investigate change in nature and quantity of domestic waste
- Changes in production of materials, resources and retailing
- Changes in food technologies

Basics to be developed throughout the topic

Concepts

- What do we need? What is waste? The inevitability of waste materials in modern industrial society
- Waste collection and disposal: an essential community service
- Waste: a problem for our planet. Issues and solutions
- Effective management of waste materials
- The Earth's natural waste disposal process, decomposition

Attitudes

- Appreciation of, and care and concern for, the quality of our environment
- Care and respect for our Earth and its resources
- Individual responsibility in the community

Environmental issues

- Waste production
- Management of waste
- Recycling

STARTING POINTS

- Start in the local community. Before commencing the topic with children, do some preliminary investigations. Find out the following from your local authority's Environmental Health Department:

How and when is domestic waste collected?
How is it disposed of?
Does the local authority have an incinerator?
Are there landfill sites in the area?
What provision is made for recycling?
What proportion of waste is recycled?
Are facilities being upgraded with new technologies?
What voluntary recycling programmes are available?
Where and when can they be accessed?

- Suitable starting points with children should inevitably focus on waste that they can relate to – domestic waste and litter. Survey the local area for waste products. Investigate household waste. Visit a bottle bank or a save-a-can scheme.

- Move on to more specialised areas for development or sub-topic work: for example, industrial waste, water pollution, nuclear waste, and waste as an issue on a global scale.

- Start with aesthetic, qualitative dimension, that is waste as a threat to the beauty of our world. Scientific aspects will inevitably follow on from this dimension, leading to a well-balanced cross-curricular topic.

ENGLISH ACTIVITIES

C37

1 Consider the aesthetic, qualitative dimension of waste in our world. This makes an excellent and rather unusual starting point for what would appear to be a topic rooted in science education. Take the children for a walk around the neighbourhood, school site or a local park. Ask them to observe the environment critically and discuss what they see. What is beautiful about the landscape? What spoils it? Ask them to write words to describe feelings about the 'good, bad and ugly' qualities of places. Ask them to draw things they have seen on the visit which make places beautiful and those which spoil their appearance. Almost certainly the environmental

problems of waste, litter, vandalism and graffiti will rank amongst the 'bad and ugly' features.

2 Write poems and creative thoughts about the 'good, bad and ugly' characteristics of places.

3 Ask the children to do factual writing about problems encountered, their thoughts on where blame lies, and on possible solutions. Such activities help to raise awareness of litter and waste as significant problems which are perhaps more complex than the children may have thought.

4 Prepare exercises and puzzles designed to

introduce a basic vocabulary of waste, necessary for a more scientific understanding and analysis. For example, ask the children to define it; to think of words that mean the same as waste (left over, superfluous, no longer needed, discarded, thrown away, etc). Do crosswords or other puzzles to reinforce categories of waste (paper, glass, metal, rubber, natural/organic or plastic) and introduce other relevant words such as decay, decompose, incineration, burial, and recycling.

5 **Copymaster 37** (Weekend throw-away) contains an activity designed to heighten awareness of waste as an issue and reinforce basic vocabulary. Ask the children's parents to co-operate with this activity. For one weekend, children should record on the copymaster all items discarded at home. Perhaps they could attach a sheet to the wall by the kitchen bin or dustbin and ask family members to jot down anything they throw away. Tabulate the results at the end of the weekend into the suggested categories. This can be done as a total or as tally counts, with suitable illustrations if space permits.

Inevitably, this activity will raise many questions as well as provide answers. Use these as important discussion points. For example, what about items like a glass bottle with a paper label that cross categories? Refine the recording sheet to take account of children's questions. Sub-divide items further into those that are natural, those made by people and those that are a mixture. Ask the children to record in pictorial sets or graphically.

6 Organise classroom debates on controversial issues related to waste, for example the dumping of nuclear waste at sea, siting of a landfill project, or of a nuclear waste land repository. Prepare arguments on both sides of the issues and debate them.

7 Help the children to design, write, illustrate and produce a classroom newspaper.

A classroom newspaper – the Waste Times

Divide the children into groups to work on various aspects of the paper including writing accounts, reports, illustrations, design and production. Aim the paper at an audience of other members of the school and the local community. The purpose of the paper may be to inform its readers about local waste matters, discuss controversial issues on the topic and advertise community involvement schemes such as recycling glass and paper.

8 Write a class letter to an established local paper, drawing attention to community recycling programmes and pledging support.

ART ACTIVITIES

1 Use photography as a starting point. Take polaroid or other photographs of environmental quality. Place emphasis on the beautiful and the ugly aspects of the neighbourhood. Use these as stimuli for discussion and writing. Photographs will give instant yet lasting impressions upon which to base writing and debate. Ask the children to make a photo montage of litter and waste in the locality.

2 Ask the children to design posters drawing attention to the danger of litter to animals. Post them around the school or in the local library.

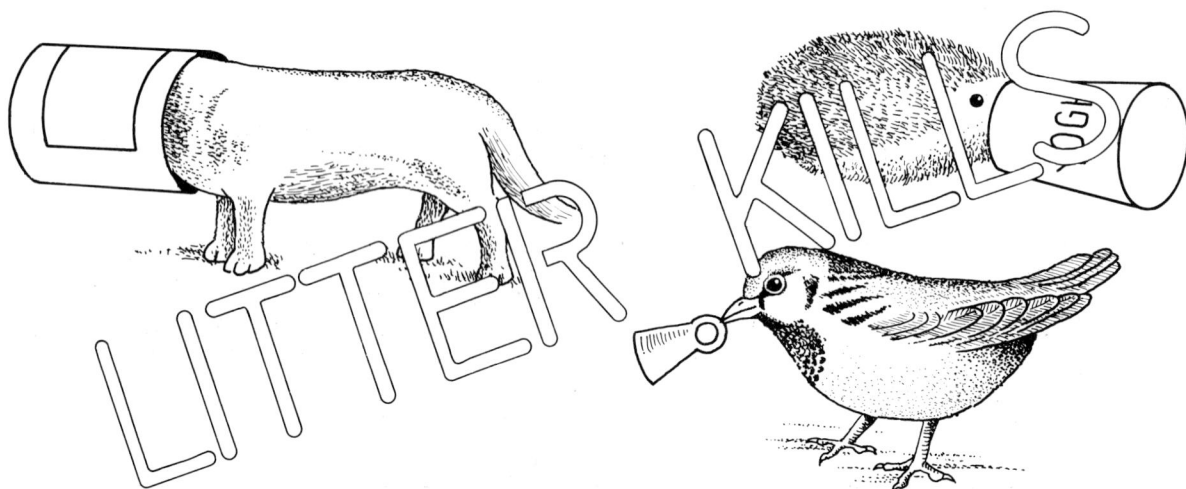

Litter can be dangerous to animals.

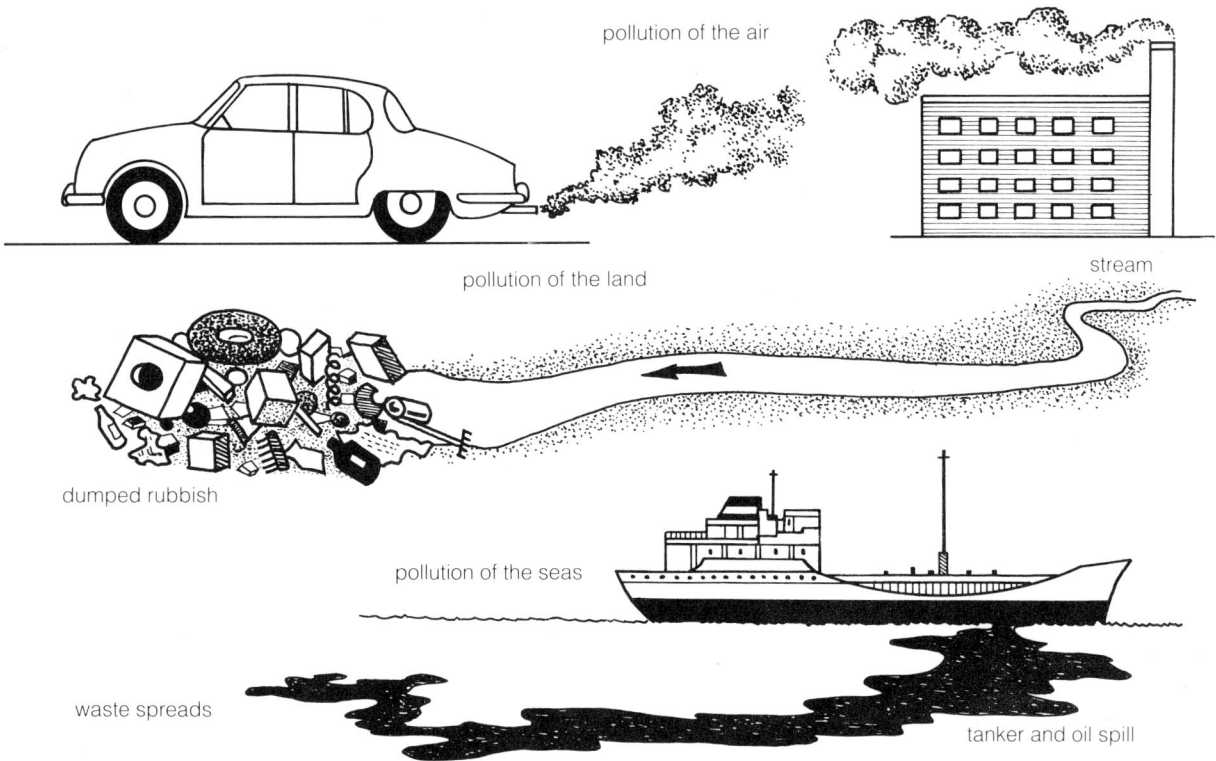

Pollution spreads.

3 View a collection of slides, videos or photographs on pollution caused by waste. This pollution may relate to land, sea or air. Contrast this with a collection of impressions of unspoilt environments. Discuss the reactions to the two visual collections. Ask the children to add to the collection by painting their own pictures.

4 Make a large collage wall frieze of 'waste in our world', dividing the background into three sections, air, land and sea. Depict various forms of pollution from waste on this background.

Use this collage as a vehicle for indicating that waste spreads: air pollution is blown across international boundaries, waste on the land is carried along by water sources, and ocean pollution spreads over wide distances. This helps children to appreciate that whilst waste may have local origins, it is in fact a global problem. Follow this up with reference to case studies. The Chernobyl disaster, for example, produced a cloud of radioactive pollution which affected many European nations.

5 Show the children how to make papier-mâché. This is a good way of using waste material for producing useful objects or artwork. Tear sheets of newspaper into tiny pieces. Put them into a bucket with very hot water (be aware of safety aspects) and beat them into a thick pulp. When the pulp has cooled, Polyfilla and plaster of Paris or wallpaper paste can be added for strengthening. Ask the children to use the resultant material like clay as a modelling medium.

6 Use waste materials such as kitchen foil and take-away food dishes to make decorations and collages.

Waste metals can still be useful.

SCIENCE ACTIVITIES

LITTER SURVEY: ROSE BANK				
quantity				
Items	Week 1	Week 2	Week 3	Total
Glass	ⵑ ⵑ ⵑ II	ⵑ ⵑ III	ⵑ ⵑ ⵑ	45
Rubber	II	III	I	6
Metal	ⵑ ⵑ II	ⵑ III	ⵑ IIII	29
Paper	ⵑ ⵑ ⵑ ⵑ ⵑ I	ⵑ ⵑ ⵑ ⵑ III	ⵑ ⵑ IIII	63
Plastic	III	I	I	5
Organic waste	ⵑ ⵑ IIII	III	ⵑ	22
				170

When collecting litter take collecting bags and gloves, and use litter tongs if possible.

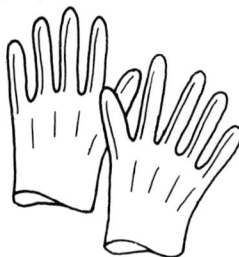

Making a litter survey

1 Involve the class in a practical investigation of waste in the school and/or local area. Look for places that are polluted with litter and rubbish. Photograph these and record the findings. This could be quantified by doing a formal litter survey – collect litter from specific areas over a certain period of time, classify it and count items in each category.

2 Ask the children to represent survey results in the form of graphs or pie charts with percentages.

My household waste:
Saturday 4th March

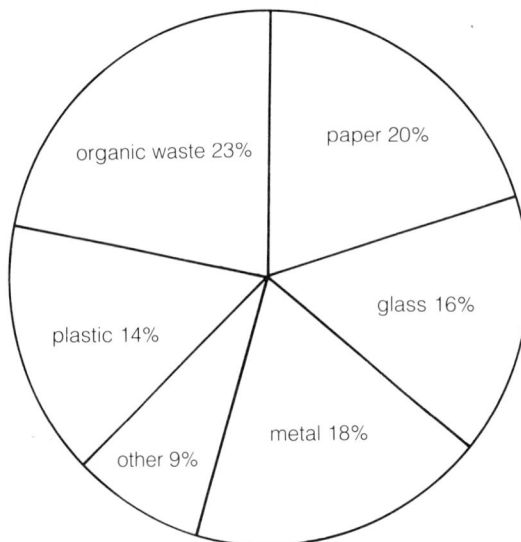

organic waste 23%
paper 20%
plastic 14%
glass 16%
other 9%
metal 18%

Total number of items disposed of = 176.

Household waste pie chart

Rusty can experiment

3 Survey household waste (see also English activity 5, page 114). Ask the children to monitor waste which their family discards on one particular day or weekend. If possible, record each item, classify it and analyse the results statistically. Record the findings in table form, on graphs or as pie charts showing percentages, as illustrated on page 116.

4 Investigate the disposal of solid household waste. Trace the journey of waste from 'bin liner to burial' (or incineration) in your local area. Help the children find out facts and figures about collection and disposal. Suggested questions for investigation are listed under Starting points, page 113.

5 Conduct experiments and investigations to find out more about the physical properties of various types of waste materials. For example, some metals such as steel are attracted to a magnet. Others, such as aluminium, are not. Food and beverage cans are made in a variety of metals. Some cans are made entirely of aluminium, some have an aluminium top but a tin-plated steel body. Their composition is very important in the recycling process. All cans can be recycled, but it is best to collect them separately. Aluminium cans are more valuable than steel ones.

6 Ask the children to test a wide range of cans with magnets to identify their composition and record the results on **copymaster 38** (Can investigation). Remind them to test both the ends of the cans as well as their bodies.

Let the children weigh the cans to see whether one type is consistently lighter. (The lighter metal is aluminium.) They should observe the cans closely and read the labels. Is there any indication in the printing which identifies what the can is made of?

Find out whether each of the cans in the sample goes rusty.

You will need
- Cans in your research sample
- A sharp nail
- A tank of salty water.

What to do
- Carefully make a deep scratch on the bottom of each can with the nail and place the cans in the tank.
- Leave them underwater for 1 week, then inspect them for signs of rust on the scratch.

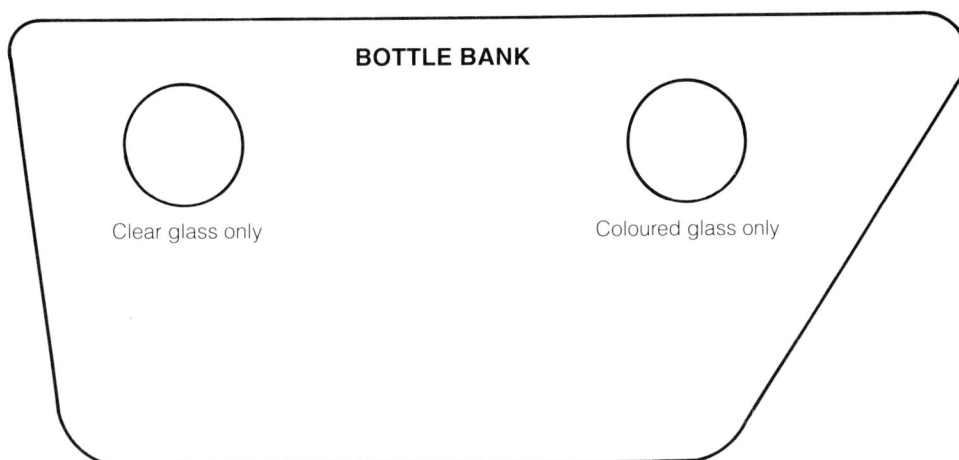

A typical bottle bank

Ask the children to use the copymaster to record results. They should tick appropriate columns, work out the totals and complete the graphs. Ask them to write sentences about the properties of aluminium and steel.

7 Find out about the energy which is needed to make aluminium and steel. Aluminium uses far more energy in initial production, most of which is used to convert ore into metal. Recycling it uses only a small fraction of this initial energy.

8 Help the children find out about the metal recycling process in your local area. How and when are various metals separated? There may be an officer in the local Environmental Health Department responsible for recycling, who could provide information or arrange a visit to a reprocessing plant. This would lead on to a sub-topic on the theme of recycling in general.

9 Take the children out to investigate recycling initiatives in the community. Ask them to map the location of bottle banks, save-a-can skips and paper collection points.

Encourage them to find out about rules for recycling. For example, bottles should be separated into clear glass and coloured glass deposits; cans should be washed and squashed. Find out the reasons for these rules.

10 Investigate properties of decay and decomposition of waste materials. Introduce the term bio-degradability. Bury a range of waste materials in damp soil, and observe the results after a period of several weeks. Is there any noticeable change in appearance and state?

11 Build a compost heap and teach the children to differentiate between organic waste that will decay and waste that will not. **Copymaster 39** (Decay of vegetable waste) may be used as a classroom exercise, or children can actually design and construct a compost heap in the school grounds. Relate learning to the cycling of nutrients in nature.

You will need
- 4 posts, measuring approximately 1 m × 10 cm × 10 cm
- Wire netting, plus staples to attach it
- Sheets of thick card.

What to do
- Fix the stakes firmly in the ground.
- Staple wide mesh wire netting around all sides.
- Insulate the sides with cardboard.
- Fill up the heap with layers of vegetable waste and garden waste, alternated with thin layers of soil and the chemical ammonium nitrate. The soil contains the bacteria and other decomposers necessary for the decay of vegetation. The ammonium nitrate helps feed the decomposers.

On the copymaster ask the children to label the layers in the heap, and consider the items drawn around the outside. Ask them to draw a green ring round those suitable for composting and a red ring round those which are not.

12 Relate the concept of biodegradability to the use of landfill sites for the burial of solid wastes. If possible, visit a local landfill facility. Help the children list the advantages of landfill as a waste disposal method. What are the disadvantages? (For example, space will eventually be limited, there will be a release of toxins from waste into the ground.)

13 Find out about the release of gas from waste. How can methane gas produced on landfills be exploited and put to good use?

Do an experiment to show that decomposing material produces gas. Take large, clear bottles and fill them with a variety of wastes buried in soil. Place a deflated balloon over the neck of each bottle, and leave for a week or two. At the end of this time, ask the

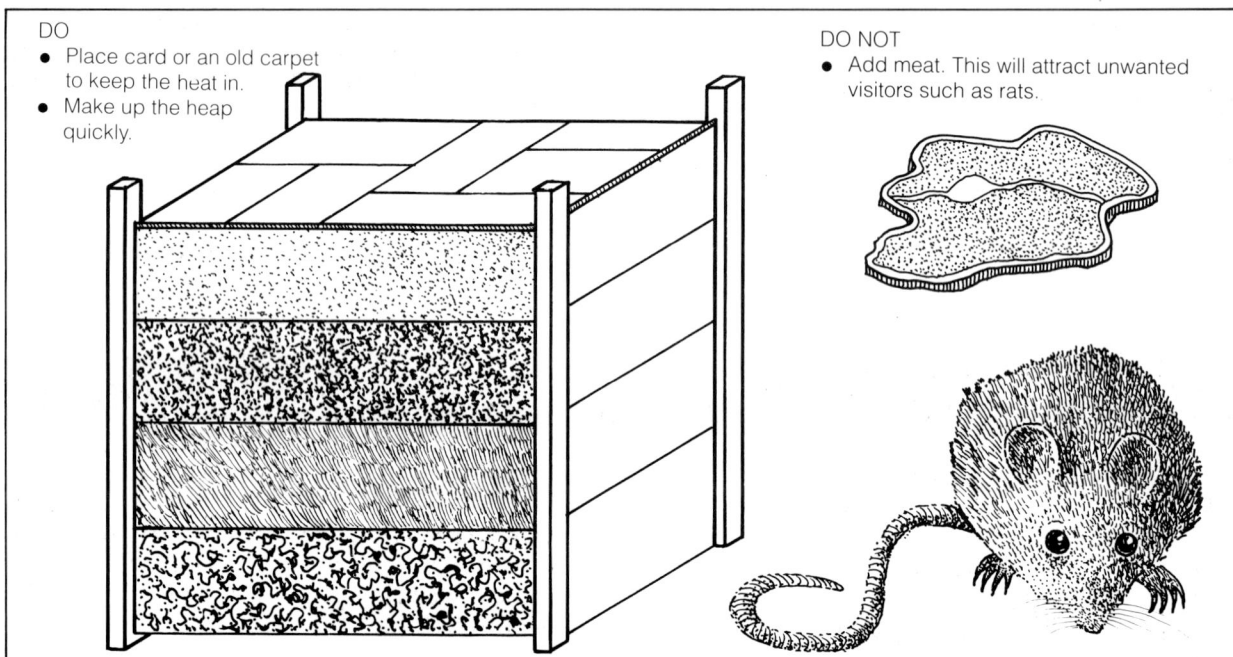

DO
- Place card or an old carpet to keep the heat in.
- Make up the heap quickly.

DO NOT
- Add meat. This will attract unwanted visitors such as rats.

Compost DOs and DON'Ts

Gas from waste experiment

children to observe the balloons. In the bottles where decomposition is taking place the balloons will inflate, showing that gas is present. Keep a control bottle with no waste, to show that its balloon remains deflated.

14 Appropriate sub-topics you could develop include soil, decomposition, underground and water. In the latter, focus on the issues of water pollution, the importance of maintaining supplies of fresh water, and

the problems of toxins escaping from landfills into water sources.

15 Find out more about one specialised dimension to the problem of waste disposal, for example the disposal of nuclear waste. This sub-topic will lend itself to broadening the issue from local to global considerations, and help children to appreciate the very controversial nature of waste as a global issue.

DESIGN AND TECHNOLOGY ACTIVITIES C40

1 Discuss the packaging of various products, for example foods. How could this be improved in order to conserve resources? Ask the children to design alternative methods of preparing foods for the grocery store shelves.

2 Ask the children to design recycling systems such as save-a-can skips, bottle banks, paper savers and litter bins. Encourage them to consider all aspects of the process including design and materials, manufacture, location, layout of whole recycling centres for convenience and practicality.

3 Help the children construct recycling systems for use in school: litter bins, bottle savers, etc.

4 Help the children write about how recycling systems in the local community could be improved. Ask them to write to the Environmental Health Department with constructive suggestions. Prepare suggestions as a result of formal evaluations based on observations and interviews.

5 Find out more about how modern technology is helping to deal more effectively with solid waste. What improvements have been made or are planned for local waste disposal facilities?

6 Consider the management policies of waste disposal. What are the alternatives to landfill? Visit a waste incineration plant. Find out how waste is sorted.

Copymaster 40 (Managing waste disposal) can be used by the children to draw and record facilities that are available in your local area. They can also add statistics and any other relevant information on new technologies. Use it as a basis for discussing the importance of an integrated waste management policy, which should include all three elements.

EFFECTIVE MANAGEMENT OF WASTE = RECYCLING + LANDFILL + INCINERATION wherever possible

HISTORY ACTIVITIES

1 Read stories set in the past, and ask the children to talk to grandparents and other elderly friends and relatives to find out how changes in household objects, foods, etc., have inevitably affected the nature and quantity of domestic waste.

2 Consider and discuss changes that have occurred in the production of materials, in resources used in manufacture, and in retailing.

3 A sub-topic on food might embrace a study of changes that have taken place in transportation, preservation and storage of foods: consider the impact of refrigeration, freezing, microwaving, the growth of take-aways and fast-foods on the nature and production of waste materials.

119

Ash waste has declined.

Plastic and metal wastes have greatly increased.

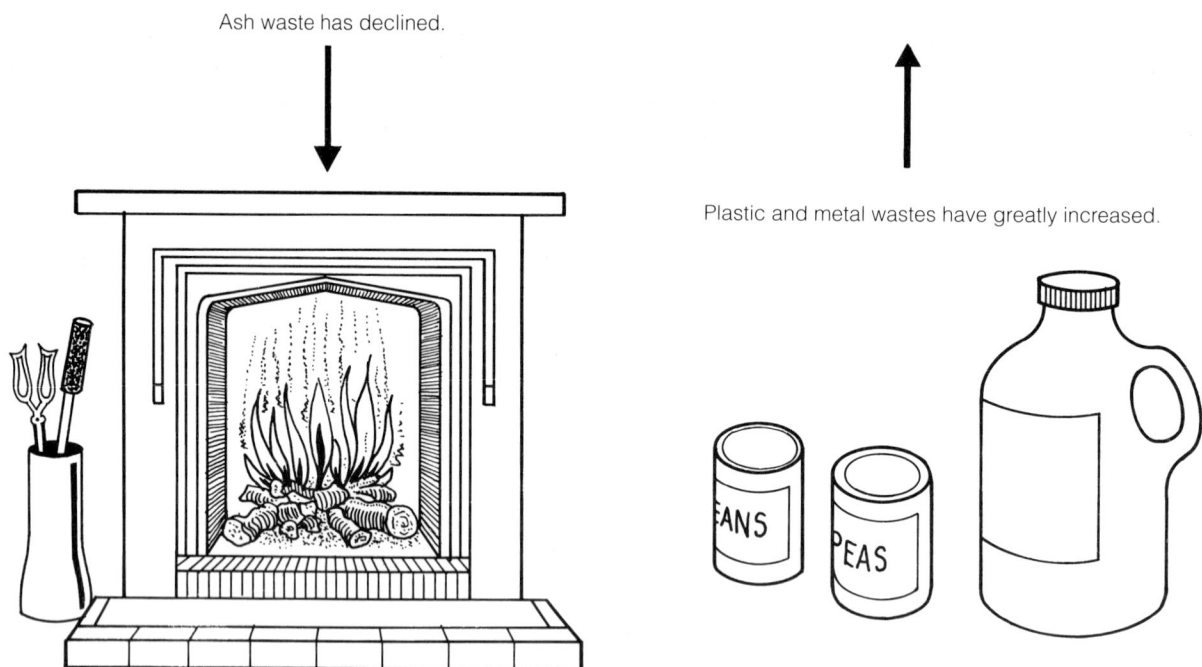

Domestic waste has changed over the years.

MATHEMATICS ACTIVITIES

C41 –42

1 Apply basic mathematical skills to everyday situations involving waste: for example, a survey of household waste will give the children the opportunity to count, classify into sets and record in numerical or pictorial forms.

2 Ask the children to calculate distances travelled by users to a recycling system (see Geography activity 1, below) and their transport costs. Let them work out the over-all costs of recycling, including the cost of establishing, emptying and managing the facilities. What are the collected goods worth? Help children carry out cost-benefit analyses.

3 **Copymaster 41** (Dustbin awards) is a board game which can be played by two or more children in the class. For greater durability, cut out the 'board', mount it on stiff card and cover it with clear plastic. Materials needed are a dice, shaker and one counter per participant. To play the game, start in the bottom right-

hand corner and proceed by shaking dice in turns and moving individual counters the appropriate number of squares forwards. When a 'special' square is landed on, there will be an instruction to move forward or backward a number of squares, depending on whether the message is positive or negative. The game is designed to reinforce messages about waste and recycling.

4 **Copymaster 42** (Waste code) contains an initial coded message about waste which needs to be translated. More complicated mathematics is then required to calculate the code and translate it to find out the contents of the dustbin.

There are endless possibilities for the children to work in pairs or groups and make up their own coded messages about waste and recycling for others to decipher, either using the code provided on the sheet, or innovative codes devised by the children.

GEOGRAPHY ACTIVITIES

1 Ask the children to do a neighbourhood recycling survey. You could take them to visit a recycling centre where there are bottle banks, save-a-can skips, etc., perhaps in the car park of a local supermarket. Let them interview members of the public with prepared questionnaires to find out:

- What they have brought to recycle
- How many objects

- How far they have travelled – where they live
- What mode of transport they used
- Whether they always recycle materials, or merely when it is convenient
- Why they recycle materials.

Discuss the results of the survey and ask the children to write about them. They will raise key issues such as

120

the convenience of recycling centres, the need for transport, motivation, etc. Ask them to draw a map showing the location of the recycling centre and plot the homes of people who visit it. They can calculate distances travelled and time taken. Consider whether people would still travel to recycle even if they had no other reason for visiting the site, for example for shopping.

2 Find out more about the reasons for and vital importance of recycling, that is, conservation of our Earth's vital resources. Investigate the geographical origins of resources, such as ores for metal manufacture, paper for trees, ingredients for glass and plastic manufacture. This activity will lead on to related sub-topics on distant lands, for example tropical rain forests (exploited for bauxite ore and trees).

3 Ask the children to make posters and write about the reasons for promoting recycling initiatives:

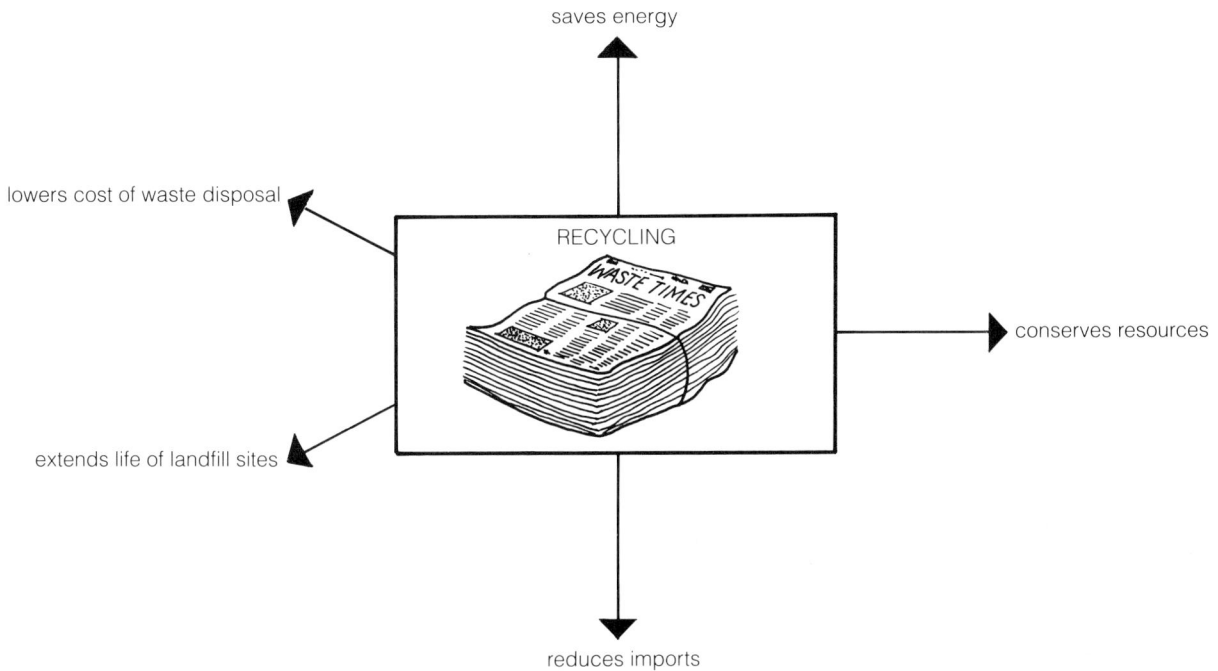

Reasons for promoting recycling initiatives

4 Record stages in production from raw materials to final products, using key words, for example:

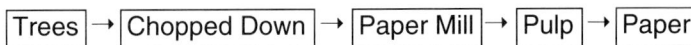

Trees → Chopped Down → Paper Mill → Pulp → Paper

From raw material to product

121

Weekend throw away

paper	metal	glass	plastic

food scraps	other organic waste, e.g. leaves	rubber	other?

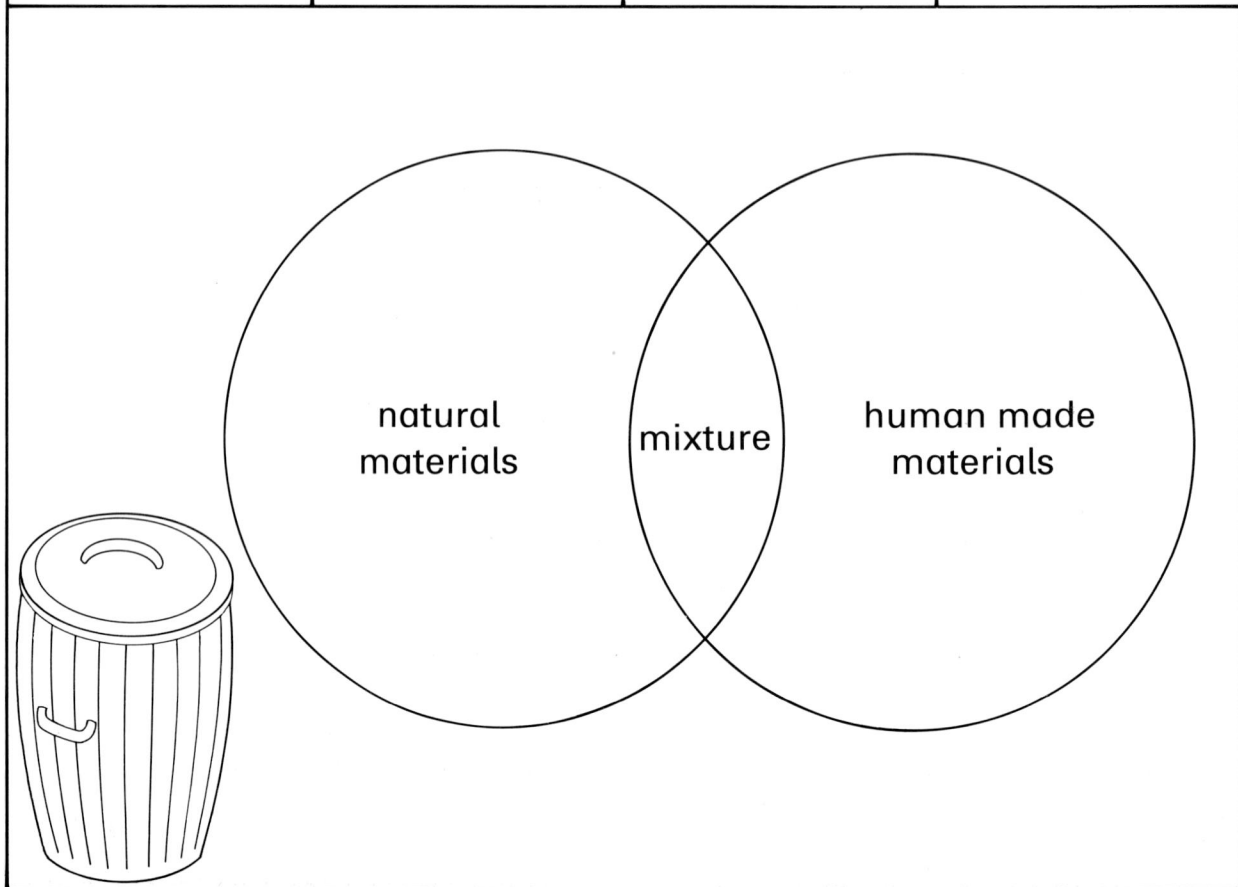

natural materials

mixture

human made materials

Can investigation

type of can	rusts	does not rust	magnetic	non-magnetic	
TOTALS					

number of cans

rust   do not rust

number of cans

magnetic   non-magnetic

Decay of vegetable waste

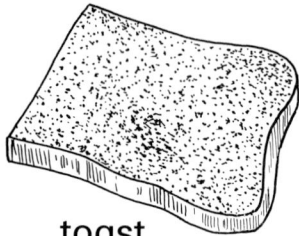
toast

tin cans

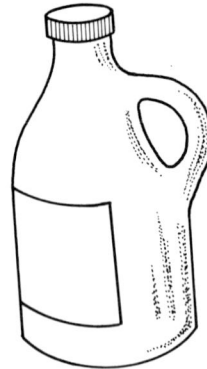
plastic bottle

potato peelings

egg shells

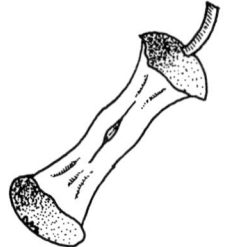
apple core

tea bags

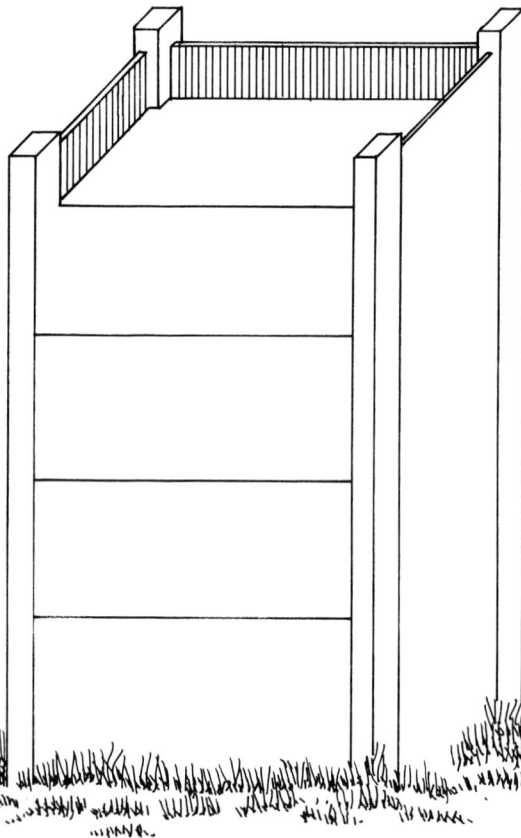

glass bottle

leaves

worn out shoes

Colour the heap and label its layers.
Draw a green ring around things you would add to your compost.
Draw a red ring around things that should not be there.

Managing waste disposal

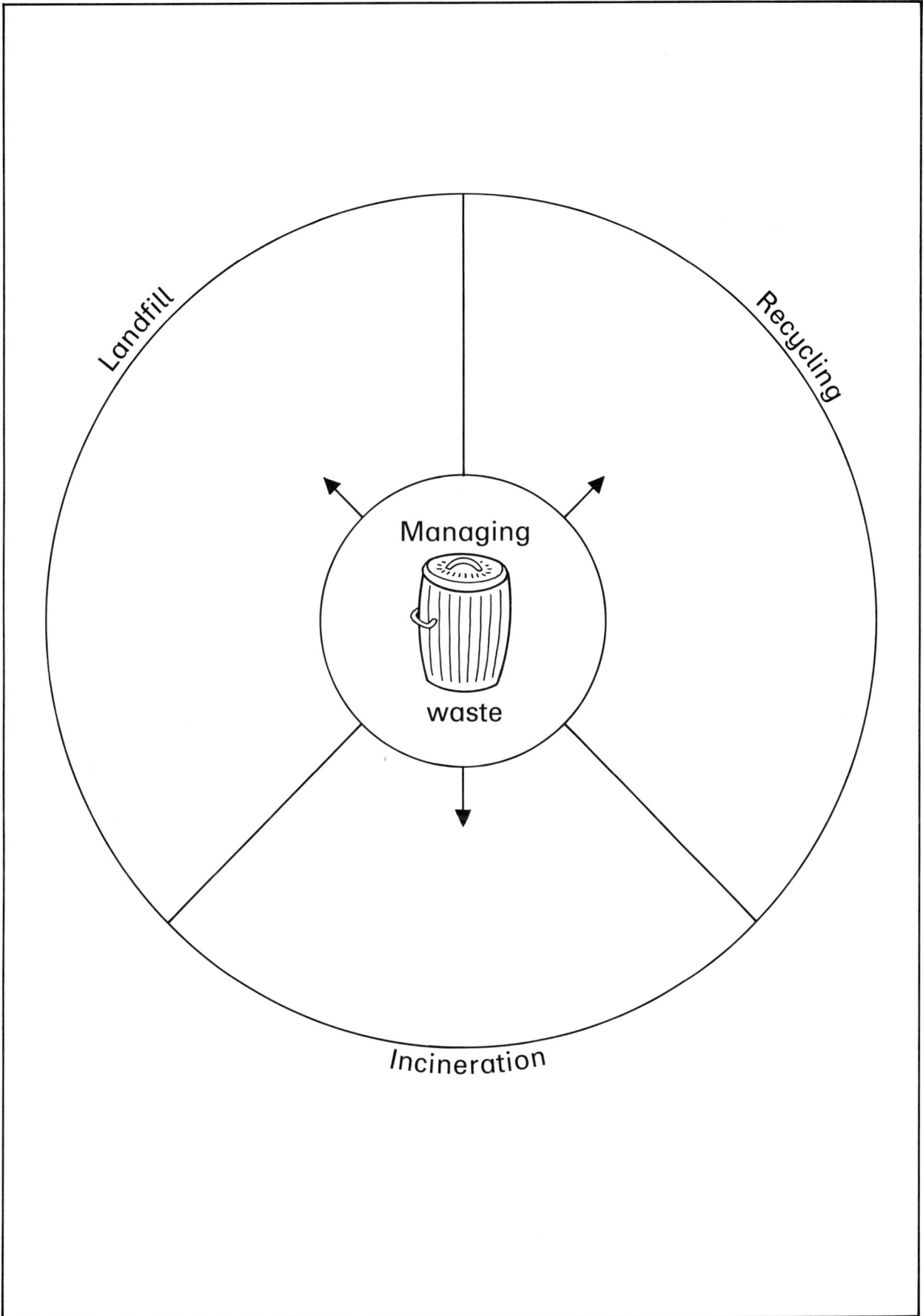

Landfill

Recycling

Managing

waste

Incineration

Dustbin awards

48 FINISH (exact throw only)	47	46 (−6) put bottle in dustbin	45	44	43	42
35	36	37 compost your vegetable peelings (+3)	38	39 buy recycled paper (+4)	40	41 throw sweet paper in street (−7)
34	33 start paper collection (+5)	32	31	30	29	28
21	22	23 (−5) buy plastic bags at grocery store	24	25	26 old tea bags on compost (+5)	27
20	19	18	17 (+7) take your own bags to shops	16	15	14
7	8 off to save-a-can (+5)	9	10	11	12	13 start can collection scheme (+6)
6 Put can in dustbin (−4)	5	4 (+6) use a bottle bank	3	2 buy packaged vegetables (−2)	1	START

Waste code

Here is the code:

a	b	c	d	e	f	g	h	i	j	k	l	m	n	o
26	25	24	23	22	21	20	19	18	17	16	15	14	13	12

p	q	r	s	t	u	v	w	x	y	z
11	10	9	8	7	6	5	4	3	2	1

Can you work out the message?

26 15 4 26 2 8	8 12 9 7	4 26 8 7 22

26 13 23	9 22 24 2 24 15 22	18 7

4 19 22 13 22 5 22 9	11 12 8 8 18 25 15 22

What does this bin contain?

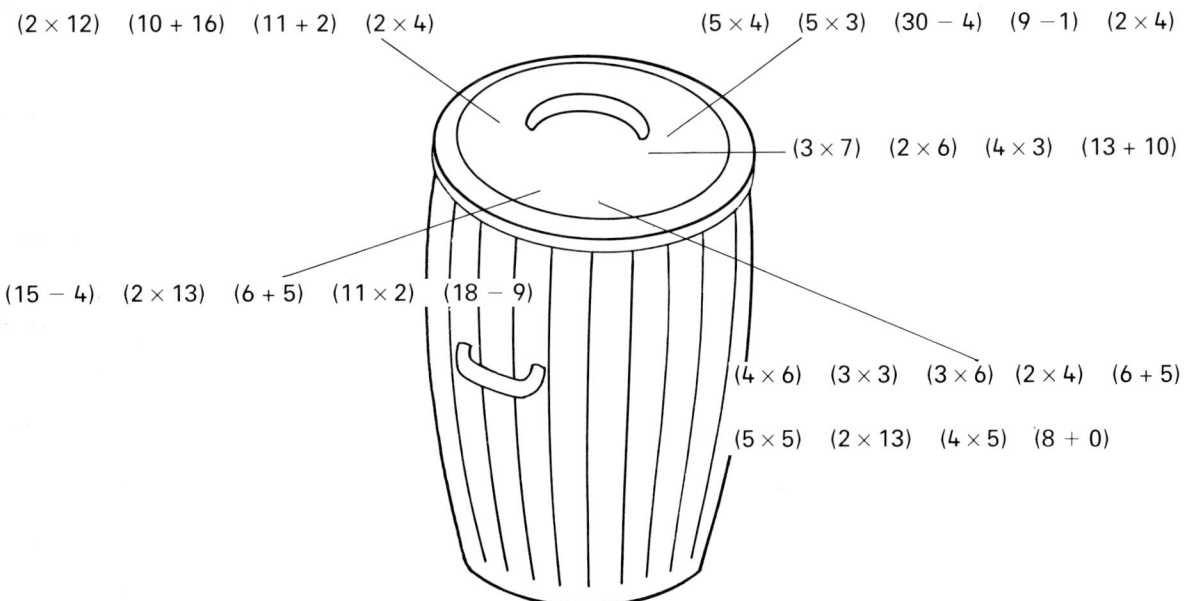

(2 × 12) (10 + 16) (11 + 2) (2 × 4)

(5 × 4) (5 × 3) (30 − 4) (9 − 1) (2 × 4)

(3 × 7) (2 × 6) (4 × 3) (13 + 10)

(15 − 4) (2 × 13) (6 + 5) (11 × 2) (18 − 9)

(4 × 6) (3 × 3) (3 × 6) (2 × 4) (6 + 5)

(5 × 5) (2 × 13) (4 × 5) (8 + 0)

Now write your own message about waste.

WORK

National curriculum links

Principal location in the National Curriculum

- People and Communities

Other areas covered by topic

- Materials, Resources, Energy ● Buildings, Industrialisation, Waste

Context of study

- The individual ● Local issues ● Global concerns

Suggested sub-topics and their location in areas of study of curriculum guidelines for Environmental Education

Sub-topic	Areas of Study in the National Curriculum						
	Climate	Soils, Rocks, Minerals	Water	Materials, Resources, Energy	Plants and Animals	People and Communities	Buildings, Industrialis-ation, Waste
World of business				○		●	●
Power/ engines			○	●		○	●
Trade	○		○	○		●	○
Leisure/ tourism	○		○	○		●	

Key   ● Principal location   ○ Part coverage

English/Economic and Industrial Understanding

- Definition of 'work' and common usage
- Sayings
- Designing questionnaires and conducting interviews
- Why people work – discussion and analysis
- Job applications/descriptions/interviews/qualifications
- Job advertisements
- Wearing a uniform
- Setting up a business
- Unemployment, inability to work
- Debates

Geography

- Global issues, e.g. trade inter-dependence of nations
- European Community
- Impact of industrialisation on the environment
- Unemployment figures
- Leisure/tourism industry
- Cultural aspects of the environment

RE

- Voluntary work
- Employment for the disabled
- Fund-raising for charity

WORK – cross-curricular links

Science and PE

- Work of machines and engines
- Concept of power
- Work of everyday instruments and objects
- How our bodies work
- Use of energy

Art

- Designing job advertisements
- Make business cards and stationery
- Advertising posters
- Photography as a medium for displaying work

History

- Impact of modern technology on employment
- Community changes in employment opportunities
- Patterns of commuting

Mathematics

- House building
- Work time study
- Holidays/annual leave

129

Basics to be developed throughout the topic

Concepts

- Work is an essential aspect of our industrialised world
- The concept is complex. It may refer to people, to inanimate objects or to processes
- There are a wide variety of reasons why people work
- Work may be paid or unpaid
- The effects of lack of work/unemployment
- The balance between work and leisure

Attitudes

- Respect for other people, their lives, activities, occupations and opinions
- Respect for those who work to help us
- Care and concern for those who cannot work
- Tolerance and open-mindedness

Environmental issues

- Similarities and differences between people and how they use their time and environments
- The impact of new technologies on jobs and communities
- Appropriate technology for different jobs and conditions
- Cultural aspects of the working environment
- The impact of industrialisation on the environment

STARTING POINTS

- Take the children for a walk into the local environment. Look for evidence of work: for example, people at work, places of work, and the impact of industrialisation on the environment.

- Focus on a particular job or industry. Invite someone to come and talk to the children about their work, for example a bank manager, a farmer, a shopkeeper or a nurse.

- Start with the *word* work: this can mean a wide variety of things. Look it up in the dictionary, and discuss how it is used in many ways in everyday speech.

- Begin with one object, for example a computer, and discuss how one machine has revolutionised the world of work and business. Analyse this change.

- Take an individual approach: ask the children what work they like doing best and what they would like to do when they leave school.

- Collect job advertisements from newspapers. Use these as starting points.

ENGLISH, ECONOMIC AND INDUSTRIAL UNDERSTANDING
C43

1. Look up the meaning of the word work in the dictionary. Discuss how it can be used to mean different things in everyday speech. Either prepare a series of sentences using the word in different ways, or ask the children to write their own sentences, showing a variety of meanings, for example:

- My mum was late for work today.
- I can't work it out.
- Running that race was hard work.
- The bulldozer is doing work.
- This kettle does not work any more.
- Let us start a topic work book.

2 **Copymaster 43** (What do we have in common?) may be used in association with activity 1 above. All the pictures are of objects or people doing work. Ask the children to write sentences about each picture. Discuss the fact that work can be physical, intellectual, mechanical or powered. Make them aware that we do work every time we make something move and when we do work, we use up energy. In everyday speech, however, work is often taken to mean the same as employment.

3 Think of sayings that are about work, for example, 'All work and no play makes Jack a dull boy'. Make children aware of the overlap between work and play, chore and fun. Do things seem like hard work when we enjoy what we are doing? What is work for one person may be pleasure for another.

4 Help the children do an inventory of work that is done by people in the school. First, ask them to make a list of people who work there: the pupils, teachers, head teacher, cooks, secretary, caretaker, cleaners. Which of these are in paid employment? Help the children write a questionnaire and interview every adult who is employed in the school. Questions could include:

- How long have you worked here?
- Who employs you?
- How many hours a week do you work?
- What are your starting and finishing times?

- Do you wear a uniform or need any special equipment for the job?
- What is your job called?
- Who are you responsible to?
- Are you responsible for the work of others?
- Could you describe what you do?
- Do you enjoy your work? What are the good and bad aspects of it?
- Why do you do this work?

5 This extensive list will raise numerous thoughts for further discussion, recording and analysis. For example, ask the children to draw graphs to show a comparison of hours worked by different people. Discuss whether these differences mean that some people work harder than others. Analyse starting and finishing times: for example, it would be inappropriate for the secretary to work very different hours from the head teacher, whilst the cleaners have to work either before or after the school day for practical reasons.

Help the children draw charts to show line management and discuss the important issue of responsibility in employment. Most people who work are employed by someone or an organisation, and have to account for what they do. Ask the children to write imaginative stories about unreliability and irresponsibility at work. What disasters could happen at school if people did not do their work properly?

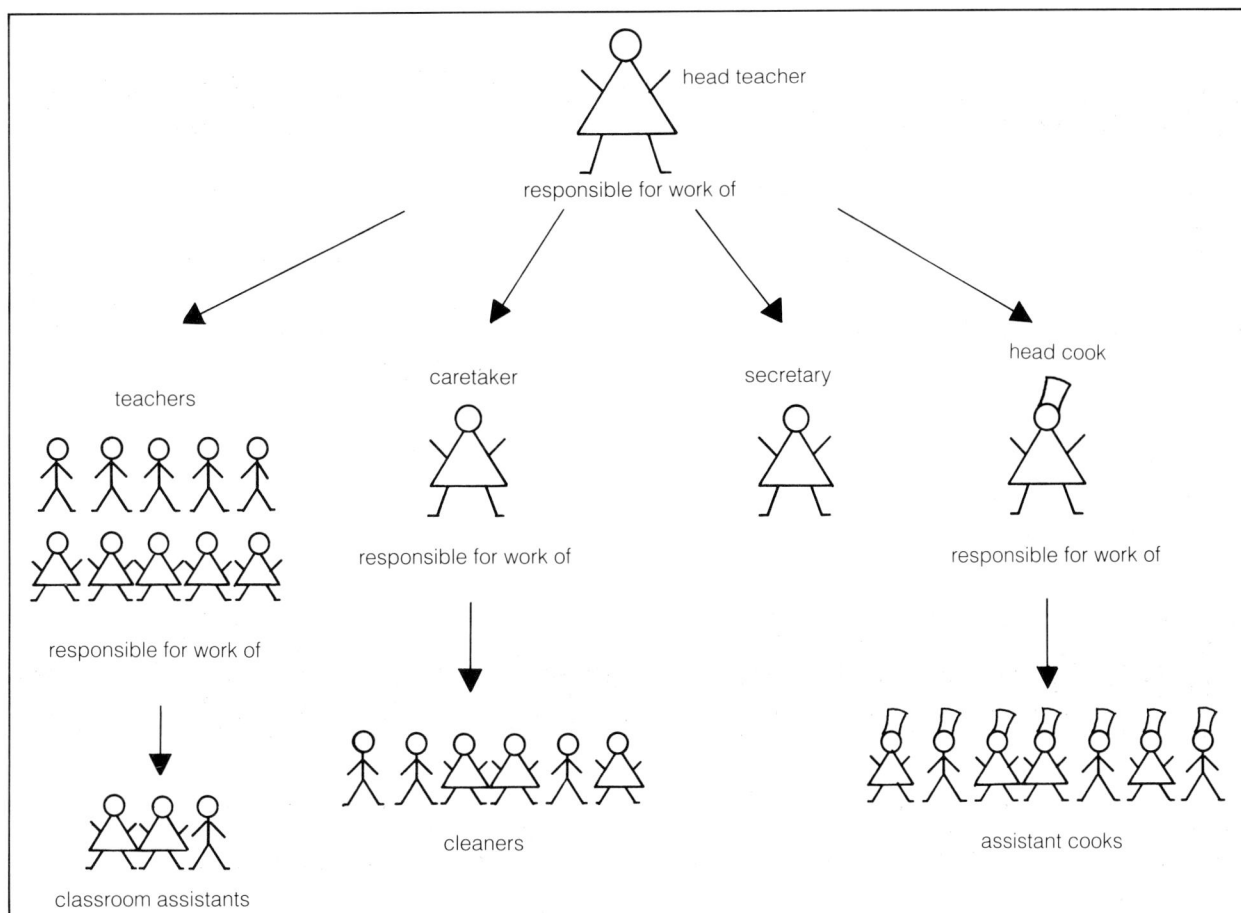

Line management in a school

131

Discuss the reasons people give for doing their work, and whether they are happy doing it. Ask the children to rank these in order of significance as given in their first and second choice answers, and then record graphically as illustrated below.

6 Ask the children to design a large wall frieze about 'Our school as a place of employment'. Ask them to write up the results of interviews, display charts and graphs, and add photographs or paintings of all people employed in the school.

7 Ask the children to find out how people apply for jobs. This raises many key issues including qualifications, job applications and interviews. If there is a Job Centre nearby, find out how it operates. Take the children to visit it at a suitable time (seek permission first) and record details of some of the jobs being advertised, what qualifications they require, and how much the employee will be paid.

8 Look in newspapers for job advertisements. See how they are organised in the paper (under employment headings?) and what information they give. Cut out some of the advertisements. Each group or pair of

Why we work at Chestnut Copse School

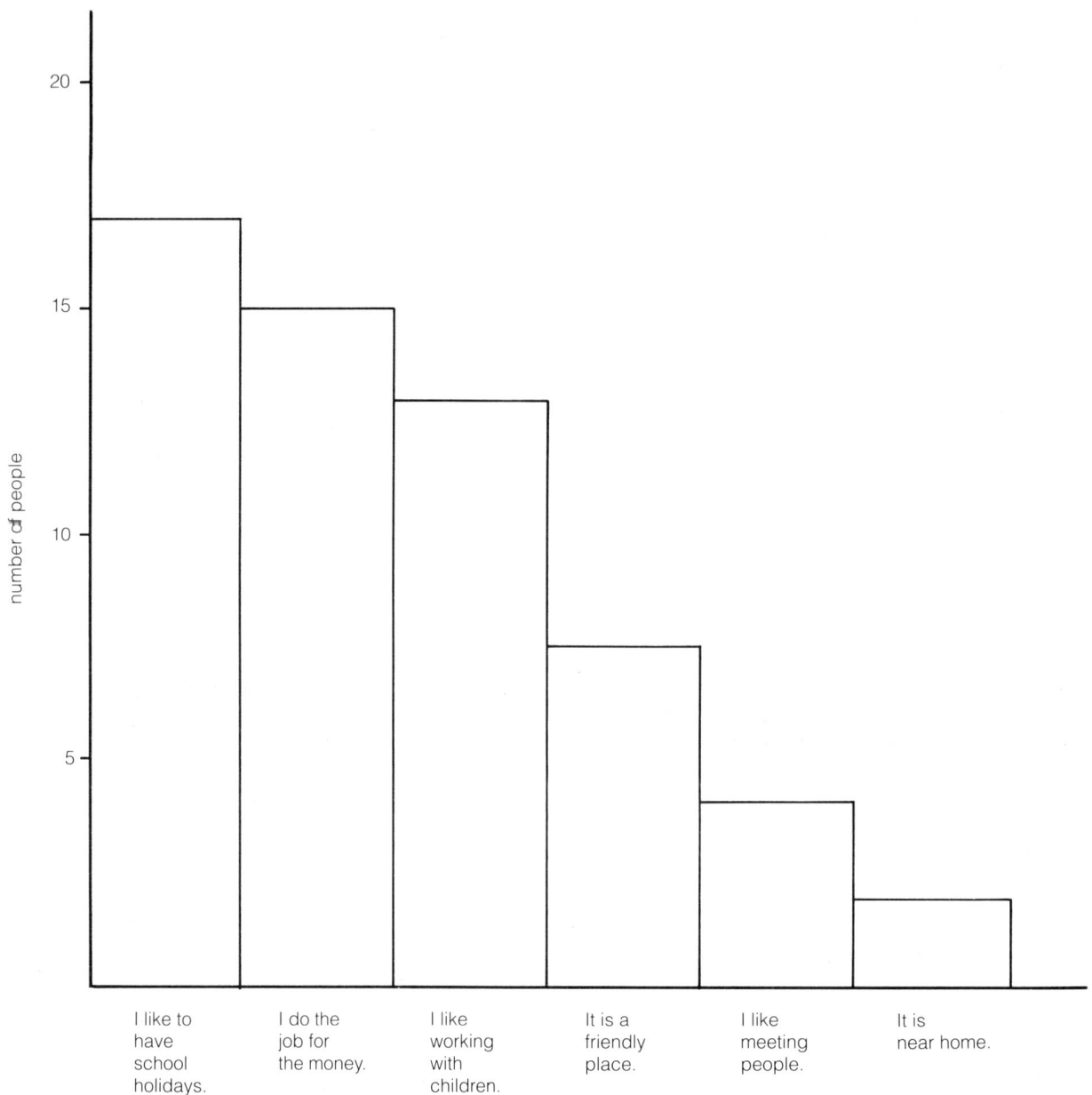

Children could summarise the interview responses graphically.

children in the class can then discuss a specific advertisement and share thoughts on who could apply and those for whom the job would not be suitable.

9 Return to your survey of jobs in the school (activities 4 and 5 on page 131). Ask the children to find out (by interview, if necessary) what qualifications the various employees needed in order to get the job. Answers may include academic and professional qualifications, as well as personal qualities.

10 Talk about the personal qualities you would look for if you were going to employ someone. Perhaps consider this generally, then write various jobs on cards, for example: a nurse, a fire officer, a night security guard, a baby-sitter, a banker.

Share these cards among the children and ask them to list qualities they would look for when employing people in these various jobs.

11 Help the children write job descriptions. Take a variety of occupations and write a description of the job which might be in the 'further particulars' of the job sent to potential applicants. Consider the essence of this – it must be a fair description, aimed at attracting the 'right' people.

12 Ask the children to write letters of application for various jobs. They could imagine they are applying for the work they would really like to do. This can be related to an investigation into the genuine qualifications needed for specific jobs. These can be researched and included in applications. Ask children to imagine that they have the necessary qualifications and write a covering letter, saying why they think they are the right person for the job.

13 Organise job interviews in the classroom. Select various occupations. Children can take turns to be the interviewee and on the panel of interviewers. Interviewers must compile a list of suitable questions, discuss the order in which they will be asked, and appoint a chairperson. When someone is appointed, the interviewers must be prepared to discuss why they thought this person was the most suitable candidate.

14 Help the children find out why some occupations require the wearing of a uniform. Invite one or more uniformed employees to come and talk to the children about the nature of their work – perhaps a policeman or policewoman from the community, the school nurse or a fire officer. Ask the children to paint pictures and write accounts of their duties. They should explain why the uniform is worn, and give details of any other equipment that is a necessary part of the job.

15 Set up a classroom or school business. There are endless possibilities, well-documented in books on business and enterprise education. For example, run a bank, or manufacture and sell a product. Involve all children in every stage of the venture, for example design of the product, feasibility study, manufacturing process, sales, accounting. It should be a genuine corporate activity. Aim to demonstrate the principles and processes involved in setting up and running a small business.

16 Invite a local industrialist, business person or bank manager to come and talk to the class about their work.

17 Discuss the all-important issue of people who are not in employment for various reasons. It is essential that the children appreciate some of the problems of unemployment. For example, many people are genuinely searching for jobs that they are able to do, but there are not always enough jobs available in a particular location. Some people do not have the qualifications necessary for the work they would like to do. Some people are physically handicapped and therefore unable to do certain work. (See also RE activities, page 137.)

18 Ask the children to do thoughtful, imaginative writing on such topics as: 'The work I would least like to do, and why', 'What I think should be the world's best paid job' and 'The world's most exciting work'.

19 Organise classroom debates on controversial issues such as the extraordinarily high income of professional sportspeople or pop stars. Are they worth it?

SCIENCE AND PE ACTIVITIES

C44 –46

1 Investigate how machines and engines work. When they work, they use up energy of some kind. It takes energy to make things move. Differentiate between energy and power. (Power means the rate at which energy is produced or used.) Machines are used to convert one form of energy into another. The more energy a machine uses in a given time, the more powerful it is, and the more energy it can provide (see Energy topic, pages 61–78).

2 Use **copymaster 44** (Where do they get their energy?) to discuss sources of energy. Differentiate between natural renewable sources (the Sun, wind) and those which depend on the Earth's finite resources. Match the working items shown with their energy source. Be prepared for ambiguities; there will

undoubtedly be questions on whether a calculator uses solar energy or electricity (battery). Discuss the advantages and disadvantages of various energy sources.

3 Extend activity 2 by doing a survey of powered objects which work at school or in the children's homes. Ask the children to make a list of items and a list of energy sources. Ask them to represent these in graph form. Which is the most popular form of energy? Analyse whether the items used are really necessary in our lives. Discuss how we could conserve energy by having fewer working machines.

4 Take a selection of useful objects and find out in greater detail about how they work. Divide the children into groups, each to take a different item and report to

133

A ball full of air bounces off a hard surface.

A deflated ball would not have the energy to bounce back into the air.

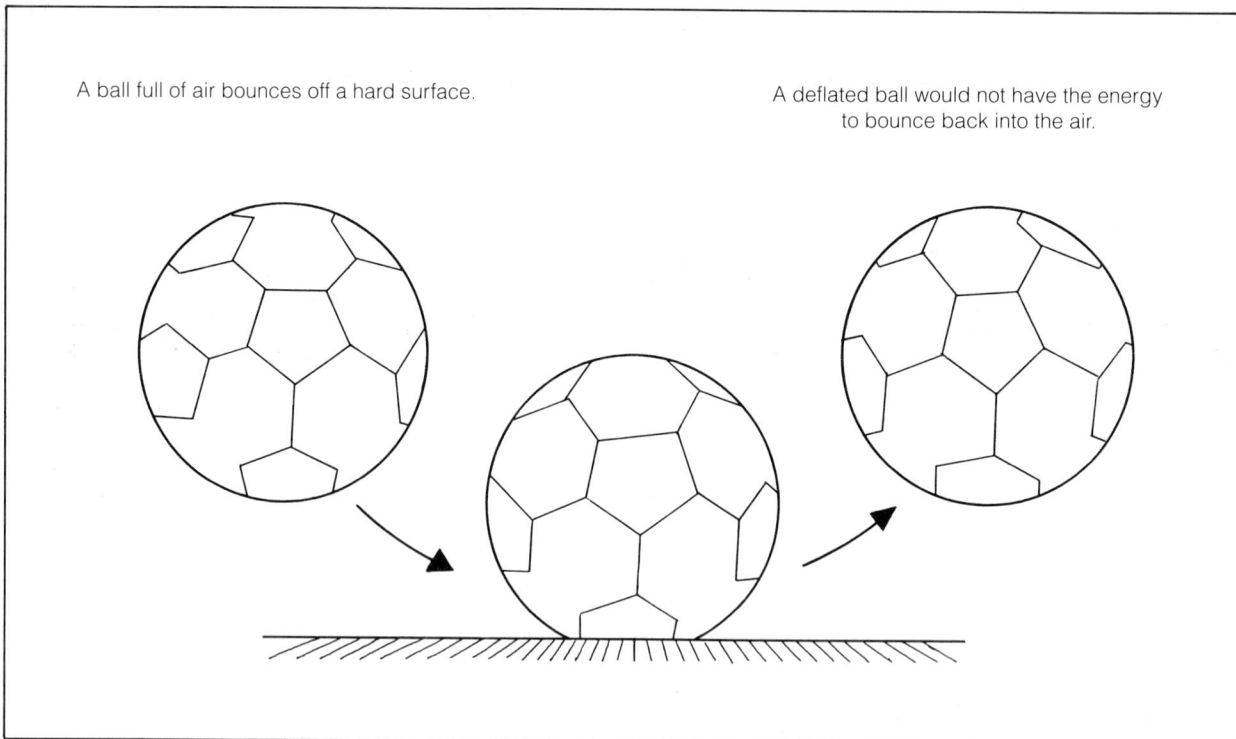

the class on its necessary parts and what is needed to make it work. For example, examine a torch.

The torch can be safely taken apart so that children can investigate its batteries, bulb, spring, reflector and switch. Ask the children to write the labels in the correct places on **copymaster 45** (How does a torch work?). Ask them to write a sentence about each part to describe its function.

5 Broaden the interpretation of work. We say that anything which functions in a particular way works in that way. Ask the children to write a list of everyday objects which work, for example a thermometer, a mirror, a pair of scissors, a fountain pen, a ball, a balloon. What do they depend on for successful functioning?

6 Discuss the importance of a ball 'working' properly. Most ball sports rely on balls bouncing off the ground. Ask the children to unscramble the letters on **copymaster 46** (Why do we all need air? So you can use us.) to identify well-known ball sports, and to complete the sentence to say what a ball depends upon for success. If a rubber ball is not completely full of air, it

will not bounce effectively. When it is full of air and hits a hard surface, the air is squeezed and the ball flattens. The force of the air then pushes it back into its original shape and the ball rises off the ground.

7 Use PE lessons to investigate how our own bodies work. When we set up apparatus for PE lessons, we move it by pushing, pulling or lifting. This is doing work. We continue to do work when we make our bodies move on the apparatus. Whenever we work, we use up energy. Investigate various forms of exercise, the amount of energy used and where this comes from (see also Energy and Food topics, pages 61–78 and 93–110, respectively).

8 Relate physical activity and energy use to different occupations. Collect pictures of various jobs, ranging from sedentary to the very demanding. Talk about fitness levels needed in certain occupations. For some jobs, being physically strong is more important than having academic qualifications. Collect information about physical training programmes which are an integral part of some areas of employment.

GEOGRAPHY ACTIVITIES ▶

1 Consider the global aspects of work. Introduce concepts such as world trade and the inter-dependence of nations in industry and business. Take a simple starting point such as a visit to the supermarket to look at the fruit and vegetable display. Ask the children to write a list of all produce on sale, sketch items and find out their country of origin (often this is stated on

the display or packaging). A survey should reveal a large number of goods that have come from outside the United Kingdom. Help the children trace their origins, and make a study of all the work involved, from source to supermarket. Perhaps divide children into groups, each to trace the path of one particular item. Present results in the form of a wall map/diagram.

Work with an artichoke, from California to Southlands Supermarket

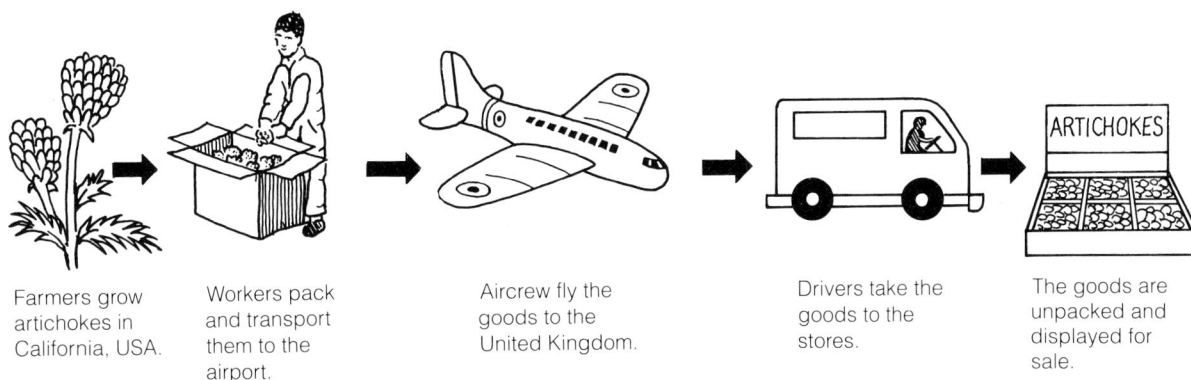

Farmers grow artichokes in California, USA.

Workers pack and transport them to the airport.

Aircrew fly the goods to the United Kingdom.

Drivers take the goods to the stores.

The goods are unpacked and displayed for sale.

Air route: San Francisco to London

Atlantic Ocean

From source to supermarket

Build up a world map with results of investigations of the various groups, showing the transport routes of the foreign produce on sale.

2 Discuss world trade, and the fact that fruits and vegetables are only one aspect of 'work' that is exchanged between countries of the world. Study energy supply and demand, for example the dependence of industrialised nations on oil exporting countries.

3 Make a case study of an international company. Find out how many people are employed, in how many countries, and what is the nature of the business or products manufactured.

4 Discuss the relevance of the United Kingdom as a member of the European Community. What effect does or will this have on trade and working with Europe?

5 Examine the impact of industrialisation on the environment. Take the children to visit and observe local factories/industrial estates. Find out the nature of the businesses and industries involved. How are raw materials transported to the site, and how are goods transported away? Make a map or plan to show the location of industrial units in the local area, and transport routes used. Calculate from maps or plans the area which is taken up by industry. Are there any signs of environmental pollution, such as smoking chimneys, or discharge of waste into water supplies?

6 If you know anyone who lives near to industrial areas, talk to them about it. Find out their views on the advantages and disadvantages of industrialisation in the area.

135

THE GOOD	THE BAD
provides employment good public transport support for local shops etc.	spoils the view of the natural landscape traffic jams on main roads etc.

The pros and cons of
industrialisation

7 Consider unemployment figures. Find out what percentage of people in our country are unemployed. Are there geographical areas of the United Kingdom where the unemployment rate is higher than others? Discuss reasons why this is the case. Ask the children to talk to parents and their friends, and find out who has moved for work reasons. Ask the children to draw a map to show other areas of the country from which families of children in the class may have moved for reasons of employment.

8 Use the expression 'All work and no play makes Jack a dull boy' as a starting point for discussion. Consider the importance of the leisure industry in our society. People who work hard need leisure activities in order to relax and take a break from work. People who are unemployed, retired or choose not to work for various reasons need leisure facilities to occupy their time. Help the children find out about the leisure industry in your own community. What job opportunities are there for people to be employed in leisure and tourism in your own locality?

9 Do a sub-topic on leisure and tourism. Find out about job possibilities such as working as a travel agent, air steward or stewardess, tour operator's representative abroad, airline pilot, city guide, leisure centre manager, coach driver, hotelier, waiter or waitress, etc. Help the children compile a directory entitled 'Work for play'. Include details of jobs in the leisure industry, draw sketches of uniforms or equipment needed, and write about necessary qualifications, personal qualities, and include a job description.

10 Consider cultural aspects of the environment, and those who work to make it a more enjoyable and beautiful place. Visit an art gallery, museum or concert hall. Ask the children to write about those who devote their lives to working with their creative talents.

MATHEMATICS ACTIVITIES

C47

1 **Copymaster 47** (Build a house) is a board game to be played by two or more layers. Cut out the 'board', mount it on stiff card and cover it with clear plastic for increased durability. A dice is required and one counter for each participant. Players take turns to shake the dice and move their counter from the number 1 (START) to number 56 when they have finished the job of building a house. Certain squares contain instructions to either move forwards or backwards a specified number of squares. Many of these instructions draw attention to problems and pitfalls of the job, for example materials not arriving on time, weather halting work, employees falling sick, etc. Use these as a basis for discussion on the hazards of work of this kind. Often we meet problems that are beyond our control, especially when work is dependent on weather conditions or the services of other people.

2 Do a sub-topic on the mathematics of working time. This may involve introducing discussion on such practices as working fixed hours, flexi-time hours, doing shift work, being on call and job sharing. Develop this by questionnaires and interviews; let the children talk to a wide range of people about the hours they work. Ask them to find out if they always start and finish at the same times each day and whether they work a precise number of hours each week/year. Other questions to include on the questionnaire could be:

● Are you self-employed, or does your employer fix your working hours?
● Does your pay depend on the number of hours worked?

Where possible, ask the children to tabulate results and draw graphs to show comparisons. In many

136

instances this may be difficult and more qualitative recording will be necessary.

3 Follow up activity 2 by going on to investigate 'time off'. How many days' holiday do the people in the sample have each year? Ask whether holiday has to be taken at a specific time. What do we mean by the term

Bank Holidays? Do people get paid for the days they are on holiday? Ask the children to draw graphs and tables to demonstrate which occupations have most and least leisure time. All of the above activities should generate much discussion and develop greater understanding of the complex world of work and employment.

ART ACTIVITIES

C48

1 Ask the children to design a job advertisement in the space provided in **copymaster 48** (Wanted!). Look at published job advertisements with them to find out what key information should be provided. Children can decide their own job or area of employment. Ask them to write a list of vital information and key words. Encourage them to think carefully about layout and design. As a whole, the advertisement should be informative, accurate and eye-catching.

2 Ask the children to design and make business

cards and stationery for imaginary businesses or for a business enterprise established in the classroom.

3 Advertise your business (see activity 2 above) by designing posters and leaflets to distribute.

4 Take photographs of people at work in the street. Make a photo-montage showing a busy high street or a working village, to show the wide range of activities going on in the community.

HISTORY ACTIVITIES

1 Let the children study the impact of modern technology on employment. Take the computer as a starting point. Let them talk to people who use computers in their work and find out what changes these machines have made to the nature of the job and to the business in general. Invite someone such as a bank manager to come and talk to the children about how computers have changed the world of banking.

2 Help the children find out what changes have taken place in employment opportunities in your community in the past 20 years. Again, parents and grandparents will be a good source of information. Find out if any industrial estates, factories or new transport facilities have been built. In rural areas, have there been

any farm developments? Assess the general trend of the community. Is it growing and developing, or are population and employment declining?

Find out which industry, business or other establishment employs the largest number of people. Help the children draw a map of their village, town or neighbourhood and show the position of any new areas of employment and indicate the original site of any establishments which have moved or closed down. Define limits for this if you live in a large town or city. If you live in a residential area, do a survey to find out the main towns or neighbourhoods to which people commute for work. Is there a changing pattern of commuting in your locality?

RE ACTIVITIES

1 Many people work for no monetary reward. Ask the children to find out which parents and friends of the class do voluntary work. Ask where they go, what they do and why they do it. Discuss the obligations which we all have to help others who are ill, elderly, or unable to do certain jobs for themselves. Tell the story of the Good Samaritan, and other stories of individuals who have devoted their lives to the service of others.

2 Help the children investigate employment possibilities for the disabled in your area. Write to a

number of businesses and industries to enquire about any special facilities which they may have for handicapped employees.

3 Find out whether your local authority has a special training or employment programme or unit for the disabled. If so, find out more about its work.

4 Organise a fund-raising venture for the severely handicapped. This serves two excellent purposes: experience in planning a classroom venture, and at the same time helping those who will never be able to work.

What do we have in common?

Where do they get their energy?

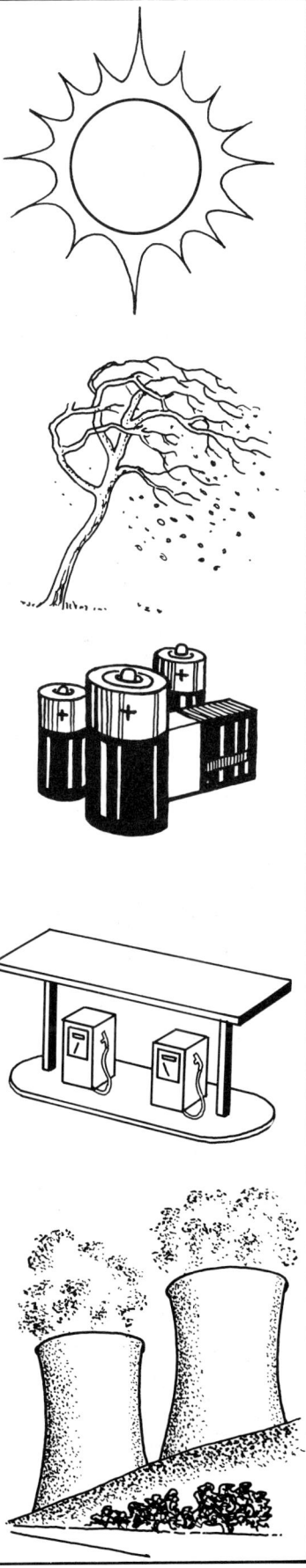

How does a torch work?

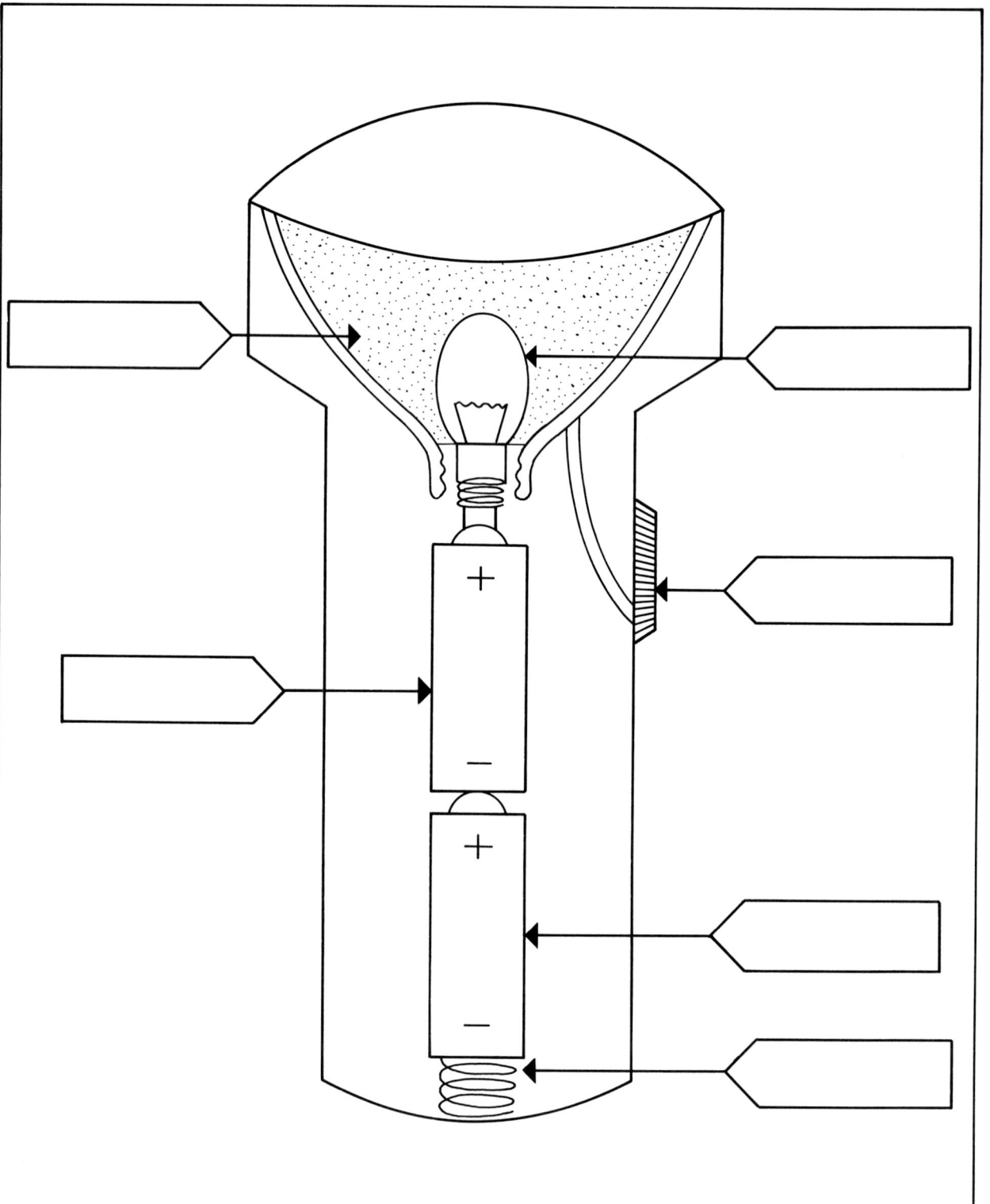

spring	battery	bulb	switch	reflector

Why do we all need air? So you can use us.

How does a ball bounce?

What games do we use these balls for?

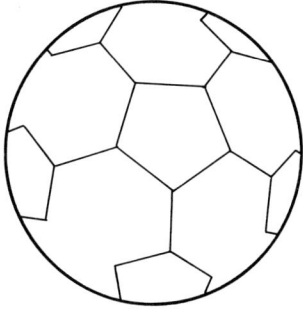

c e o r s c

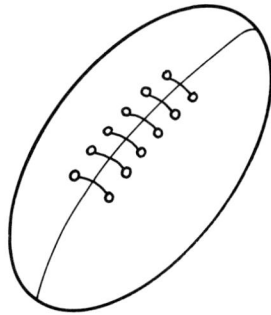

u g r y b

e n s i t n

l e v a l o b l y l

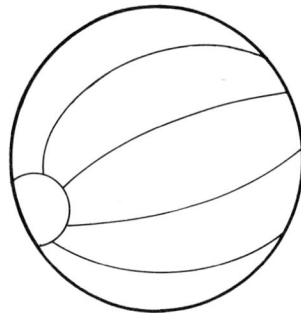

e l l n a t b

A ball bounces when it is full of ____.

Build a house

1	2	3	4	5	6	7
START Off to build the house		Brick order delayed. Go back to start		Bricks delivered as special order. Move on 4		Snow holds up work. Go back 3
14	13	12	11	10	9	8
			Foundations laid. Advance 6			
15	16	17	18	19	20	21
			Bricklayer off sick. Go back 5			
28	27	26	25 Walls complete. Advance 5	24	23	22
29	30	31	32	33	34	35
Plumber leaves for a better paid job. Go back 3				Roof tiles don't arrive. Go back 5		Employ new plumber. Advance 4
42	41	40	39	38	37	36
	Windows in. Advance 4			Electrician off work after accident. Go back 2		
43	44	45	46	47	48	49
				Electrician works overtime. Advance 5		
55	54	53	52	51	50	
FINISH Purchaser likes house.					Tidy garden. Advance 1	

Wanted!

WANTED: Reliable employee

Send letter of application and c.v. to:

_____

_____

_____

_____

OCEANS

National curriculum links

Principal location in the National Curriculum

- Water

Other areas covered by topic

- Materials, Resources, Energy ● Climate ● Plants and Animals ● People and Communities
- Buildings, Industrialisation, Waste

Context of study

- Global concerns

Suggested sub-topics and their location in areas of study of curriculum guidelines for Environmental Education

Sub-topic	Areas of Study in the National Curriculum						
	Climate	Soils, Rocks, Minerals	Water	Materials, Resources, Energy	Plants and Animals	People and Communities	Buildings, Industrialis- ation, Waste
Pollution	O	O	●	O	O	O	●
Global warming	●		O	O	O	O	O
Water life	O		●		●	O	O
Water power	O		●	●		O	

Key ● Principal location O Part coverage

144

Geography

- The planet's oceans
- Routes of explorers, voyages of discovery
- Sea level, lands above and below
- Crossing the oceans – oceans as 'barrier'
- Maps of rock pools
- Food from the oceans/the fishing industry
- Benefits from oceans
- Ocean pollution
- Management of global commons
- Climate/global warming

Science

- Fresh and salt water
- Tides and waves
- Food chains and webs
- Ocean transport
- Resources from the sea bed
- Ocean life at various depths
- Alternative energy

Design and Technology

- Water power

OCEANS – cross-curricular links

English

- Moods of the sea
- Art work and literature
- Factual writing
- Ocean vocabulary
- Endangered species – campaigns
- Underwater cities

PE

- Water sports

Mathematics

- Fish prices
- Mail service – costs and analysis
- Ocean holiday – detailed planning and costings

Basics to be developed throughout the topic

Concepts

- Water is essential for life
- Seas and oceans support a vast array of life forms, including endangered species
- Seas and oceans are a valuable resource for human life which must be conserved and protected
- Oceans are part of our planet's 'commons' and require international management

Attitudes

- Care and concern for the environment and all living things
- Care and concern for conserving the Earth's resources
- Independence of thought on environmental issues
- Respect for empirical evidence and rational argument

Environmental issues

- Water conservation
- Causes of water pollution
- Problems of water supply
- Renewable sources of energy
- Management of resources
- Destruction of natural habitats and endangered species

STARTING POINTS

- Consider the part that oceans play in our own lives – notably for holidays and to provide food. Start by considering the variety of fish that we take and eat from the seas of the world.
- Visit a fishmonger or the fish counter of a supermarket. Find out the names of the varieties of fish on sale, where they came from, and how they reached the point of sale.

- Read or tell stories associated with oceans and ocean life. Make a collection of suitable tales, poems and pictures.
- Look at films about life in the ocean
- Make a visit to the seashore or to a fishing port.

GEOGRAPHY ACTIVITIES

C49
–51

1 With the children, study a globe and maps of the world. Talk about the surface of our planet, and the fact that a greater proportion of it is covered by water than by dry land.

2 Study the routes of early explorers who sailed across the world's oceans. Ask the children to trace their paths on the globe. For example, follow the journey of Magellan who sailed from Spain in 1519 and proved that the Earth is round. His fleet sailed down the coast of South America, across the Pacific and Indian Oceans, around Africa's Cape of Good Hope, and back to Spain. It is therefore possible to travel all the way around the world on the oceans, without crossing land.

3 Having studied a globe and world maps, ask the children to record the names of the major oceans of the world on **copymaster 49** (Oceans all around us). Use it also for discussing the nature of maps; talk about why a globe is the most realistic world map. Since globes are a model of the round shape of the Earth, then all distances and sizes can be true scaled versions of reality. Look at flat maps of the world. These must artificially flatten the real round Earth. Compare world maps of different projections. Point out that some countries seem proportionally bigger on some than others. Despite differing projections, the fact remains that three quarters of the surface of our planet is covered

146

with water. Discuss why this is always coloured blue on world maps and globes.

4 Develop map work by asking children to consider what is beneath the oceans' surface. Most children will understand that land is not flat: it has mountains and valleys, but they will assume that the sea bed is perfectly flat like the sea shore. Point out that there are in fact more mountains, deep canyons and volcanoes under the oceans than on dry land. Talk about how to represent these on a piece of paper: we might view them from above (in plan/map form) or from the side (cross-section).

5 **Copymaster 50** (Islands in the deep) introduces the important concepts of sea level, above and below, as well as giving practice in basic map work skills such as the use of scales and keys. Ask the children to look at the scale in the key and find the sea level. Land above this, (that is, the land of the islands) is labelled A. Ask them to colour this in green on the map. Land below the level of the sea is graded according to depth. Ask them to colour this (sections B–E) in deepening shades of blue. Explain that the map as a whole shows two tropical islands and the surrounding area of sea.

6 Ask the children to think about what these islands would look like if we viewed them from the side. Ask children to draw a cross-section, showing sea-level and the two areas of land above it.

7 Explain that on all maps, elevation, that is height of the land is measured from sea level. Cartographers show land height by using a coloured key and lines called contour lines.

8 Ask the children to find out where the highest land on Earth is. (Mount Everest in the Himalayas reaches 8708 metres (29 028 feet) above sea level).

9 Talk about the oceans as a 'barrier': they separate people and nations. There are many occasions when people and goods need to travel across them. Ask the children to imagine that they need to travel from the United Kingdom to Australia. Talk about ways of doing this. Visit a travel agent and find out the routes that air and sea transport might take. Ask the children to look for transport routes on the globe and prepare an itinerary. Which countries would they fly over in an aeroplane? Which oceans would they cross? Children could be divided into groups, some to investigate routes of air travel to the other side of the world, and some to investigate surface routes (see also Mathematics activity 4 page 154).

10 As well as maps of global scale, include small-scale map work activities. On a visit to the seashore, investigate rock pools. (This could be done as an imaginary, classroom-based activity if a visit is not possible). Ask the children to use graph paper to make a map of a rock pool. They should divide the area into squares (using string stretched across the pool attached to stakes in the ground if this is a genuine field investigation). They can record where the main areas of

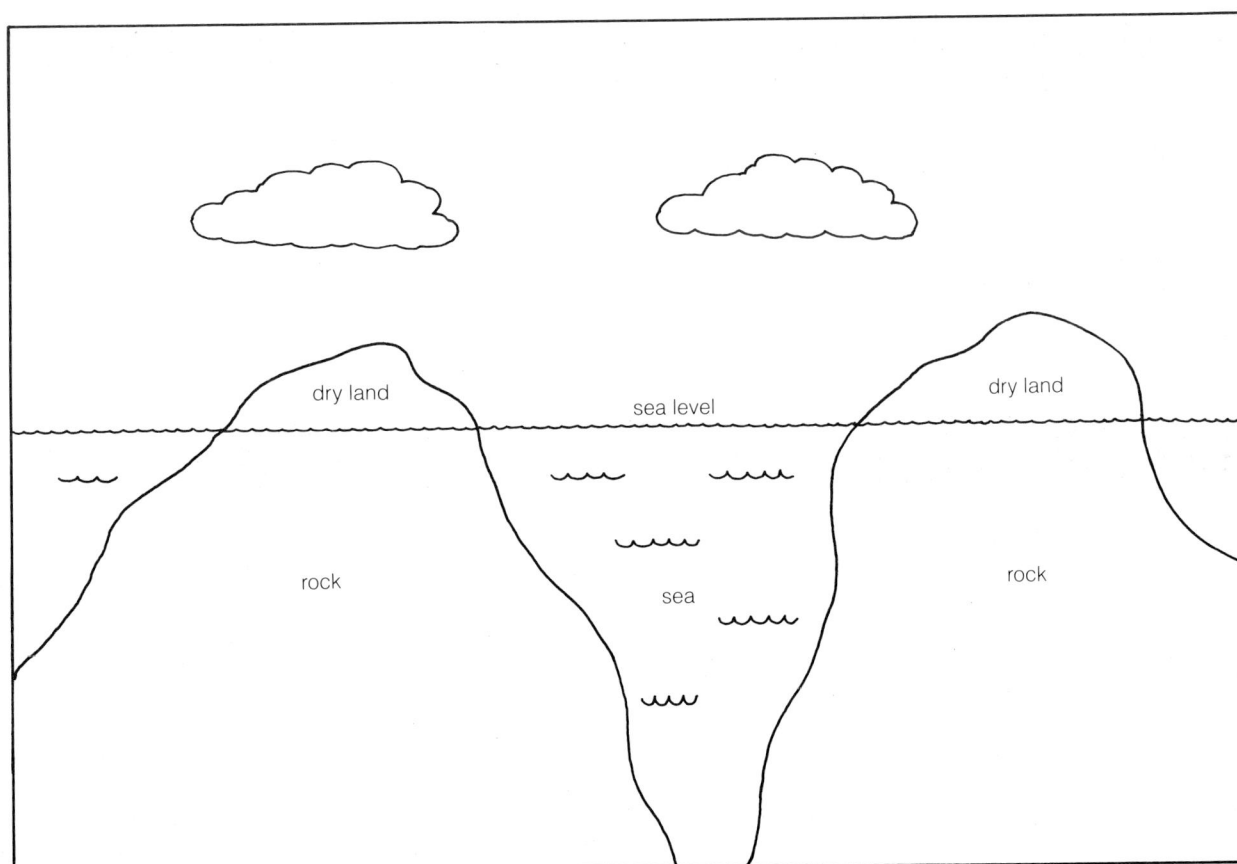

Above and below sea level

147

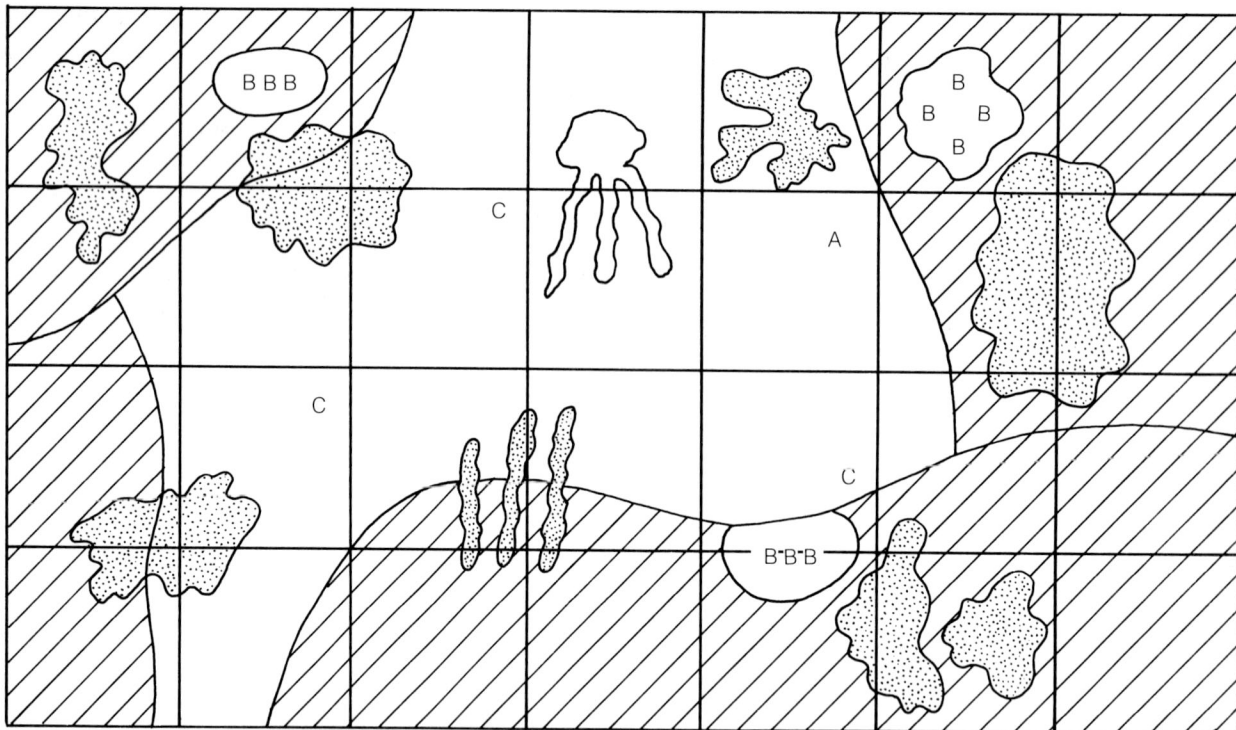

Key

rock (colour grey)

Weed (colour green)

Mapping a rock pool

seaweed are growing and where the rocks are. Ask them to devise a key to show these as illustrated above.

Ask the children to make a list of all the animals spotted in the pool. Record these as symbols or as a lettered key. Identify them in the key:

A	Crab
B	Areas of limpets
C	Anemone
	etc.

11 Do a sub-topic on 'food from the oceans'. A good starting point is a visit to the fish counter of a supermarket, a fishmonger's store or a fish-and-chip shop. Find out what varieties of fish are on sale and if possible where they were caught. Record details of prices (see Mathematics activities 1 and 2, page 153).

12 Investigate the fishing industry. Use a map of the British Isles and locate well-known fishing ports. If possible, visit a port and let the children observe boats, warehouses and look for evidence of what happens to the catch. Ask the children to paint pictures of different kinds of fishing vessels – drifters and trawlers. Find out what size and shape of nets are used, and how long they are out at sea. Other questions to investigate will include the following:

- What varieties of fish are caught in drift and trawl nets?
- How far out to sea do the boats go?
- What happens to the fish on the boat?
- How are the nets lowered and raised?
- What happens to the fish once they are landed?

13 Help the children make a large wall collage to show fishing boats at sea. Use a real net and arrange it in an appropriate shape under the water. Add collage fish and sea birds following the catch.

14 Help the children find out how lobsters and crabs are caught. Add some lobster pots to the fishing collage.

15 Do a class survey to find out how often fish is eaten. Which varieties? Where do families buy it? Is it bought ready cooked? How is fresh fish prepared? Ask the children to draw bar charts to record the results as in the example below.

16 Discuss the nutritional value of fish. They are really good for us, being high in protein and low in fat (see also Food topic, page 93–110).

17 Introduce the key environmental concept of over-fishing. Huge modern fishing fleets catch so many fish that many traditional fishermen cannot catch enough to earn their own living. Also, many species of fish are becoming rare or even endangered species. Talk about the importance of international co-operation aimed at conserving fish, the 'harvest of the seas'.

Fresh or ready cooked?

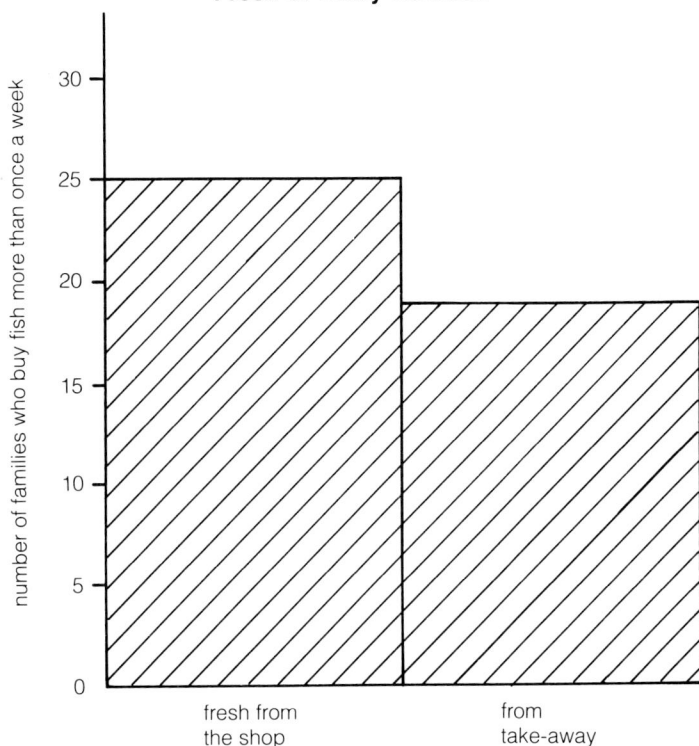

How do we usually cook fresh fish?

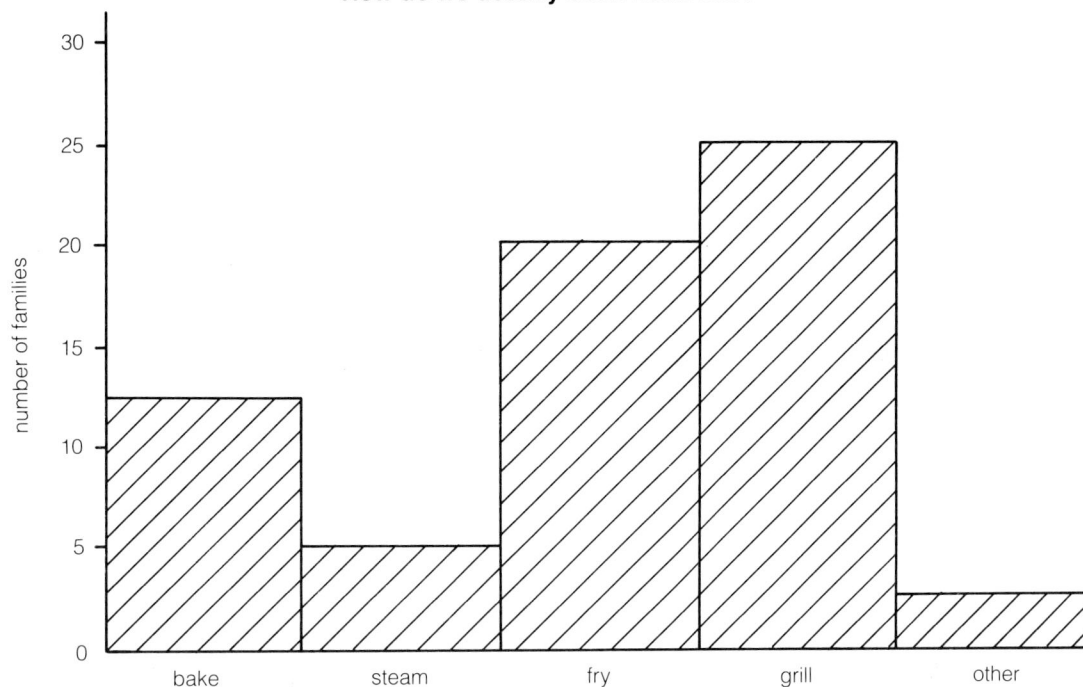

18 Find out about any other edible forms of ocean life. Ask the children if they would like a seaweed diet. Point out that for some nations in the world (such as Japan), seaweed is a staple part of the diet. Use international recipe books and investigate how seaweed may be used. If you live in a large city, it may be possible to buy dried or prepared seaweed – particularly from Chinese or Japanese supermarkets. If so, let the children taste it! Seaweed is full of nutrients. Many people believe that it is the food of the future, containing medicinal properties.

19 Ask the children to write down all the good aspects of ocean life on our Earth. For example, we can obtain food from the oceans, play water sports, they are beautiful to look at, we can take holidays at sea and on the seashore, the oceans play a vital role in the water cycle and are home for many fascinating forms of life. Ask the children to write accounts and paint posters of the 'benefits of the oceans'. Then consider what might spoil this vital habitat.

20 Do a sub-topic on pollution at sea. There could be three major strands to this: pollution from land-based activities, from oil disasters, and from the dumping of nuclear waste in the oceans. Some 80 per cent of marine pollution is derived from the land, for example through sewage and industrial waste. Help the children draw diagrams to show how this finds its way into the oceans through the water cycle (streams and rivers).

21 Find pictures of large oil tankers. Many weigh as much as 200 000 tons. If an accident occurs at sea, huge quantities of oil may spill into the water. Ask the children to write about the many consequences of a disaster of this kind: millions of sea creatures and plants will die and oil may wash onto the land, spoiling beaches and killing sea birds and creatures of the shore.

22 Read about oil disasters that have actually happened. What were the consequences? Who took responsibility?

23 Help the children find out what other poisonous substances are carried out to sea. Some countries use the sea as a dumping place for radioactive waste. Investigate how nuclear waste is prepared for burial at sea. Where is it taken to? Consider the opinions of those who believe that this is a safe thing to do, and those who disagree.

24 Introduce the key environmental concept of the oceans being 'global commons', that is, they do not belong to any one nation. Ask the children to write about whose responsibility they think it is to manage the seas. Ask them to write a 'global treaty' for keeping the oceans safe and clean. Discuss the importance of co-operation between nations over such matters as fishing and pollution.

25 Do a sub-topic on climate related to the oceans (see the topic on Weather, page 12–29). Consider the issues of acid rain and the greenhouse effect. Find out how global warming would affect sea levels. Try to find out what will happen to the coastline of the United Kingdom if world temperatures continue to rise, the polar ice caps melt, and ocean levels rise.

26 Ask the children to write imaginary stories about 'The day the sea invaded the land'. Whilst based on the children's imagination, these may reflect real events of the past (for example in East Anglia) and predictions for the future.

27 Discuss the sheer beauty and fascination of certain geographical wonders of the sea, such as the Great Barrier Reef.

Ask the children to locate the Great Barrier Reef on a map of the north east coast of Australia. Find out how it was formed, how large it is, and about the fascination of life there. Use reference books to identify the plants and animals shown on **copymaster 51** (Home on the Great Barrier Reef). These can be coloured. This could be a preliminary exercise to making a large Barrier Reef wall frieze, depicting many more forms of life.

How pollution from the land reaches the sea

150

SCIENCE ACTIVITIES

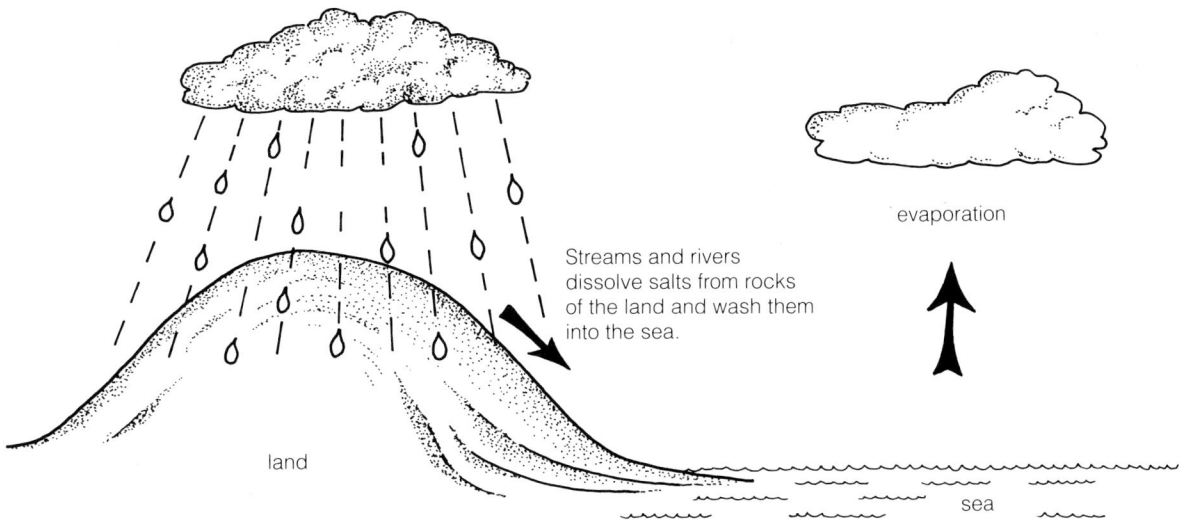

The water cycle

Streams and rivers dissolve salts from rocks of the land and wash them into the sea.

evaporation

land

sea

[1] Help the children find out how ocean water differs from fresh water of the land. Demonstrate how salt dissolves in water. Relate this to an understanding of the water cycle.

[2] Do an experiment to demonstrate why oceans do not freeze easily.

You will need
- 2 plastic containers (for example, ice cream tubs)
- Tap water and salt.

What to do
- Fill both containers almost to the top with water.
- Add three tablespoons of salt to one of them and stir until this has dissolved.
- Label and place both containers in a freezer, or in the freezing compartment of a refrigerator.

- Observe them every half hour; record which freezes first.

Repeat the experiment, this time adding three tablespoons of salt to one container and six to the other. Label the containers once again. Which freezes first?

[3] Another way in which oceans differ from land-based ponds and lakes is that they are always moving. Help the children find out about tides and waves. What causes the sea to rise and fall each day? Are tides useful or dangerous? High tides bring needed deep water into harbours and ports so that fishermen and sea travellers can sail in and out. However, they can be hazardous, causing floods and washing people and boats out to sea.

[4] Ask the children to draw wave diagrams. Waves are caused by the wind. They get bigger and bigger until they turn over and 'break'.

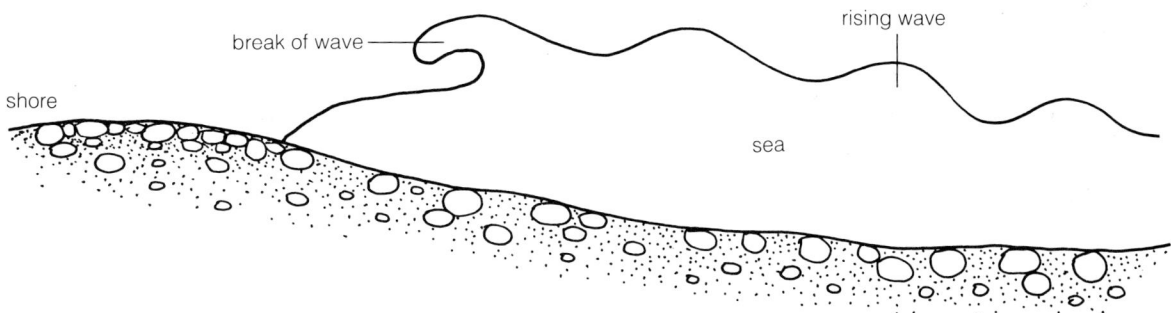

break of wave

rising wave

shore

sea

A wave diagram

151

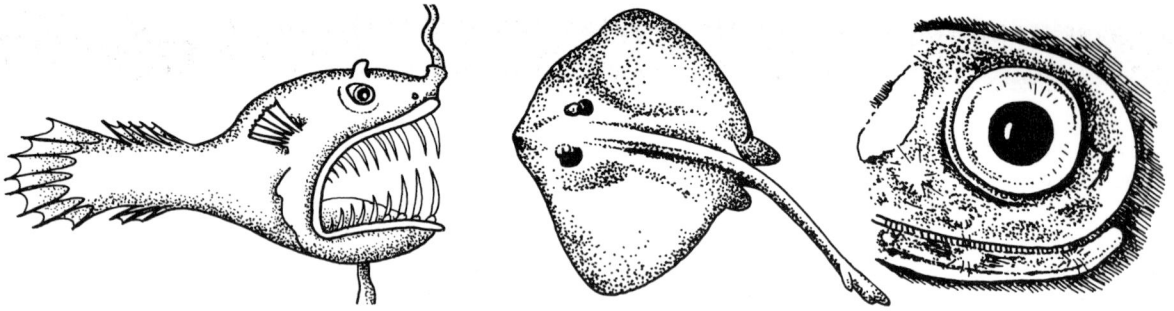

Life on the ocean bed

5 Encourage the children to find out about life in the ocean depths. Draw cross-section diagrams, divided into three layers – 'near the surface', 'mid-depth', and 'the deep sea'. Add appropriate plants and animals. Point out that these are not fixed depths, but that certain creatures are always found nearer the surface, whilst others like to live in the dark on or near the sea bed. Questions to investigate include:

- How deep down are fish caught?
- Why is it so dark on the ocean bed?
- Can people reach the bottom of the ocean?
- Why do plants have no roots?

6 Write about adaptation techniques of ocean bed forms of life. These will also make fascinating pictures to paint. In the deep sea, it is very cold and very dark. There are no plankton.

7 Find out about feeding in the ocean environment. The basic form of life is plankton – millions of tiny plants and animals which live near to the surface. Many of these are so small that they cannot be seen with the naked eye. They need sunlight for photosynthesis, and so are not found in the dark depths. Investigate plankton (if you cannot visit the sea, they live in fresh water too). Place some sea water on a microscope slide. Ask the children to draw what they observe and try to identify common species.

8 Draw ocean food chains and food webs. Use **copymaster 52** as a basis for this activity, then the children can construct their own webs, perhaps by arranging pictures stuck on cards or creating mobiles. This copymaster is useful for introducing basic vocabulary, for example phytoplankton (plant plankton) and zooplankton (animal plankton). Ask the children to draw arrows between the illustrations showing the direction of food movement. Note that people form part of the web. Note also that one illustration may have more than one arrow (for example, small fish, large fish and mammals all have an arrow to the fishing boat).

9 Collect pictures of different forms of ocean transport – investigate those which move across the surface (ocean cruise liners, cargo boats, fishing vessels, small pleasure craft, etc.) and those which can go down into the water. Ask the children to paint submarines. Find out who uses them, why they are used, how deep they can go and how long they can stay under water. Ask the children to write stories about life on a submarine.

10 Help the children find out what other resources we may derive from the sea, such as oil and mineral deposits. A great deal of the world's fuel comes from the sea bed. Look for pictures of undersea coal mines, oil drilling platforms and gas platforms. Investigate the jobs of people who work in such operations. How is the fuel brought from rocks so deep under the sea? How is it carried to the land?

11 Let the children learn about diving equipment and ask them to draw pictures of all that is necessary to keep people alive underwater.

12 Consider the potential of the oceans as a source of renewable energy (see also the Energy topic, page 61–78). This may take the form of tidal energy or wave energy, both of which rely on movement of water to generate electricity. Relate this to the key issues of conservation of finite energy reserves, and the need to develop new sustainable sources of power. The world's oceans are a vast untapped resource. Discuss why they are not more widely used. What are the problems of harnessing wave and tide energy? Examples include dealing with very high waves and strong winds in bad weather and the destruction they may cause.

Common species of plankton

152

DESIGN AND TECHNOLOGY ACTIVITIES

1 Make a waterwheel to demonstrate that moving water has power.

You will need
- A circle of silver foil
- Scissors
- A thick stick.

What to do
- Mark eight slits at regular intervals around the edge of the circle of foil (the wheel), extending three quarters of the way to the centre. Cut along these slits carefully.
- Bend the eight corners forward to make the paddles of the wheel.
- Make a small hole in the centre of the wheel and push the stick through.
- Hold the wheel under a gently running tap, and watch it turning round.

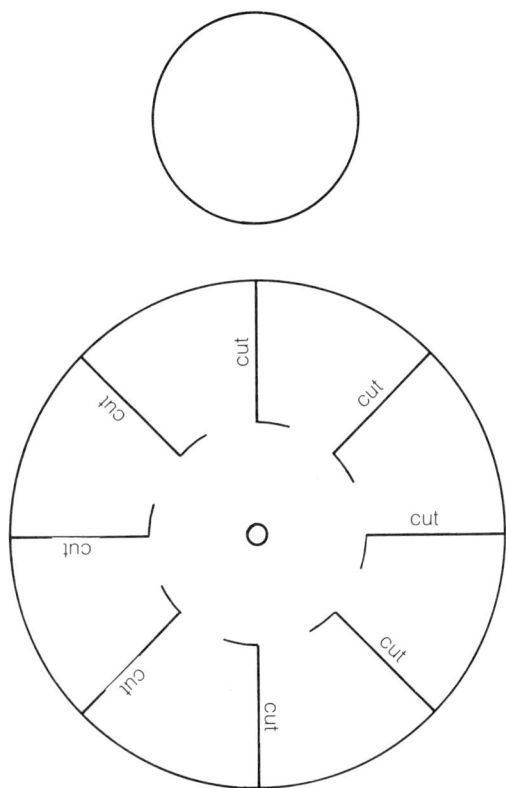

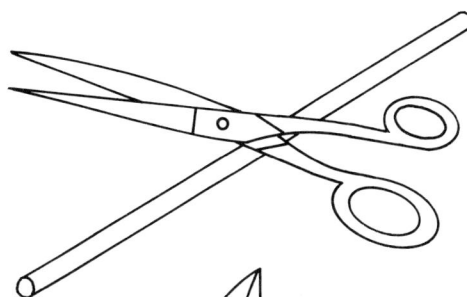

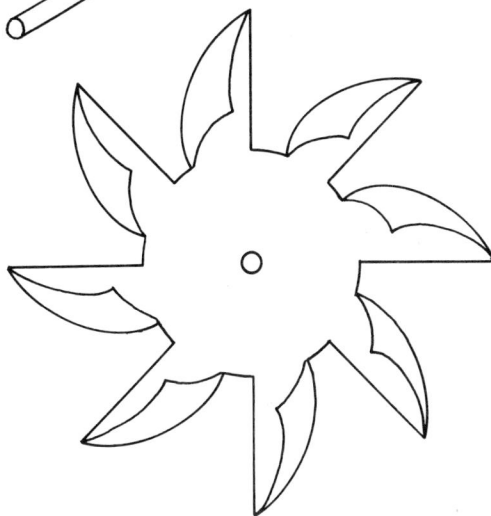

MATHEMATICS ACTIVITIES

1 Ask the children to record the prices of various fish in the supermarket or fishmongers. How are fish sold: by weight? Per fish? Do basic number work using this data.

2 Ask the children to try to work out why some fish are more expensive than others. What factors affect price? Do prices vary depending on the time of the year? Ask them to record changes from week to week.

3 Relate the Oceans topic to an investigation of mail services between nations. Find out from the Post Office what alternatives there are for mailing a book from the United Kingdom to the USA. Compare costs and anticipated duration of air and surface delivery. If the children have contacts in other countries, ask them to send letters by air and surface mail. Ask the recipients to let you know how long the letters took to arrive.

153

4 Ask the children to plan an 'ocean' holiday, then make a 'holiday book' to include details of all aspects of preparation for such an undertaking. They can illustrate their book with pictures from travel agents' brochures. Choose a holiday on an island or on a cruise liner. The children could work in groups, with each group organising details of a different destination. The book should include records of the following:

- The location, its climate, sights to see, etc.
- How far away it is
- How to get there (travel times, distance of home from airport, sea port, etc.)

- Speed of travel
- Cost of travel
- Cost of accommodation
- Details of other expenditure (insurance, food, leisure, etc.)
- Total cost of holiday for the family or group.

The book could also include accounts of what items need to be taken, and what activities might be undertaken during the holiday.

This activity should help children appreciate the sheer size of oceans, and the scope of world travel.

PE ACTIVITIES ▶

1 Do a sub-topic on water sports. Find out about equipment needed, and where you might go to learn surfing, water-skiing, diving, speedboat racing, etc. Collect pictures of these activities. Ask the children to write about what they would like to learn if they had the chance, and why. Perhaps there may be people in children's families or the local community who take part in these sports. If so, invite them to bring some equipment and talk to the class.

ENGLISH ACTIVITIES ▶

C53 –54

1 Use pictures, films and photographs as a basis for discussion on the 'moods' of the sea. Compile lists of words relating to contrasting moods: angry, dark, tempestuous, strong, powerful, tranquil, calm, gentle, soothing, lapping, etc.

2 With the children analyse how the moods of the sea have been represented by authors and artists. Take the children to visit an art gallery and observe sea/ocean paintings. Read poems and stories which portray the 'character' of the oceans. How has this been portrayed (use of colour, choice of words, style of writing, etc.)?

3 Ask the children to write stories about 'The shipwreck', 'Storm at sea', 'The powers of the waves', 'The calm after the storm'.

4 Ask the children to create poetry from 'wave words': splish, splash, crash, lap, wash, splosh, etc.

5 Let the children learn vocabulary associated with classification of ocean life. Use this in word games and puzzles. For example, take one interesting form of life, such as whales, sharks or dolphins.

6 **Copymaster 53** (Shark words) teaches the class name *Chondrichthyes*, the family of sharks (also sawfish, skates, rays). Ask the children to colour the various sharks, then make as many words as possible from the letters of the word *Chondrichthyes*. Set this as a class or group challenge to see who can make the greatest number of words. The children can then use reference books, an important skill in itself, to find out more about the sharks shown. Ask them to write accounts of the life and dangers of shark-infested waters.

7 Ask the children to write stories about the adventures of a seagull. What would it be like to have a bird's-eye view of the ocean?

8 Ask the children to write factual accounts about endangered species, persuading others to take individual action on behalf of the protection of marine creatures. Find out about the activities of organised campaigns such as 'Save The Whale'. What have such campaigns achieved? (In 1982 the International Whaling Commission agreed to ban commercial whaling for a period of five years, commencing in 1985). Whaling still continues in some nations, but on a much smaller scale than before. Contact organisations such as Greenpeace and World Wide Fund For Nature for information.

9 Ask the children to colour in the picture on **Copymaster 54** (Ocean 3000) which introduces one of our world's most intriguing questions: Could human populations ever inhabit underwater cities? Discuss why this is an important issue, and not merely science fiction. Human numbers are increasing dramatically, and inhabitable space on our Earth is limited. Ask the children to write about 'Underwater city, year 3000'. How do the people breathe? How do they find food? Do they travel?

Ask the children to paint larger pictures of various aspects of the sea bed city. Help them create a wall frieze of this imaginary environment. While doing this, it might be interesting for the children to consider that with the wonders of modern science and technology we probably know more about the surface of the moon than we do about our planet's sea beds. Ask the children to write a caption for the frieze: for example, 'Our future needs the oceans'. This will serve as a reminder that while we may never build cities in them, we certainly need to take care of the oceans of our planet.

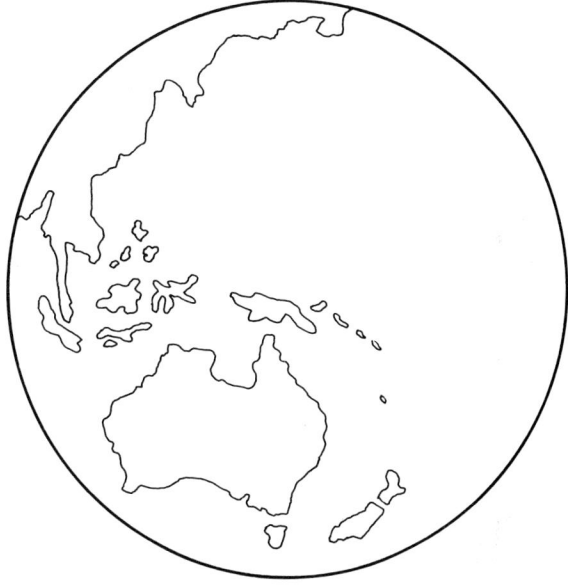

Nearly three quarters of the surface of our planet is covered with water. This is in the world's seas and oceans, filling large hollows in the ground.

Unscramble the names of the Earth's major oceans.

T A A I T L N C

A C I P C I F

D I I N A N

R T A I C C

C T A R A T N C I

Islands in the deep

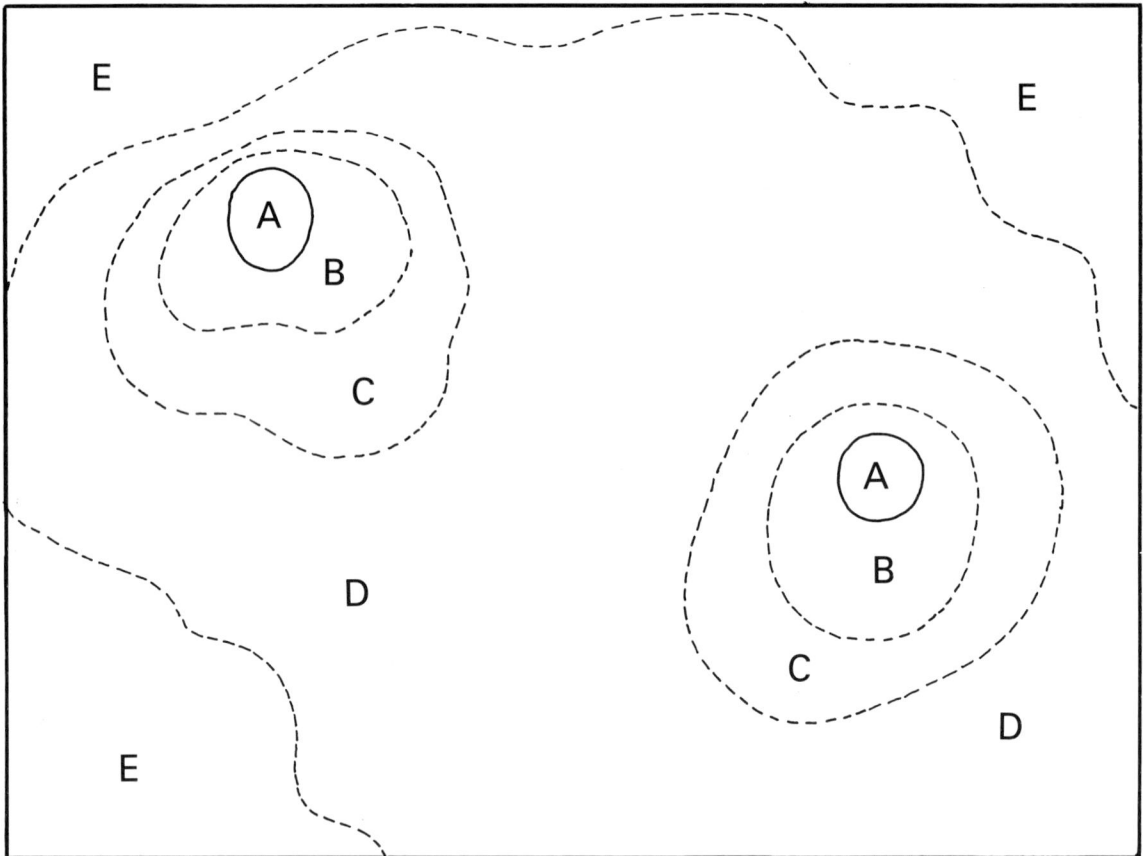

Key

Sea level

A	100 metres above sea level	
B	100 metres below sea level	
C	200 metres below sea level	
D	300 metres below sea level	
E	400 metres below sea level	

Colour A in green and B⟶C⟶D⟶E in deepening shades of blue.

Home on the Great Barrier Reef

The Great Barrier Reef on the north-east coast of Australia has around **3000** animal species.

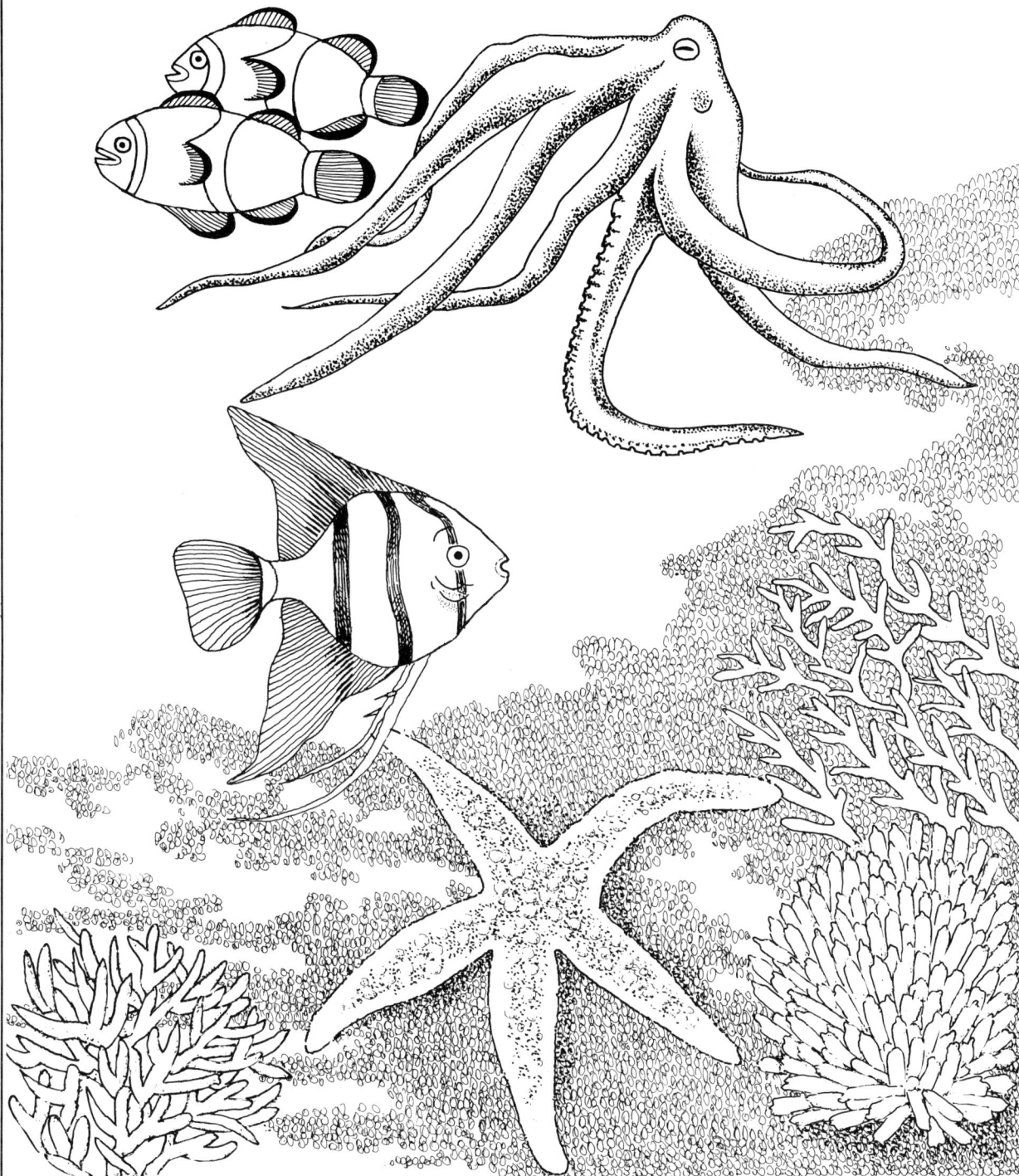

How many plants and animals can you identify?

Ocean food web

Who eats whom?

phytoplankton

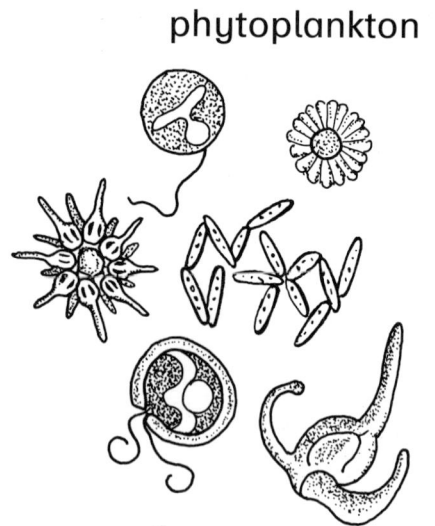

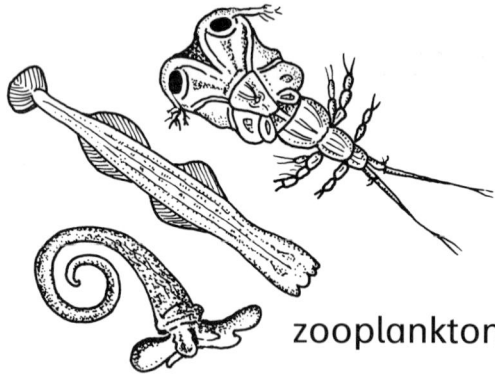

zooplankton

small fish

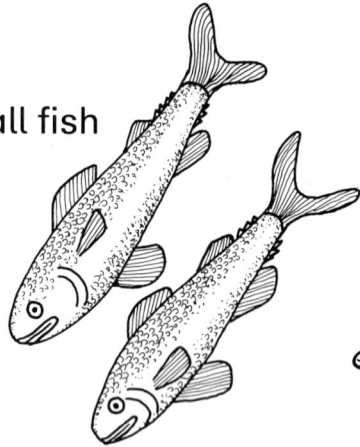

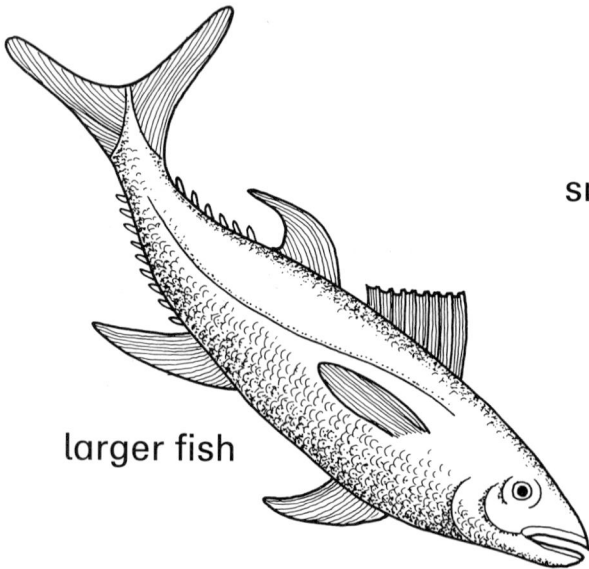

larger fish

people

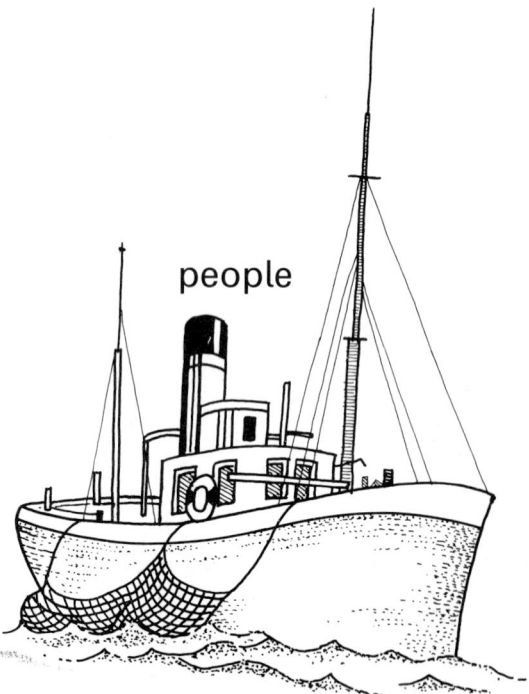

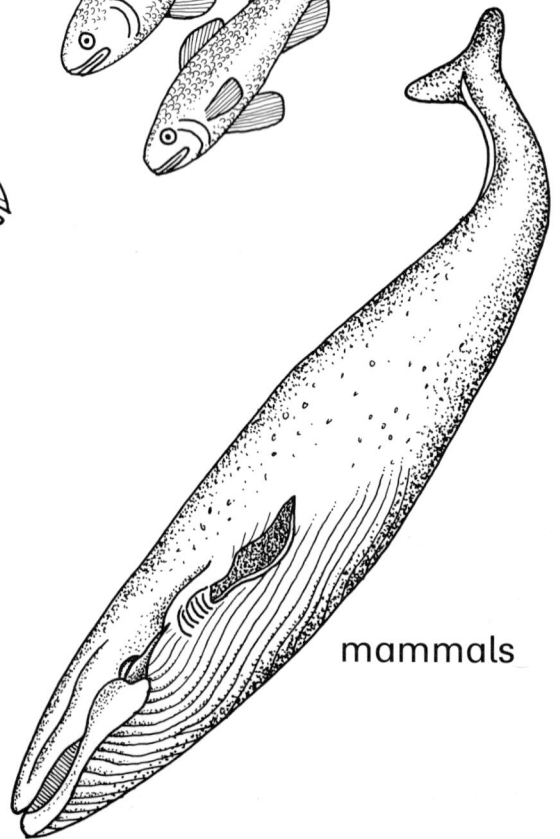

mammals

Shark words

Sharks belong to the class called

CHONDRICHTHYES

How many words can you make from the letters of this name?
What other creatures belong to this class?

Ocean 3000